The Community College Presidency

To Peggy, Brandt, and Andrew

THE COMMUNITY COLLEGE PRESIDENCY

George B. Vaughan

Piedmont Virginia Community College

American Council on Education • Macmillan Publishing Company
NEW YORK

Collier Macmillan Publishers
LONDON

Macmillan Publishing Company
A Division of Macmillan, Inc.
866 Third Avenue, New York, N. Y. 10022

Collier Macmillan Canada, Inc.

Library of Congress Catalog Card Number: 85-28663

Printed in the United States of America
printing number
        2   3   4   5   6   7   8   9   10

Library of Congress Cataloging in Publication Data

Vaughan, George B.
  The community college presidency.

  Bibliography: p.
  Includes index.
  1. Community college presidents—United States.
I. Title.
LB2341.V34 1986   378′.111   85-28663
ISBN 0-02-933170-6

Contents

———◆———

Foreword

━━◆━━

The Community College Presidency will undoubtedly become one of the landmark books in the slowly growing body of literature about the American community college movement. Far too little research has been conducted about the leaders of these uniquely American educational inventions. Community, technical, and junior colleges enroll over 10 million students each college year. Some 55 percent of all college freshmen begin their college education in one of these colleges. Community colleges have, in many ways, captured the hearts and imagination of the American public.

Study after study has determined that the way each college responds to various challenges and opportunities, indeed the quality of the college itself, is to a great extent dependent upon its chief executive officer. George Vaughan has included here some sound and well-crafted pieces for the largely unfinished jigsaw puzzle that depicts the two-year college in America.

Vaughan has already been labeled by his peers and colleagues as the "resident historian" of the American community college. In articles and books such as *The Community College in America: A Short History,* published by the American Association of Community and Junior Colleges, he has traced and analyzed the growth and development of these institutions. No other community college president has been more active in research and writing. In this book he turns his vibrant interest and skillful writing to his own profession, the community college presidency. It will be no surprise to those who know George Vaughan as not only an excellent community college president but also as a highly qualified researcher and interpreter in this field — that this work is the most far-reaching study ever undertaken on the two-year college presidency. Vaughan has collected not only demographic data but also the opinions and attitudes of two-year college presidents, their spouses, their colleagues, and their boards of trustees. From an immense collection of personal data, he has explored, with an insider's understanding and an outsider's objective eye, every facet of the professional role, the preparation, the hopes and dreams, and the perceived failures of these men and women. In the past 30 years, they have built and now steer, through increasingly troubled waters, the largest single segment of American higher education.

It is in the chapter "Satisfactions, Failures, and Prestige of the Presidency" that one most clearly sees the position of the two-year college president as quite different from that of the president of a four-year college or university. It will not be news to community college observers that one of the greatest psychic rewards these presidents experience is that of providing access — of opening the door of opportunity for many individuals who can find it only in a community, technical, or junior college. Readers who are not themselves two-year college presidents may understand for the first time the pressures on the chief executive officer of an institution deeply intertwined with the community it serves, and governed by a lay board from, and often elected by, that community.

A topic of long-time interest for Vaughan is presidential stress and burnout. Readers will find in *The Community College Presidency* a first-hand glimpse of what happens to men and women who live in, to judge from the metaphors used, a fishbowl and the eye of a hurricane. We hear descriptions of such stress, not only from presidents themselves, but from their spouses, and, in some cases, from their children. Of equal importance are the examples of what some successful presidents do about presidential burn-out.

I suspect that, if published alone, the material on "The President's Spouse" would become immensely popular. It should be must reading for every person hoping to become a two-year college president. It should be annual reading for every two-year college president and his or her spouse. Never before has the role of the community college presidential spouse been so thoroughly described. Vaughan details the responsibilities, the satisfactions, and the frustrations of these "partners." It must be noted that there are now over 100 women serving as the chief executive officers of community, technical, and junior colleges.

The author offers the first detailed look at leadership as it pertains to the community college presidency. He examines characteristics and skills presidential leaders believe are important to the successful president. The chapter on leadership offers trustees a checklist of characteristics they should look for when seeking a president for their institution.

This book will be of inestimable value to several categories of readers. Students of the community college will gain new insights into the institutions they study. Prospective college presidents will learn more about the joys and pains of serving as a community college president. Community college trustees will learn much about the part they can play on the leadership team of two-year colleges, as well as the impact of their support or non-support on their chosen leaders. Trustees should use it as a guide for understanding the community college presidency, especially the president of the community college which they serve. All community, technical, and junior college presidents should buy a copy of the book for themselves. If they do not, the board of trustees should buy it for them as a token of trustee understanding of an important but often thankless job.

The Community College Presidency will, I suspect, be an immediate bestseller among the aforementioned groups of readers and will certainly attain considerable long-term popularity. The full value of the book will likely come later as this rich lode of information about the community college presidency is continually mined and explored by researchers and scholars who should know more about the pioneering leaders of these "opportunity" colleges. George Vaughan is to be commended for developing an absolutely stunning "insider's" view of some important but lesser-known leaders in American higher education.

> Dale Parnell
> President and
>   Chief Executive Officer
> American Association of
>   Community and Junior
>   Colleges

Preface

———◆———

As the first major publication about the community college presidency, this book is devoted to providing an understanding of an important but often neglected subject. Most presidents, trustees, would-be presidents, faculty members, scholars of higher education, and others interested in the community college have little or no knowledge about who has led these institutions, who is leading them now, and, perhaps even more significant, who will lead them in the future. This volume is a major step toward filling that void. Moreover, I believe such a study is the only way by which the concept of the community college can ever be fully grasped.

The frank discussions herein by presidents, faculty members, trustees, spouses, deans, and others open avenues for comprehending the presidency that simply have not been available in the past. For example, before now, a dean or vice president who has wanted to become a community college president has had little or no guidance as to what routes to follow. Trustees, while certainly having had a "gut" feeling of what they sought in a president, have had, prior to this volume, little guidance on what characteristics and skills to look for in a potential president or what to expect of that important part of the presidential team, the president's spouse (the role of the spouse is discussed in some detail).

The president's function in governance has been difficult, at best, to define. This study explores the role, especially as it relates to unions on campus.

Although statistics on presidential tenure make it quite clear that not many presidents will devote their entire career to the presidency, few presidents actually plan for life after the presidency. Why are such a small number of presidents prepared to pursue an equally rewarding career after leaving the post? The issues are carefully examined.

I conducted the almost 100 interviews at intermittent periods between July of 1982 and April of 1985. The result, rather than a snapshot of the presidency, is an evolutionary picture: times change — so does the presidency. For example, in 1982, the primary issue was a lack of funds. By 1985, while still a major issue, this had been put into the broader perspective of institutional mission. The presidents were now dealing with reduced funding in a more orderly fashion than was done in the near-panic years of 1982 and early 1983.

Although this is a book about the community college presidency, it is more than that. It provides an understanding of the community college — its successes, shortcomings, evolution, and future — that can only be gained through understanding the presidency. My deepest hope is that trustees, spouses, faculty, staff, scholars of higher education, and anyone interested in the community college will find this volume a key to understanding such a complex entity in America's highly diverse and loosely structured system of higher education. My greatest desire is to help my presidential colleagues know their own roles more fully and thereby find more of the rewards and fewer of the frustrations associated with the presidency.

Chapter 1 provides a brief overview of the community college presidency and a glimpse at those individuals who currently occupy the position.

In Chapter 2, the family backgrounds of today's community college presidents are discussed. A major conclusion reached is that the men and women occupying this position are highly motivated individuals who have often moved well beyond the educational, economic, and social levels of their parents. By studying the socioeconomic background of today's presidents, one is better prepared to understand the attitudes of these individuals and the roles they have played in shaping the community college in America.

Chapter 3 is an exploration of various paths to the presidency. It offers guidance to trustees who are seeking presidents and to deans and vice presidents who are aiming for the position. In this chapter, some of the doubts, fears, and satisfactions associated with the presidency are also examined. The question is asked and answered: "Are community college presidents happy in their position?"

A seemingly simplistic but important question — "What does a community college president do?" — is considered in Chapter 4. One thing that a successful president must do is interpret and promote the community college's mission. Trustees, presidents, faculty, and others discuss exactly how successful presidents have been in this regard. The pressures and influences brought to bear on the president's office are also discussed.

Chapter 5 provides an in-depth analysis of who calls the shots on campus. Are governing boards "out of control" as has been suggested by some studies on the four-year college and university presidency? Have unions taken over the governance process? And what is the role of the faculty in this process? The various segments of the college community are placed in the total perspective of the campus environment. The president's role in governance is defined and clarified.

Chapter 6 deals with the satisfactions, successes, and failures of the community college presidency. It is also, to the best of my knowledge, the first look ever at the prestige of the office. In this chapter, presidential leaders candidly discuss how the community college rates vis-à-vis some of its undertakings.

The next chapter leaps into that rarely discussed topic, presidential stress, which may in some individuals lead to burnout. Causes of burnout are examined, as are ways of combating stress and how most presidents handle the pressures. One highly successful ex-president explains why he decided to "hang it up."

Chapter 8 is a ground-breaking look into the world of the community college spouse, a world that has been largely ignored by trustees, presidents, and, in some cases, the spouses themselves. The roles that spouses choose to play are grouped into four general categories. A brief look is also taken at the effects the woman's movement has had in this area. This chapter also comprises the personal, insightful, and, at times, provocative perspective of one spouse on what it is like "being there." The observations presented in this chapter demonstrate how the community in which the college is located influences the role of the spouse. A major contribution of this chapter is a description of the complexities of juggling the roles of community leader, mother, professional person, and spouse.

In Chapter 9 that vital ingredient, leadership is considered. Drawing on the works of Warren Bennis, James MacGregor Burns, Michael Cohen and James March, Clark Kerr, James Fisher, and others, this chapter places presidential leadership in the total scheme of things. Also detailed are the personal attributes, skills, and abilities required of the successful president.

Chapter 10 elevates the study of the presidency to a more philosophical level, although the practical aspects of the position are never abandoned. Tenure in office, professional activities, and the postpresidential careers are thoroughly explored. An example of combining the practical with the philosophical is found in the discussion of how presidents view the ability to produce scholarly publications.

The final chapter is a brief postscript on my observations of some of the characteristics and attitudes of the community college presidency.

Methodology

Several approaches were used in conducting the study. I drew upon my 14 years of experience as a community college president and as an observer of higher education in deciding what questions to ask, whom to interview, and in interpreting the information gathered.

I conducted interviews with 96 individuals. All were done in person, with the exception of one which was conducted by telephone. Among those interviewed were presidents, trustees, spouses, faculty members, administrators, and national leaders associated with the community college. (I transcribed all of the interviews myself; while time-consuming and somewhat arduous, it gave me a much better understanding of what was being said than would have been the case had someone else done the work.)

I conducted a Career and Lifestyles Survey (CLS) of 838 presidents of public two-year colleges that were at the time members of the American Association of Community and Junior Colleges. Five hundred and ninety-one (70.5%) of that number returned valid surveys. Those receiving the CLS survey were asked to identify the two top community college presidents in their state, excluding themselves. Individuals identified by their peers as the outstanding presidents were considered to be leaders in their respective states if they received as many as five votes or if they received the largest number of votes (with a minimum of two votes) in their states. Seventy-five presidents met the criteria; two states had three presidents who received five or more votes, and some states did not have any who met the established criteria.

I asked these 75 presidents to complete a Leadership Survey (LS). Sixty-eight (84%) of the 75 returned the completed LS survey. The recipients of this survey were asked to name the two community college presidents, excluding themselves, whom they considered to be the outstanding community college presidents in the nation. Ten presidents received three or more votes from the 68 individuals who returned the survey. Nine of the ten had been identified as leaders in their respective state; this would seem to validate the peer review process used for identifying leaders. Forty-eight of the spouses of those 75 presidents identified as leaders expressed an interest in completing a Spouse's Survey (SS). Thirty-eight (79%) of the 48 returned the survey. In an attempt to determine if the spouses of leaders viewed their role differently from the role of those presidents' spouses not so identified, a systematic sample comprising 107 spouses of presidents not identified as leaders were surveyed. Fifty-four (51%) of these returned the survey.

(Throughout the text, material based on the written surveys will be followed by their abbreviations in parentheses: CLS, LS, or SS.)

The term president is used throughout the volume, although some of those surveyed and interviewed have titles such as chancellor, superintendent-president, or director. Only presidents of public institutions were surveyed. With one minor exception (organizational membership), no attempt was made to distinguish between male–female, white–minority, or other categories of presidents. The study did not deal with financial compensation. Only those presidents who were "survivors" were interviewed. In other words, with two exceptions, no attempt was made to interview people who had left the presidency. The two exceptions left the position voluntarily, one through retirement and one to enter another field. Some of the quotes from the spouses were written comments taken from the Spouses' Survey.

Finally, this study is not a comparison of the two-year college presidency with the four-year presidency; nor is it a comparison of the spouse of the two-year college president with the spouse of the four-year college president, although in both instances an occasional comparison was made when it was felt it added to the understanding of the community college presidency.

Acknowledgments

Without the willingness of the many individuals who agreed to be interviewed, this book could not have been written. No one who was asked to participate in an interview refused; everyone interviewed took the meeting seriously, talked candidly, and brought a unique perspective to the presidency. The interviews bring life to the volume that would be missing if the study had been approached differently.

When I first considered studying the presidency, I asked David Riesman, Henry Ford II Professor of Social Sciences *Emeritus,* Harvard University, for advice on how to proceed. He gave of his advice freely and I followed it as closely as possible. In every instance the advice proved sound. He also commented on the material dealing with the role of the president's spouse. I deeply appreciate his advice and encouragement.

Arthur Cohen has influenced my career in one way or another since 1972 when he published my first manuscript through the Educational Resources Information Center (ERIC) for Junior Colleges. Since that time, I have called upon him regularly. Again, I must say thanks to him.

Joe Kauffman, a new-found professional colleague and scholar supreme on the college presidency, agreed to read the manuscript without having ever met me. His insights were invaluable. He transferred his knowledge of the four-year presidency to that of the two-year in a way that placed both in perspective. My desire is to meet him and thank in person for his many contributions. Meanwhile, I hope this deep expression of my gratitude will suffice.

Martha Turnage, a friend and colleague of 16 years standing, is now Vice President for University Relations at Ohio University. Her keen insights into, and knowledge of, the community college helped me greatly in identifying several unique contributions of the community college president.

Robert Templin is Academic Dean of Piedmont Virginia Community College. As dean, he is competent, loyal, challenging, and respected by the entire college community — someone any president would indeed be fortunate to have on staff. He is an excellent critic of what the community college can and should be. He challenged me, cajoled me, and pushed me to the limits. Bob, thank you. I am more than fortunate to work with you; I am indeed blessed.

Roberta Ostar, a scholar on the role of the spouse of the college and university presidency, offered critical comments on my chapter on the president's spouse. Indeed, she prevented me from making a major mistake in my analysis.

In addition to Dean Templin, several individuals at Piedmont Virginia Community College made significant contributions to the volume and to my mental health. Pat Buck, Secretary to the President, was helpful in every way possible, including holding the office together for the two months I was on leave. Linda Ragland was always concerned with deadlines and did her part to see that I met them. Pyror Hale made a number of insightful comments on the chapter dealing with stress and burnout. She brought her discipline of psychology to bear on the chapter and gracefully reminded me that I must not exceed my field of expertise. Ed Pittman prepared the illustrations for the chapter on leadership. Joe Jenkins read several chapters from the "layman's perspective," as he put it, and helped me guard against becoming too esoteric in my discussions. Indeed, the entire faculty and staff made very effort to keep the college running smoothly while I was on leave.

Frank Doherty, who, at the time the surveys were being conducted, was a graduate student at the University of Virginia

(UVA) served as research assistant on the surveys. He was invaluable in helping to design them and evaluate the results. Linda Little, a graduate student at UVA, was very helpful in designing and analyzing the LS survey. She contributed the format used in the illustrations in the chapter on leadership.

Members of the staff of the American Association of Community and Junior Colleges (AACJC) were very supportive in bringing the volume to fruition. Dale Parnell, president of the Association, gave his time, his knowledge, and his support to the project from beginning to end. Bernie Luskin also worked to see that the book would become a reality. Jim Gollattscheck did all that I could hope for and more. He read the entire manuscript and offered valuable comments; he served as the liaison person between the American Council on Education (ACE) and the AACJC. More important, Jim served as a sounding board and friend throughout the project.

William Meardy of the Association of Community College Trustees gave his support to the study.

James Murray of ACE committed himself fully to the project at an early stage. He has been very helpful and without him the book would not have been published by the current publisher. Lloyd Chilton, Executive Editor at Macmillan, has been very helpful. I am indeed fortunate to be able to work with someone with his vast experience. He has answered all of my questions and has given me a sense of security that was missing prior to my beginning to work with him.

Joan Pitsch, Editorial Supervisor at Macmillan, has been very helpful. Her effort to keep me informed of the status of the volume was greatly appreciated.

Members of the Presidents Academy of the AACJC were both an inspiration and a source of knowledge to me as I conducted the research for the study. Mike Crawford and Larry Tyree were especially encouraging throughout the development of the book. My presidential colleagues and the deputy chancellor in the Virginia Community College System were a constant font of inspiration and information.

All presidents have many people to whom they must answer. Among those I answer to is Jeff Hockaday, Chancellor of the Virginia Community College System. Jeff realizes that, if the professional person is to be successful, he or she must be encouraged to pursue professional interests. His concern extends much further, however. He deeply appreciates what I do; without his support, I would not have taken on this project while occupying my current position.

The Piedmont Virginia Community College Board has helped at every opportunity. Since its members first became aware of my interest in preparing such a volume, I was encouraged to take a few minutes at each board meeting to bring the members up-to-date on my progress. Without a supportive board, no president can hope to succeed, much less conduct a major study of the presidency.

A note of thanks is due to my brothers and sisters and their spouses who saw me through the "lean" years, "took me in, and fed me when I was hungry."

How does one thank one's spouse for the moral support needed to complete a book? One thanks her for her encouragement, understanding, and inspiration. But to thank Peggy for these things would be grossly inadequate, for she did much more. She read the entire manuscript many times, correcting the grammar, asking questions, and making sense out of chaos. She brought a depth to the volume that I could not have achieved alone.

Finally, in addition to Peggy, my two sons Brandt and Andrew have encouraged me to complete the study and have been patient beyond what one could ever hope for from two teenage boys. As with Peggy, their love and support have always been the key to whatever success I might have enjoyed in my career and in completing this volume.

The Community College Presidency

CHAPTER 1

A Brief Overview

Today's community college president is a symbol of that group of Americans born of blue-collar parents and reared in blue-collar homes, who either lived through the tail-end of the Great Depression or who had heard enough stories about it to influence forever their values. While many of today's presidents were too young for service in World War II, their values were shaped, if not by the war, certainly by the ferment in American postwar society. At the war's end, these young men and women were ready to take advantage of America's unprecedented affluence. They were also to be caught up in the great democratization movements within the country, which climaxed in the rights movements of the 1960s. The democratization of American society also made possible the development of a nationwide network of public community colleges.

In spite of the vastness of the community college movement, little is known about the men and women who served in the movement's vanguard (even less is known about their spouses). Today's community college presidents are philosophically, emotionally, and, in some cases, spiritually geared to serve as presidents of "the people's college." The growth of community colleges in the 1960s and 1970s provided the perfect setting for today's presidents to expend their energy, vent their emotions, and preach their cause. Never in the history of the nation was the time more propitious for so many individuals to make a major statement on the future shape of American higher education and ultimately on American democracy. Indeed, community colleges brought about a meeting of the individual and the institution rarely seen before in America.

The family background of today's community college presidents is revealing. Most fathers of current presidents either did not finish high school or finished but did not attend college. A similar pattern exists with the mothers of today's leaders. The parents' occupations tend to follow their educational levels. What do family backgrounds tell us about today's community college presidents? One thing we know is that their leap to the top was in spite of, or perhaps because of, their blue-collar background.

Competing with others who would like to be president, today's presidents reached their current position through a number of avenues. Three are identified and discussed: the serendipitous route exemplified by the president who claims that "the escalator came by, I got on and rode it to the top"; the plan exemplified by those presidents who enrolled in graduate programs for the explicit purpose of preparing to attain community college administrator, and higher; and the opportunistic path, which is exemplified by those presidents who saw the opportunities associated with the community college as "the best game in town." Of course, level of education, mentors, and personal attributes and skills played important roles in deciding who was to be president.

Some surprises awaited the presidents once they assumed office, the most important of which was finding out exactly what the job entailed. New community college presidents quickly discovered that there were no "how-to" books on being a successful president. The romantic ideal of the president as academic leader soon gave way to the reality for most presidents. They suddenly discovered that legislators, business leaders, faculty, unions, and practically everyone else wanted a piece of the presidency and that many were willing to generate enough pressure on the office to get, if not a piece of the action, certainly the president's attention and time. Time became as elusive as academic leadership. Yet leadership remains a major aspect of the successful president, although it is a different type of leadership from that envisioned by today's leaders prior to their assuming the post, the majority of whom had followed the academic route.

Today's community college president must balance the seesaw that is loaded with the concerns of faculty, students, staff, and, last but not least, trustees. Special interest groups bring both opportunities and problems to the president's office. Shifting roles for governing boards means shifting priorities for both the trustee and the president. Today's presidents must be sensitive to the delicately balanced board–president relationship and see that it is clearly understood by all parties. Inheriting a bureaucratic organizational structure, today's leaders have successfully dispelled the myth that they are enshrined at the top. Indeed, one of the important conclusions reached in this volume is that they have successfully married the bureaucratic structure with participatory governance. Yet no sooner did presidents come to grips with mating collegiality and bureaucracy than unions came to campus. Are unions a real threat to collegiality or is fear of them similar to the fear of the dark at the top of the stairs? Presidents and others provide some interesting commentary on the subject.

What are the satisfactions, successes, and failures associated with the community college presidency? Presidents, trustees, faculty, and others were asked that question. The answers reveal, among other things, that today's presidents are relatively happy with their position, that they do indeed subscribe to the community college philosophy, and that they believe that the keystone to that philosophy is open access. Also apparent is that today's presidents have failed to interpret and articulate the community college's mission effectively and consistently to its various constituents. The prestige of the presidency is examined and found lacking when compared with the four-year presidency. The prestige associated with the presidency can influence funding, prestige of the institution, and job satisfaction, although few presidents felt that the prestige of their position had anything to do with their own satisfaction with their office.

Stress resulting in burnout is one of the hot topics of the 1980s, and community college presidents are prime targets. Most presidents, however, handle stress so well that burnout is not a major threat. On the other hand, some presidents cling to the "Superman-Wonderwoman" idea of the presidency and continue to try to present an invincible appearance, especially to faculty and trustees. The observations of spouses on presidential stress are revealing and should help leaders put stress in perspective, both for themselves and their spouses.

A detailed examination of the spouses' role reveals that many are confused and frustrated. In some cases, the woman's movement has clarified roles; in other cases, it has simply added to an already ambiguous situation. Spouses speak out about trustees, often in a somewhat bitter tone. One spouse, in a separate section, brings her own perspective to what it is like "being there." Her observations on the evolving nature of the spouse's role are revealing and enlightening.

In attempting to understand the presidency, to use the words of one president, "In the final analysis it all comes down to one word: leadership." Leadership is elusive; however, here it is defined and examined in terms of the community college presidency. Presidents rank integrity, judgment, courage, and concern for others as the top personal attributes the successful presidential leader should possess; the most desirable skills and abilities are producing results, selecting qualified people, resolving conflicts, communicating effectively, and motivating others. Potential conflict between the personal attributes and skills and abilities is examined, as are the levels of leadership presidents seek in their subordinates. For example, presidents believe it is more important for the staff, rather than the president, to be good team players.

Finally, the questions "How long is too long to remain in one presidency?" and "Is there life after the presidency?" are discussed. Views on length of tenure varied, but the conclusion was that the mythical five-to-seven years is no longer a valid measurement, especially if a president wants to be a leader in the field. Indeed, community college presidents who are singled out by their peers as leaders have been in their current position over nine years; those not so identified have been in their jobs for slightly over five years. The news is not heartening for those presidents who seek another position that is equally rewarding in terms of pay, prestige, and challenge. Most presidents either do not have, or do not take, the time to prepare for a profession after the presidency. Moreover, the educational backgrounds of most leaders are such as to limit their future career choices.

This is but an outline of the complexities surrounding the community college presidency. The major conclusion of the volume is that the nature of the American community college can only be truly appreciated through an understanding of its most important leader. The remainder of this volume is devoted to bringing about that understanding.

CHAPTER 2

An Intimate Profile of the Presidency

Community college presidents help to chart the educational, social, and economic life of thousands of communities across the nation. They lead institutions that enroll approximately five million students in credit courses each year and serve an estimated four million individuals in noncredit activities. Many of these pupils are from lower socioeconomic groups and many are minorities and women, groups whose members might not be able to attend college if the community college did not exist. The men and women who serve as presidents of the nation's public community colleges head schools that spend billions of dollars each year and employ approximately 270,000 full-time faculty, librarians, counselors, and administrators, as well as a large number of support staff and part-time faculty. These officers also interact with other community leaders to make decisions that affect the lives of millions of workers.

In addition to being an important position, the community college presidency is an interesting one, often failing to fit the stereotype associated with the college presidency. Occupying that middle ground in the educational hierarchy between the public school superintendent — indeed, some of today's presidents came to the presidency from this post in the public school system — and the four-year college or university president, the position is often ill-defined. A partial explanation is that it is relatively new in the scheme of things. Another complicating factor in delineating the office is that community college presidents are likely to spend more time than do their four-year counterparts with external constituents who are members of the local financial, business, political, and educational communities. The community college president is usually more active in the local Chamber of Commerce than in a professional organization devoted to an academic discipline. Interviews reveal that, after the mandatory reading of *The Chronicle of Higher Education* and the *Community and Junior College Journal,* these leaders often turn to business publications for their professional reading.

The community college president fails in other ways to fit the image that the public often associates with the status of a college president. One study revealed that less than 15 percent of community colleges provide homes for their presidents (Nicholson, 1981, p. 41), a sharp contrast to four-year schools where it is assumed that the college furnishes a house on campus (some college and university presidents, however, did choose to flee the campus during the student protests of the 1960s). Not living in a college-owned house on campus has many implications, especially in regard to entertainment, the role of the spouse, and the "sense of family" often associated with institutions of higher education.

Community college presidents differ from the stereotype in other areas. Rarely do these officers have dormitories to oversee or large sums of money to raise from private sources (although there is some evidence to suggest that the latter may be changing). Rarely do they have an active alumni association or a "box" for athletic events. Rarely can these leaders take leisurely strolls on an ivy-covered campus for the purpose of talking with students, practically all of whom are commuters and many of whom attend college part-time and at night. And rarely do they find that the large number of the part-time, working, older adult students who make up so much of the student body show more than a passing interest in campus governance, much less in the office of the president.

Should community college presidents work to resemble more closely their four-year counterparts? The answer is, "Probably not." While assuming a presidential "persona" might make the public image of the community college president more recognizable, simply to emulate certain aspects of the four-year post for emulation's sake would be a mistake. It would ultimately take away from some of the community college's uniqueness, a uniqueness that helps it to fulfill its mission. On the other hand, a price is paid for not fitting the stereotype. As will be discussed later, the two-year presidents suffers from a lack of prestige when compared with their four-year colleagues.

The time to take a closer look at the community college presidency is at hand. The position of the community college president is well into its second generation: over 50 percent of the presidents have been at their current level for five years or less. Thus the "typical" president is no longer the founder and builder of colleges so typical of the 1960s when so many community colleges opened.

The path to the presidency is also changing. Serendipity often played a major role in deciding who became a president during the period of rapid growth. Today, however, the presidency is often viewed as the culminating point of a career that has been years in the making.

Why study the community college presidency? Attempting to understand the community college without understanding its most important leaders, is, at the risk of being accused of engaging in a bit of hyperbole, tantamount to trying to understand the American Revolution without studying Jefferson and Washington. To expect the community college to provide effective leadership in the years ahead without a better concept of how its leaders function, would be like asking Machiavelli to write *The Prince* while ignoring Cesare Borgia.

A starting place for studying the community college presidency is a closer examination of the individuals who occupy the position. Who are today's presidents? Where did they come from and where are they going? With whom do they socialize? What is their relationship with that middle-class American phenomenon, the service club? What do they do for recreation? Do they go on vacations? And, if so, do they take work along? Did they come from blue-collar homes? If so, did this fact influence their ascent? Do they send their children to public institutions of higher education? To community colleges? Or do their children go to private colleges, an indication of what some would call social climbing? These questions were some of those explored in the Career and Lifestyle Survey (CLS) discussed in the Preface. Answers to these and other questions provide an intimate profile of the community college president.

Family Background

In seeking to understand the community college presidency one might well begin with the presidents' backgrounds. Major indicators of a family's socioeconomic status are the educational level and occupation of the father, assuming the father is the head of household (Karabel, 1972; Jencks, 1972, pp. 73–80; London, 1978, pp. 1–28).

In the case of today's community college presidents, over 51 percent of their fathers did not finish high school; almost 29 percent finished high school but have no formal education beyond that level. In other words, 80 percent of the fathers of the current community college presidents never attended college. Slightly less than 2 percent have an associate degree; slightly less than 8 percent have a bachelor's degree, and less than 8 percent have either a master's or doctor's degree. A very small percentage received other degrees and awards such as a law degree or that of a certified public accountant (CLS). Based on the educational level of the father, one can conclude that the great majority of today's presidents grew up in working-class homes. But the father's education is only one indicator of the family background of today's presidents.

The educational level of the mothers is also revealing. Almost 40 percent of the mothers have less than a high school education; another 38 percent finished high school; almost 6 percent received an associate degree, 10 percent a bachelor's, and slightly over 3 percent received master's or doctor's degrees. As with the fathers, a small percentage received other degrees and awards

(CLS). The mother's educational level, then, is similar to the father's and does nothing to change the image of the blue-collar background of the majority of today's presidents.

PARENTS' OCCUPATIONS

The occupations of the fathers of the current presidents are also revealing. The largest single occupational category was in the field of administration and management. Almost 18 percent of the presidents listed their father's occupation in this category. It included a number of positions such as foreman, textile manager, accountant, standards engineer, construction superintendent, general contractor, banker, and a number of other positions which, according to the father's educational level, required a high school diploma or less. More than 14 percent of the presidents listed their father's occupation as in agriculture; almost 8 percent were salesmen; over 8 percent were in construction; more than 9 percent were in manufacturing production; and almost 6 percent were in service occupations. Approximately 13 percent indicated that their fathers held jobs in such fields as teaching, law, and the sciences, which normally require a bachelor's degree or above. The remainder worked in any number of occupations, few of which normally require more than a high school education (CLS). The father's occupation would also support the thesis that most of the current community college presidents came from blue-collar homes.

The occupation of the presidents' mothers also sheds light on the background of today's presidents. Almost 60 percent of the mothers were homemakers, according to the presidents. The next largest categories were educators (less than 10% of the mothers fell into that category) and administrative support, which includes secretaries (slightly over 9%). Three percent of the mothers were in health-related fields, including nursing (CLS). As with the fathers, the mothers' occupations indicate that most presidents grew up in blue-collar homes.

What does it mean that less than 50 percent of the presidents' fathers finished high school, and that the majority of the president's fathers and mothers were in positions that are traditionally

associated with the working class? How, if at all, do these facts
and figures influence the presidency?

Significance of Family Background

One thing that can be concluded from the foregoing information
is that today's presidents are high achievers. There are data to
further illustrate this point. A 1971 study of public school
teachers found that the fathers of teachers came from the following backgrounds: 19.3 percent farming; 8.4 percent skilled;
25.7 percent skilled-semiskilled; 5.5 percent sales; 22.1 percent
managerial and self-employed; and, 18.9 percent professional or
semiprofessional (Chesler and Cave, 1981, p. 161). Another
study concluded, "Anyone studying teaching during the sixties
was bound to encounter men whose fathers were on the fringes of
the economy during the Great Depression of the thirties" (Lortie, 1975, p. 36). The fathers of today's community college presidents fall within the boundaries described in the two studies.
Therefore, while it is not unusual for first-generation college
graduates to go into education, it is not common for them to
"leapfrog" to the top of their profession, as did the community
college presidents. Moreover, as will be seen later, many did so at
a relatively young age. One can conclude that most of today's
presidents were somehow able to extricate themselves from the
great mass of people associated with the community college,
including those who were interested in assuming positions of
leadership, and acquire the top leadership posts themselves. In
addition, these presidents could be viewed as the leading edge of
a new generation freed from the Depression and World War II
and catapulted to high office by rapid social, economic, and political events.

A study of their family background may also help to explain
the missionary zeal exhibited by many community college presidents. Anyone who has ever attended the annual meeting of the
American Association of Community and Junior Colleges
(AACJC), or practically any other gathering of community college leaders, must surely be either impressed, stunned, or turned
off by the shear force and magnitude of the rhetoric emanating

from the speakers. Speakers refer to the community college movement (the use of the word "movement" itself has an evangelical ring to it) as a "holy crusade," "America's unique contribution to higher education," "America's hope for the future," and "the most dynamic segment of all of education." Of course, there is the ever-present phrase "the people's college," a term widely used to describe the land-grant institutions during the 19th and early 20th centuries but which has become synonymous with today's community college in the minds of many of its leaders. For example, anyone who attended the closing session of the 1981 session of the AACJC annual meeting must surely have been impressed with Bill Priest's introduction of Edmund Gleazer, retiring president of the AACJC and the speaker for the evening. Priest, former Chancellor of the Dallas Community College District and longtime community college leader and mentor to leaders, provided a description of Gleazer which left no doubt as to how Gleazer viewed "the movement." He described Gleazer as "a super evangelist preaching the community and junior college cause" who "preached a community-base" and "inspired us all." Priest further described Gleazer as having a "magnificent vision" and noted that "he hurled himself into the fray with evangelical fervor." Gleazer himself resorted to evangelical metaphor in his speech that evening. He used as his text the biblical question "Can anything good come out of the town of Nazareth?" Gleazer pointed out that, just as much good has come out of the movement that had its humble beginning in Nazareth, so, too, has great benefit come out of the humble beginning that resulted in today's community college.

Community college presidents, many of whom were either deans or presidents during the 1960s and 1970s, entered the profession at the height of the "movement." The presidents, many of whom had scaled the professional ladder to heights beyond which might have been expected or likely, considering their family backgrounds, were prime candidates to be swept away by the "evangelical fervor" described so eloquently by Priest. These presidents tied their future inexorably to that of the community college, realizing that the president must play a key role in its success.

The backgrounds of the current presidents might also help to explain the defensiveness of community college leaders when criticized (Cohen and Brawer, 1982, pp. 342–365; Johnston, 1980, pp. 43–45; Astin, 1983, p. 122; Vaughan, 1979, p. 11). Since the majority of the presidents did not grow up in a home with college-educated parents, it is unlikely that they were accustomed to the "point and counterpoint" type of discussions that one expects to occur routinely in homes where the parents have college degrees. While the presidents' own educational background would be expected to take them into the realm of conflicting ideas, it is likely that the home background would continue to influence their thinking, especially when many presidents probably see the community college as the institution *they* would have attended had one been available when they were growing up; indeed a large number of today's community college students come from backgrounds similar to those of the presidents (Cohen and Brawer, 1982, p. 40; Karabel, 1972; London, 1978, pp. 2–8). The combination of heading one's "own college" and viewing that college as serving one's "own kind of people" would seem to create a defensive stance among many presidents and would explain in part the unwillingness of many community college leaders to examine their institutions critically. On the one hand, community college presidents could be said to resemble lawyers, doctors, and most other people in that they do not take readily to criticism of their profession. On the other hand, some presidents view the reluctance to subject the community college to critical analysis as a major failure of its leadership.

Finally, the family background of today's presidents might help to explain their ready acceptance of the community college's comprehensive mission and especially their willingness to embrace occupational-technical programs as a major part of that mission. Leonard V. Koos, an early junior college leader and mentor to future leaders, felt that preparation for the occupations (or "semiprofessions," as he called them) was a major purpose of the junior college as early as 1925 (Koos, pp. 20–21); the American Association of Junior Colleges endorsed occupational-technical training as an important part of the junior college mission as early as 1941 (Vaughan, 1984). It was not until the 1960s, however, that these programs achieved hegemony in the community college (Cohen and Brawer, 1982, pp. 191–222). Obviously, there were many factors that contributed to the rise of occupational-technical education in the community college. The point to be made here is that community college presidents not only accepted these programs but embraced them as a part of their overall goal and promoted them with the same fervor they devoted to the rest of the mission, a situation that might not have been the case had more of their parents been college graduates who inculcated the future presidents in the liberal arts.

Mobility

It is interesting to note that almost half (45%) of the presidents are currently presidents of colleges in the state in which they finished high school (CLS). This information might be an indication that 45 percent of the presidents have remained provincial in terms of their environment. On the other side of the coin, one can say that over half (55%) were willing to leave their home state and take a less provincial outlook. This two-sided coin provides little information other than that which is speculative. Does it serve the community college well that almost half of the presidents "stay close to home?" Many community colleges have a regional if not local person at their head, a situation that may be viewed as highly desirable considering the commitment of community colleges to serve the region in which they are located. But it is conceivable that appointing presidents who grew up in the area or in the region might be an undesirable practice. This is especially true in rural areas where the community college is the only avenue to higher education for much of the population and is one of the very few entities in rural America charged with, in theory at least, challenging the status quo. My own six-year term as president of a rural college showed me that the status quo often translates as people bound by the myths and prejudices of the past. As one president expressed it, "Home-grown presidents are more likely to be subjected to local political pressures, more likely to appoint local faculty members, and are more likely to perpetuate the lies of the past." As with so much else about the community college presidency, a great deal depends upon the individual president. Thus, while it is interesting to note that almost half of the community college presidents work in their native state, going beyond a conjecture of the impact of this situation would be counterproductive.

A more useful statistic in understanding the presidency is whether current presidents are willing to leave their current position and, if so, why. Table 2.1 summarizes the responses regarding presidents' willingness to move.

Are the presidents who are in the state in which they finished high school as likely to move as those who are in states other than the one in which they finished high school? Of the presidents responding to the question regarding moving, over 58 percent who are in a state other than the one in which they finished high school are very likely or likely to move within the next five years; in contrast, 41 percent of those who are presidents in the state where they finished high school are very likely or somewhat likely to move. In other words, almost 60 percent of those presidents who are working in the state where they finished high school are content to stay where they are (CLS). It would seem, then, that serving as president in one's home state is appealing to many presidents. It might be that having a president from the area or region in which the college is located does indeed contribute to the provincialism of some community colleges, a shortcoming of the community college, according to some critics.

TABLE 2.1 Presidents' Willingness to Leave Their Current Positions in Relation to the Number of Years in Present Position

| | LIKELIHOOD OF MOVING FROM PRESENT POSITION | | | | | |
| | VERY LIKELY | | SOMEWHAT LIKELY | | NOT LIKELY | |
YEARS IN POSITION	n	%	n	%	n	%
0 to 5	75	25	109	37	113	38
6 to 10	29	24	36	29	58	47
11 to 15	10	11	20	22	60	67
16 to 20	8	19	6	14	29	67
More than 20	0	0	0	0	12	100

What else do the above statistics tell us about the presidency? For one thing, the longer a person is in a position, the less likely he or she is to move to a new one. Those presidents who have been in their position from one to ten years are very likely or somewhat likely to move within the next five years. The percentage of presidents who are very likely to move is about the same for those who have been in the presidency from six to ten years (23.6%) and for those who have been in it from one to five years (25.3%). The somewhat-likely- and not-likely-to-move figures might be more revealing; less than 30 percent of those presidents in the six-to-ten-year category are somewhat likely to move; over 47 percent are unlikely to move. Almost 38 percent of those in the one-to-five-year category are somewhat likely to move and only 38 percent are unlikely to move within the next five years. In summary, 62 percent of the presidents who have been in their current position for five years or less are somewhat likely to move within the next five years.

Based on my own experience with the presidency, and based on the large percentage of presidents with five or fewer years of experience in their current position who are likely to move within the next five years, the following conclusion seems valid: *many individuals are willing to assume a presidency with which they are less than satisfied in order to break into the ranks of the presidency. The majority of these presidents are looking for, or at least dreaming of, another position from almost the beginning of their current presidency.* The longer one stays in the position, the less likely it is that he or she will initiate a move.

The size of the college seems to be a factor in a president's decision to move, although it does not appear to be as important as one might assume. Table 2.2 illustrates the relationship between the size of a college and the president's willingness to move.

The desire of the presidents of smaller colleges to move is based on motives other than just the size of the college, although college size tends to coincide with what the presidents see as reasons for moving. Some of the expressed motives for moving other than size of college per se are: a search for greater challenges (although some presidents of small colleges will debate

TABLE 2.2 President's Willingness To Leave Their
Current Positions in Relation to the Size of the Institution

| | LIKELIHOOD OF MOVING FROM PRESENT POSITION | | | | | |
| | VERY LIKELY | | SOMEWHAT LIKELY | | NOT LIKELY | |
FTES° ENROLLMENT	*n*	%	*n*	%	*n*	%
Fewer than 1,000	29	24	39	33	51	43
1,001 to 3,000	57	23	74	29	120	48
3,001 to 5,000	10	13	28	36	39	51
5,001 to 7,500	16	32	8	16	26	52
7,501 to 10,000	4	20	4	20	12	60
10,001 to 15,000	3	12	9	38	12	50
15,001 to 20,000	1	12	4	50	3	38
More than 20,000	1	17	1	17	4	66

° Full-time equivalent students.

whether the challenges are greater in a small or large college); boredom with the smallness of the college; the pressures resulting from knowing everyone personally and seeing them almost daily; higher salaries at larger institutions; and the cultural and educational opportunities available in urban and suburban areas that are not normally available in rural areas.

Those presidents who indicated that they were very likely to move within the next five years were asked to give their reasons for wanting to move. While the answers ran the gamut (go into private business, move to a warmer climate, been here long enough, spend more time with the family, fed up with public education, seek a four-year presidency, return to teaching, frustrated, fed up with the board), the overwhelming response was the desire to move to a larger community college, usually in an urban area. With very few exceptions, those who wanted to move to a larger college had been in their current position for fewer than ten years; a large percentage had been in their present office for five years or less; 17 had been in their current job for two years or less (CLS). These data further document the conclusion that many presidents who assume a presidency keep their mental bags packed and are "already looking upon arrival."

Educational Level of the Presidents

As might be expected, the great majority of today's community college presidents (over 75%, or 443 of the 591 responding to the CLS survey) have doctoral degrees: almost 44 percent of them have the Ed.D.; almost 32 percent have a Ph.D. in various fields, including education. Perhaps the surprising figure is that 24 percent of the presidents do not have doctorates. Indeed, slightly over 17 percent have master's degrees; in other words, 101 of those responding to the survey have a master's degree as their highest degree. Three presidents have only bachelor's degrees. The remainder have educational specialist degrees, law degrees, and various other degrees and awards (CLS).

Knowing what percentage of the presidents hold what degree is helpful in understanding the presidency. For example, a degree in education does not characteristically carry as much weight or as much prestige on many campuses as does a Ph.D. in an academic discipline. In contrast to the typical community college president who has a doctorate in education, one study of four-year presidents found that of those presidents involved in the study, 80 percent had Ph.D.s in an academic discipline, a prerequisite to being accepted by the faculty in the colleges studied (Benezet, Katz, and Magnusson, 1981, p. 23). In contrast, 77 percent of the community college presidents with doctorates have their highest degree in education, and although almost 32 percent of them have Ph.D.s, a large number of the Ph.D.s are in education rather than in an academic discipline (CLS).

Certainly there is nothing wrong — and much right with — college presidents getting their degree in education, especially from programs in higher education that emphasize management, finance, and human relations. However, as noted above, degrees in education do not have the weight in academic circles that degrees in academic disciplines carry. This is in spite of the fact that, as one source notes, since World War II the academic study of higher education has developed as an applied field of study and is becoming increasingly important for the preparation of middle-level administrators. The same source, however, is careful to point out that most four-year college and university presidents have neither studied higher education nor administration, nor do they have degrees in higher education (Kauffman, 1980, p. 39).

The President at Home

Ninety-two percent of the 591 presidents responding to the question on marital status reported that they are married. Almost 2 percent are single, 4 percent are separated, less than 1 percent are divorced, and almost 1.5 percent are widowed (CLS). The percentage of married presidents is high when compared to the total adult population. On the other hand, no presidents fall into the young adult category, a category that has the largest percentage of unmarried adults. (Almost nothing is known about the role of the spouse of the community college president. In order to fill this gap regarding the presidency, a later chapter is devoted to interpreting the role of the spouse. For now, the discussion will center around the president and other family members, with only occasional references to the spouse.)

The president's family often extends beyond the president and the spouse. Sixty-five percent of the presidents have children under the age of 18 living at home; 72 percent have children over the age of 18. Forty percent of those presidents with children under the age of 18 expect at least one child to attend a community college, and 40 percent expect at least one child to attend a public four-year institution; of those with children over the age of 18, 57 percent had at least one child graduate from a community college, and 72 percent had at least one child graduate from a public four-year institution. Of those with children over age 18, 9.4 percent had at least one child graduate from a private college or university; of those with children under the age of 18, 11 percent expect at least one child to attend a private institution of higher education. Thirty-four percent of those with children under the age of 18 are unsure of their children's plans regarding higher education (CLS).

The Education of Offspring

If having one's children attend a public institution indicates support, community college presidents are strong supporters of public higher education. Furthermore, the small number of presidents' children attending private institutions indicates that most presidents are not on a social track that leads to their children attending a private college or university. However, which college the child of a community college president attends can present some problems for the president, spouse, and children, that most families do not have to face. For example, if the child chooses to attend the flagship state university or a private institution instead of the community college, the president is often accused of advocating the community college for everyone's child except his or her own. The situation is similar to the reason vocational education has often had a hard time selling itself: "Vocational education is great — for someone else's child." Presidents face the same criticism.

There are, however, legitimate reasons why the children of presidents do not attend the community college, few of which have anything to do with the type of education the child would expect to receive at the community college. The most obvious reason is the same one that so many young people give for wanting to go away to college: simply getting away from home. The interviews revealed a number of other explanations of why the offspring of presidents do not want to attend the community college. One prominent factor is that the children do not want to attend the community college where one of their parents is president. Another reason given by a college president in the South was that his father and his grandfather had attended a particular college and it was just assumed that if he had a son he too would attend that college (the same applied to his daughter, for it was assumed that she would attend the same college that her mother had attended). One president noted that he had encouraged his son to work hard in school in order that he could get into his state's most prestigious university; consequently, when the time came to choose a college (the son had applied himself and got high marks), the father could not then say "Hey, sure you worked hard and have good grades, but I want you to go to the community college." Perhaps the most important reason for children of presidents not attending the community college is that the children are taught that by age 18 they ought to be able to think for themselves, which includes having a major say in where they attend college. That decision may or may not be to attend the community college. However, the fact remains that for whatever reasons the children of community college presidents decide not to attend the community college, the president is likely to feel some pressure, especially from his or her colleagues whose children have attended or plan to attend the community college.

Time Away from the Family

Most people concede that college presidents are busy people. An indication of just how busy is revealed in the Career and Lifestyle Survey. Fifty-six percent of the presidents indicated that they work over 50 hours a week, including time spent on professional entertaining. On the other hand, over 73 percent of the presidents spend fewer than 10 hours a week doing various types of community services, which is perhaps less than perceived to be the case by the faculty and segments of the public.

Presidents do not feel that they are able to spend enough time with their families. Indeed, a common complaint among presidents and spouses is the lack of time presidents devote to their families, especially if they have children at home. (Many presidents interviewed stated that if they had it to do over again, they would spend more time with their families.) The Career and Lifestyle Survey reveals that 65 percent of the presidents have fewer than 20 hours a week with their families and 25 percent fewer than 10 hours, excluding the time spent sleeping. Thirty-six percent indicated that they pass fewer than 10 hours alone with their spouse, other than time spent sleeping; almost 70 percent spend under 20 hours a week alone with their spouses, excluding sleeping time.

Social Activities

Social activities and acquaintances are important to both presidents and spouses of presidents. Table 2.3 provides a summary of the social contacts of the presidents and their spouses. Certainly the social groups listed in Table 2.3 are not mutually exclusive; one assumes both presidents and spouses see any number of

TABLE 2.3 Distribution of Social Contacts of Presidents and Spouses

TYPE OF ACQUAINTANCE	PRESIDENT		SPOUSE	
	n	%	*n*	%
Childhood Friends	31	5	41	8
Colleagues	421	73	222	42
Neighbors	286	49	328	62
Club Friends	277	48	200	38
Church Friends	286	49	285	54
Other Friends	219	38	232	44

Note: The number of responses exceeds the number of cases since the categories are not mutually exclusive. The percentages shown are of the number of cases. For example, 31 (5%) of the presidents who responded reported social contact with childhood friends. These same presidents also reported social contacts with at least some of the other categories of friends.

combinations of the above, as well as literally hundreds of other members of society.

While the above observations do not make a definitive statement regarding with whom the presidents and spouses spend their time, patterns are nevertheless clear enough to give a fairly good picture of the president while "off duty." As is the case with most professions, the president's colleagues play an important role in the social life of the president and the spouse. An observation worth noting is the relatively small amount of time presidents spend with childhood friends, especially when one considers the number who are presidents in the state in which they finished high school. Is it possible that the high achievement level of the presidents places them at a distance from their friends of the blue-collar past?

The President "Off Duty"

While it is difficult for most community college presidents to divorce themselves from their position, most presidents do spend some time "playing," in spite of (or perhaps because of) their busy schedules. Approximately 32 percent of the presidents belong to a country club; however, club membership might not be all fun and games, for over 80 percent of those who belong to a country club use it for professional entertaining. Presidents engage in a number of sports, with golf topping the list (almost 39% indicated they play golf); the next most popular sport is fishing (34% of the presidents fish); next is jogging (31%). Twenty-five percent of the presidents swim and almost 25 percent play tennis. Nineteen percent ski and over 17 percent hunt. An interesting point is that, at the bottom of the list of sports categories, was the traditionally blue-collar sport of bowling, with slightly over 7 percent of the presidents indicating they bowl (CLS). Obviously, many presidents engage in more than one sport and, just as obviously, the above categories do not cover all of the sports they play. There appears to be nothing about the presidents' physical activities that would indicate they engage in any sports that would not be expected of people in similar positions. As will be discussed later, many presidents see physical activity as one important means of combating stress.

One important form of community contact for many presidents, and in a sense community service, is membership in a service club. In many cases service club membership "comes with the job"; that is, in many areas, especially rural ones, it is assumed that the president will join a local service club. Service clubs form a point of contact with the business and professional communities and provide an important source of social contact for presidents and their spouses.

The Career and Lifestyle Survey revealed that 86 percent of the presidents belong to one or more service clubs. By far the most popular service club is the Rotary: almost 65 percent of the presidents indicated that they belong to Rotary International. A distant second is the Kiwanis, with slightly over 14% holding membership; next came the Lions Club with slightly over 6 percent of the presidents belonging; slightly over 1 percent of the presidents are members of the Ruritan Club. Only 1.6 percent belong to the Jaycees, which is not surprising since most current presidents have passed the eligibility age for membership. Some 31 percent of the presidents are in service-type organizations not listed above. Only 24 percent of the presidents belong to more than one service organization. While considered a fraternal organization rather than a service club, the Masons have over 11 percent of the presidents as members.

Although no attempt was made to distinguish between male and female presidents, organizational membership requires that a distinction be made. Many males still belong to "males-only" service clubs, the top-ranked Rotary being a prime example. Forty-six female presidents were asked to list the predominately female organizations to which they belong. Nineteen (41%) of the females responded. The most popular organization to which female presidents belong is the Delta Kappa Gamma, comprising 42 percent of those responding; next was the American Association of University Women with 36 percent; 26 percent belong to the Business Women and Professional Club; 21 percent to the National Organization for Women; and 21 percent to the American Association of Women in Junior and Community Colleges, an affiliate council of the AACJC. A number of other organizations were listed; those female presidents responding belong to more than one organization. Of note is the fact that the organizations listed by female presidents are more cause-oriented than contact-oriented, the latter being the case with many male-dominated organizations.

In addition to service club membership, serving on the board of directors of the local Chamber of Commerce is an important civic activity for presidents, both male and female. While statistics are not available on how many presidents currently serve on Chamber boards (most Chamber boards rotate their membership on a regular three-year basis), the interviews, personal contacts, and observations reveal that membership on the local Chamber board is important to the college president and that the president often takes an active role in Chamber affairs, including serving as president. Most Chambers play a key role in industrial development; the community college often joins the Chamber's efforts in attracting industry. Since business and industrial development is important to the employment of community college graduates, and since job training and retraining is an important role for many community colleges, the Chamber – president relationship is one manifestation of the larger community college – business and industry partnership.

Understanding the background of community college presidents should help one to understand their leadership role and, therefore, the community college itself. The outstanding political scientist and historian, James MacGregor Burns, suggests that "if we know all too much about our leaders, we know far too little about *leadership*" (Burns, 1978, p. 1). The contention here is that as yet we know almost nothing about our most important community college leaders and, that in order to understand the role of the president, we need to know more about the people who fill the presidency. It is hoped that this chapter is a step in that direction.

CHAPTER 3

———————◆———————

Attaining the Presidency

The previous chapter presented a number of facts, figures, and observations which give a profile of the personal side of the community college president. It is a profile that no president is likely to fit in its entirety, but one that most presidents will not only recognize as being valid, but one to which most can relate. The present chapter moves from the more personal side of the presidency to the professional side; or, simply put, this chapter takes the president from the relatively safe environment of the home to the more dynamic and sometimes risky environment of the president's office.

Avenues to the Presidency

The Career and Lifestyle Survey confirmed what most people familiar with the community college have suspected all along: the surest way to the presidency is through the academic pipeline. The survey asked the presidents to list their position prior to assuming their first presidency. Of the 590 presidents who answered the question, 226, or slightly over 38 percent, had served as chief academic officer in a college prior to assuming the presidency. In addition, 72, or 12.2 percent, moved into the presidency from a position of vice president; while the vice presidents did not list their previous areas of responsibility, many function as the college's chief academic officer. As one can see, then, over 50 percent of today's presidents were either deans of instruction (the title varies, but this title is most commonly used to describe the college's chief academic officer) or vice presidents prior to assuming their first presidency. Another 4.6 percent of the presidents were deans of community services (again, the title varies, i.e., dean of continuing education) prior to assuming their first presidency. While the dean of community services is rarely the chief academic officer, the person filling this position is nevertheless on the academic side of the fence. Thus additional strength is given to the argument for the academic route as "the road to the presidency."

Certainly the academic deanship or vice president paths are not the only avenues to the presidency. Slightly over 15 percent of the current presidents entered the presidency from a variety of positions, including assistant to the president, Title III coordinator, director of admissions and records, director of personnel, athletic director, division chair, faculty member, and acting president. And these are just some of the positions. Fewer than a dozen presidents came to the presidency from jobs outside of education, such as attorneys-at-law and corporate officers (CLS).

Regarding the more traditional tracks to the presidency, 7.8 percent of the presidents had been deans of student services (the title given to the chief student services officer varied) prior to assuming their first presidency (CLS). Several of the presidents interviewed felt that the student services route to the presidency gained importance during the "student revolts" of the 1960s and early 1970s.

Very close to the student services path to the first presidency was that of the public schools, with the superintendency as the dominant jumping-off point. Slightly over 7 percent of the current presidents came to their first presidency from the public schools (CLS). This avenue for the presidency has narrowed significantly over the years. A 1960 study reported that over 24 percent of the junior college presidents came from positions in public school administration. Of the colleges included in the

1960 study, one third were private junior colleges; however, none of the private college presidents in the study came from public schools; thus the data are comparable with the current information (Hawk, 1959–60, p. 345). A study conducted in the period 1970–71, limited to public junior college presidents, found that 13.8 percent of the presidents were supplied by the public schools (Wing, 1972, p. 4). These data suggest that public school administration is no longer a major path to the community college presidency. Part of the decline can be explained by the movement of the public community college into the camp of higher education and away from being identified as an extension of the public schools. Another reason is that qualified candidates are available within the ranks of community college personnel and, therefore, it is no longer necessary to turn to the public schools in order to obtain experienced administrators.

Following the public schools, the next most popular route to the presidency is via the chief business officer: almost 5 percent of the current presidents came to the presidency from that position (CLS). The belief persists among many of the people interviewed that governing boards turn to the business officer to fill the presidential vacancy during times of fiscal crisis. More will be said about this later.

Four-year colleges and universities furnished 4.4 percent of the current presidents. Those coming from four-year institutions occupied any number of positions, including dean, president, department chair, and faculty member, prior to assuming the community college presidency (CLS). Just as the percentage of presidents coming from public school administration has declined, so has the percentage coming from four-year colleges. The 1960 study reported that 15.2 percent came into the community college presidency from positions in four-year institutions (Hawk, 1959–60, p. 345); the 1970 study reported the percentage at 14 percent (Wing, 1972, p. 4.) The reason for the decline in the four-year school as a source is probably the same as one of the reasons given for the decline in the number of public school administrators: the community college now has experienced administrators and apparently sees no reason to turn to four-year colleges for its presidents.

A final avenue to the presidency, while relatively small, is worth looking at briefly. Approximately 1.7 percent of the presidents held state-level positions within the office or agency responsible for coordinating, and, in some cases, directing and controlling, community college activities at the state level. The positions at the state level carried titles such as chancellor, vice chancellor and director, among others (CLS). During the late 1960s and early 1970s, a time when faculty had little or no say in the selection of the president, working at the state level was seen by some community college professionals as an important route to the presidency. Considering the growth in the number of jobs at the state level and the small number of people moving to their first presidency from state-level positions, the avenue now seems relatively unimportant in the total scheme of things. Part of the reason for a lack of popularity of the state-level route might be that most state-level offices are primarily concerned with performing regulatory and control functions; consequently, those who work at the state level are "branded" with an image of wanting to control things. Although that image may not be deserved, it is nevertheless one that constitutes the kiss of death with most faculties and, therefore, the same vis-à-vis the presidency, for today few presidents are employed without faculty involvement, and, in some cases, faculty approval. On the other hand, it is quite possible that those who work at the state level are satisfied with their positions and are not seeking a presidency. Moreover, in those states with statewide systems of community colleges and a statewide governing board, the chancellor's position is often viewed as a more desirable position than is that of college president, especially if the presidents in the state "report to" the chancellor. Regardless of where the truth lies, the fact remains that working with the community college's state-level office is not an important path to the presidency.

To summarize, the percentage of today's community college presidents who assumed the presidency from a position within the community college ranks is approaching 90 percent. Only the relatively small number coming from the public schools (7%) and four-year institutions (4.7%) departed from the pattern to any degree and, based on the decline over the years in the number of presidents using these routes, it is highly likely that they will become even less important in the future. The 1.7 percent coming from state-level positions are likely to be viewed as coming from "within the ranks." A danger in the movement to select almost all presidents from within the community college ranks is one of "inbreeding." A trustee who served as President of the Association of Community College Trustees (ACCT), the community college's national organization for trustees, fears inbreeding so much that he suggests that community colleges turn again to the public school superintendency as a major source for leaders.

From within the institution, the clear path to the presidency is through academics, with the academic deanship by far the most popular route. The insignificant number of presidents who came from business, industry, the law, and other sources outside of education gives lie to the myth popular in some circles that community colleges have turned more and more to the "captains, or at least lieutenants, of industry" for their chief executive officers.

Behind the Statistics

While statistics tell an important part of the story regarding the track to the community college presidency, they do not tell the full story. Indeed, statistics tend to say more about the "how" than the "why." In an attempt to determine why individuals assume the presidency, those interviewed were so queried. While the routes were rarely clear-cut, three major paths emerged.

SERENDIPITY

Serendipity played an important role in the lives of a number of presidents who assumed the presidency during the 1960s. As one president put it: "The escalator came by, I got on and rode it to the top." Riding the escalator to the top was more dominant among those presidents who assumed their position during the 1960s than among the newer presidents for two reasons: first, there were not enough experienced community college administrators around to meet the demand for presidents during the

1960s; and, second, leadership programs for training future community college presidents were just beginning to get underway. For example, the first grants to establish Junior College Leadership Programs were funded by the W. K. Kellogg Foundation in 1960 (see "Planning").

One president's experience, while perhaps not typical, serves to demonstrate how quickly things were moving for the community college in the 1960s. He notes: "I was trained at Harvard to be a big city school superintendent. I moved to a superintendency of 6,000 students. Just before the first meeting with the board broke up, the chairman said, 'Oh, by the way, we are starting a community college next year and you will be in charge of it too.'" Another was a public school administrator who assumed the presidency believing that the college was to be a part of a "K–14 system" but found that it was a part of the state's system of higher education and therefore under the governance of the board of regents. Along the same line, and also illustrative of the developments taking place in the 1960s, was the president who wanted to get into public school administration. He took a position as the head of an industrial education center which later became a technical school, and which is now a comprehensive community college.

Another movement in the 1960s that tended to play a serendipitous role for some of today's presidents was the transformation of two-year branches of four-year institutions into comprehensive community colleges. One person who served as president of three community colleges and is now working in a state office for community colleges "backed into" the presidency through the door of a branch college. "Actually, I had no idea of becoming a community college president. I was asked to head a branch campus and thought it would be a dandy place to get some administrative experience and then maybe I could go back to the main campus as an associate dean. After two years, the branch became a comprehensive community college with no connection with its former university." Serving as a branch college director, dean, or whatever title was used, would appear to have been a good training ground for community college presidents, since the majority of the students were local and commuted to college. The branch colleges, however, were not normally comprehensive institutions. Similarly, they should not be confused with the many public junior colleges in the 1960s that broadened their mission and changed their names to include "community."

Another president noted that he got into the presidency because of luck, not design. Another suggests that he was "in the right place at the right time." He was in graduate school when the Kellogg money came along. "The Kellogg fellowship for training future community college leaders paid a little more than my assistantship and I switched from public school administration to community college administration." Although the Kellogg support just "came along" for this president, the Kellogg-funded community college leadership programs played a significant role in making it feasible to plan for the presidency and therefore would not normally fall under the "serendipitous" umbrella.

PLANNING

A second pattern that emerged as a route to the presidency was the planned approach. A number of presidents planned their careers in a way that would ultimately lead them to the presidency. This approach assumes that there is an identifiable track to the office of president, both in terms of experience and academic preparation. As discussed previously, this assumption is correct to a large degree. The validity of the planned approach is further documented by the small number of presidents entering the presidency from outside the community college field. Moreover, today more people have experience as community college administrators and more people are academically prepared for the presidency than was the case when community colleges were opening weekly; therefore, planning for the presidency is probably essential for most people today, especially since the opportunities to "back into the presidency" are not as available as in the past.

One president who had been in his position for less than two years when interviewed exemplifies the planned approach to the presidency. He confided: "You have to understand that ever since I got out of my master's program and took my first job, it was with the goal of some day being a community college president. If

I could be anything I wanted to be I would be a community college president." Another president "had a mentor in Illinois who provided me with a role model. I liked what I saw him doing. The presidency offered me an opportunity to work not with just student services, not with just finance, and not with just instruction. I could work with the entire college; that umbrella was very appealing to me so I worked to get a presidency." Another president also noted that he became a president because he planned it that way. He was one of the first Kellogg fellows at Florida State University and was told upon entering the program that its purpose was to prepare graduates to be community college deans and presidents. This person's first position upon leaving graduate school was that of academic dean.

A major factor in permitting individuals to prepare for the community college presidency in the 1960s and early 1970s was the funding of the Junior College Leadership Programs by the W. K. Kellogg Foundation. On March 4, 1960, the Kellogg Foundation announced that it would support a number of university centers devoted to the training of two-year college administrators. By the time the program ended in 1974, 485 persons had been fellows in the program (Perkins, 1980). The Kellogg grants made it possible to receive the doctorate in higher education with an emphasis upon community college administration at ten (later expanded to 12) major universities. Among the universities receiving the initial Kellogg grants were Florida State University, the University of Florida, the University of Michigan, Michigan State University, Teachers College of Columbia University, the University of Texas, the University of California at Berkley, the University of California at Los Angeles, and Stanford University. The majority of the original Kellogg-funded centers still serve as major avenues for those persons wanting to enter an academic program for the purpose of preparing to be community college administrators. A 1970 study found that 49 percent of those presidents surveyed "had probably" participated in an activity funded by the Kellogg Foundation (Wing, 1972, p. 16). The current Leadership Survey revealed that 16 percent (10 out of 63) of the current presidents among those identified as leaders by their peers were Kellogg fellows, a significant number considering that the Kellogg leadership program ended over ten years ago.

DISSATISFACTION AND OPPORTUNITY

A third pattern, and one that tends to combine the other two, might be called the dissatisfied or opportunistic approach. This approach applies to those presidents who were dissatisfied with the public schools or the universities and saw the community college as a new and refreshing approach to solving educational problems. The dissatisfied or opportunistic approach also includes those who were unhappy with the leadership on their own campus and who felt that they could fill the role of president more adequately than could others. As shown by their comments, those who entered the presidency because of dissatisfaction appear to be more aggressive in their pursuit of the presidency than those who entered it through either the "escalator approach" or through the planned approach. They also saw the community college as providing a place for fulfilling dreams, their own as well as those of students. This category offers some candid insights and rarely discussed motives which drive some people to seek the presidency.

One president sums up her attitude as follows: "As a community college faculty member, I found that people got in my way when I wanted to do something. I don't like for people to get in my way, so I decided to join them because I couldn't lick them. Once I decided to join them, I found other people in bigger and better administrative positions in my way, so I became a president." Another who was unhappy with the way things were being administered on his campus felt that he could do a better job. Acting upon his dissatisfaction, he went back to graduate school at age 44 in order to prepare for the presidency. He then found a person who he felt could help his career and went to work for him before moving into the presidency.

Two others left public school superintendencies because they believed in the community college's mission and saw it as an opportunity to assume a leadership role. Another person worked as a program officer for a major foundation for 15 years and in a government position for two years prior to assuming the presidency. He saw the community college presidency as offering flexibility as well as an opportunity to integrate technical programs with the liberal arts.

One president was disillusioned with both elementary education and university education. After being inspired by a community college leader whom he respected and with whom he had worked, he cast his lot with the community college. Another president said he started thinking about how to get the middle group of high school students into the educational mainstream 30 years ago when he was a high school principal. He framed his concept of the community college before he even knew what a community college was; he, too, saw in the community college opportunities that were not available in secondary education.

One leader feels he owes the community college a great deal because "it picked me up when I had very little direction, very little guidance, and I was grateful to those who had helped me. When I got the chance to work in the community college, I thought I had achieved the ultimate accomplishment of my life." Another simply saw the presidency as providing the opportunity to do some things he wanted to try. The president of one of the nation's largest community colleges saw the growth occurring in the community colleges and believed that he could advance quickly if he entered the field.

Obviously, many people enter the presidency in a rather routine way. One who was dean for five years found her college with a vacancy at the president's level. The previous president had deliberately taught her about the presidency and taught her well, she surmises. When the vacancy occurred, she was at a point of having to go after the presidency or face the reality of seeing a new person come in and perhaps change much of what she had worked to achieve. In a sense she combined the three approaches: she was in the right place at the right time; she had a Ph.D. in higher education from a Kellogg program; and she seized upon the opportunity to become president when a vacancy occurred.

The Selection Process

One should not take this discussion to mean that obtaining a community college presidency is routine or automatic. The truth of the matter is that obtaining the presidency is a rather complex affair, and the number of minimally qualified applicants for any one presidential vacancy often numbers well over 100.

Sunshine laws apply to community college presidential vacancies just as they do to four-year presidencies; therefore, some potential applicants bypass those states with strong sunshine laws. In an attempt to get a better understanding of how candidates view these laws, a telephone interview was conducted with a "final-three" candidate who had just withdrawn from consideration for a position in a state "where everything is wide open and the newspapers are in on everything," according to the candidate. When asked if he would go through the application process again he replied: "It would probably affect me. I think that there are states that are more enlightened than this one. There is no question that sunshine laws keep a number of good applicants from applying unless they want everything about them and their life public knowledge immediately."

Many search processes tend to eliminate those individuals with strong opinions, for these individuals are likely to offend either the faculty, board, or some other group. Candidates are ruled out for showing the poor judgment of wearing boots to the interview; because they are internal candidates; because they are not familiar with the college and the people it serves; and the list goes on.

One example may serve to illustrate the complexities of pursuing the presidency. A candidate was being interviewed for a presidency in a Rocky Mountain state. While he and the board chairman were having dinner, the candidate ordered a Coors beer. The board chairman became verbally hostile; it seems that he was a strong union advocate and did not take kindly to "his" potential president ordering a beer brewed by the antiunion Coors brewery. While the candidate ultimately got the presidency, he got a lecture from the board chairman; he also got a Budweiser beer. The points are that a lot more people are seeking the presidency than get it, and it does not take a major faux pas on the part of the candidate to be eliminated from consideration for the position.

The avenues through which the individuals entered the presidency were not related to the size of college. The distinguishing factor is that those presidents who had been in their position for the shortest period of time had, almost without exceptions, made definite plans to enter the presidency. In other words, the planned approach is the most common avenue today. Plans include getting the appropriate administrative and academic experiences. On the other hand, many long-time presidents either "backed into the position" or saw the opportunities available in the position and went after it, often without prior community college administrative experience or without benefit of an academic program which specialized in preparing them for the presidency.

Comments on Avenues to the Presidency

Why do so many community college presidents come from within the community college ranks? Do board members prefer that future presidents be from the academic side of the fence? Whom do faculty members want as their president? Where do current presidents see their successors coming from and why? Has the avenue to the presidency changed over the years? Some brief comments follow.

One veteran trustee who has conducted and continues to conduct presidential searches for a number of colleges across the nation was philosophical in his observations on the avenue to the presidency: "When we created colleges at the rate of one a week, people came into the presidency from all sorts of levels and backgrounds. It was proved to me at that time that people can succeed from a lot of different backgrounds." The fact that so many of today's presidents came to the presidency from any number of positions would support his observation that people can succeed from a variety of backgrounds. The trustee has not lost the pragmatism that he had during the period of rapid growth, however, for he comments further, "Today, as we do presidential searches, it is inevitable that people with experience have a leg up in the process, especially if they have presidential experience."

The most telling part of the conversation with the trustee is about the avenue to the presidency and offers a clue as to why the academic route is the major avenue to the presidency. The trustee declared that he would have to look very hard at someone with a student services background if someone with a strong academic background were available. While he would consider a dean of business before one from students services, he indicated that his clear choice would be the academic dean.

Perhaps one reason for the low ranking of the student services position as a route to the presidency lies with the attitudes associated with the position. One dean of student services, when asked what he viewed as the chief path to the top office, replied: "I know what it is *not;* it is not through the dean of student services." While it would be a mistake to conclude too much from one dean's attitude, the comment may nevertheless be symbolic of how deans of student services and others view their job in relation to the presidency. For example, based upon personal observations and conversations with a number of presidents and deans, it would appear that, when the president needs a stand-in for an important engagement, it is usually the chief academic officer who is chosen. The signals given off by such acts are obviously picked up by the faculty, the board, and, more important, by the other deans. In much the same vein is the symbolism (many experts on power see it as much more than symbolism) associated with the tendency to locate the academic dean's office near the president's office and the dean of student services' office near the students. Along the same line, when asked who their chief confidant was on campus, of the various answers received, almost 25 percent (137 presidents) named the chief academic officer as their chief confidant, whereas only 2.7 percent (16 presidents) named the chief student services officer (CLS). The assumption is that the chief academic officer is turned to most often because in an academic institution most of the problems and opportunities exist in the academic area, an assumption with much basis in fact. Whatever the reason for the perception, the symbolism is the same: the president "huddles" most often with the chief academic officer, a fact that is apparent to the college community.

Faculty members tend to favor the academic officer as the successor to the president. As one faculty member notes, in order to become a president, a person must have a good reputation with the entire college community, including the board, and show evidence of educational leadership. While this faculty member would not exclude the chief business officer or chief student services officer, he feels that the chief academic officer has the edge, especially in establishing credibility with the faculty. Another faculty member, reverting to the stereotype too often associated with faculty, claims that she does not care where the president comes from as long as he or she is "pro-faculty," a stance the chief academic officer would normally take. Yet another notes that she would feel more comfortable with the academic dean becoming president than she would with either the chief student services officer or the chief business officer.

Some presidents see their role as mentor as an important part of their job. Even so, most presidents would not presume to groom their successor, at least not overtly. However, every president interviewed except one sees the academic route as the main road to the presidency; consequently, it appears likely that, if a president is asked to recommend someone for a presidency (either at the present college or at another institution), it will be an academic dean who is recommended.

The academic choice has much logic to it, some of which has already been mentioned. Presidents tend to see the academic officer as the person, other than the president, with a broad perspective on how the total college operates. At least one president offers the opinion that neither the dean of student services nor the dean of business has the broad perspectives needed to be successful as a president. Another president believes that those characteristics that make a person an outstanding dean of student services — such as a somewhat "laid back" attitude toward problems and a tendency to view student problems as "the only problems worth worrying about" — work against the chief student services officer getting the presidency, and against succeeding if he or she does indeed obtain the presidency. All presidents interviewed agreed that, regardless of what route a person follows to the presidency, financial knowledge and administrative experience are prerequisites to assuming the position.

Has the path to the presidency changed over the years? Some people believe that during certain periods of crisis or perceived crisis the board turns to persons with specific talents not normally associated with the academic area to fill the presidency. Several of those interviewed commented that the student services route was popular during the period of student unrest in the mid-1960s and early 1970s. However, an analysis of the current situation does not support the belief that current presidents who were chief student services officers prior to assuming the presidency were chosen during the period of student unrest. Today's presidents who were previously deans of student services have been in their current positions for an average of 7.5 years, with one president having been a president for 31 years; the median number of years in their current position is 6 (CLS). It does not appear that there was any great movement toward turning to the dean of student services as a major source of presidents, or, if the movement existed, no large number of those selected remain in the presidency. Since student unrest rarely approached the boiling point on most community college campuses in the 1960s and early 1970s, it is unlikely that there was ever any real or perceived need to "control" the students.

The "crisis" theory also centered around the chief business officer's position: the board turns to the chief business officer in times of financial instability, so goes the theory. Just when a financial crisis occurs is difficult to pin down and certainly varies from state to state and from campus to campus, but it is generally conceded that the "new depression" in higher education began in the late 1970s. Those presidents who were chief business officers prior to assuming the presidency have been in their current position for an average of slightly over seven years, with one president occupying the position for 33 years; the median number of years is five, thus giving credence to the claim that the business officers' position gained slightly in popularity as a route to the presidency about the time of the financial crisis in higher education (late 1970s and early 1980s) (CLS).

Some of those interviewed saw choosing the business officer to serve as president as an expedient measure that often does not work. One long-time observer whose business it is to see that presidents and boards work well together noted that, for the most part, recruiting financial experts for the presidency has not worked out in the long run. Most of them are not viewed as educational leaders and, consequently, in the final analysis do not have the credibility with the academic community that is required of the successful president. A veteran president noted that by turning to financial experts the board is looking for "short-term solutions to long-term problems," and it just does not work unless the finance person understands much more about the community college than its financial operation.

The track to the presidency has changed over the years but more in degree than in kind. A 1960 study points out that 42 percent of the public junior college presidents came from positions within the junior college ranks (Hawk, 1960, p. 345). A 1970 study reported that 59.4 percent of the presidents worked in the community college prior to assuming the presidency and that 22.5 percent of those came to the office from the academic dean's position (Wing, 1972, pp. 4–5). Today almost 90 percent of the presidents come from within the community college ranks and as many as 50 percent are likely to come through the academic ranks.

While the above comments might tend to discourage student services or financial deans from aspiring to the presidency, in every instance the observations on the presidency were qualified: many presidents and trustees noted that they knew outstanding presidents who had come to the presidency from positions of finance and student services, as well as a number of other positions. It should be somewhat encouraging to those academic, student, and business deans who want to be president that *no one* interviewed saw any important route to the presidency other than through one of the three deans' positions. Moreover, no one ruled out any avenue to the presidency as being invalid. All agreed that obtaining and retaining the presidency depends to a large extent on the qualifications, personality, drive, attitude, and other attributes of the individual — characteristics that help a person to succeed in any position of leadership.

Being There

How do community college presidents view their role once they assume the presidency? Are they happy in the position? Is the position what they thought it would be? How is the president viewed by faculty members, trustees, and others? The following observations on the office of the president give some indication of what one can expect.

No one can ever fully anticipate the responsibilities and limitations of the college presidency until he or she has been there. Assuming the presidency is further complicated by the fact that all colleges are different. As one source puts it, too much has been written and said about college and university presidencies which implies that there is "some singular, definable office called a presidency" (Carbone, 1981, p. 79). While it is recognized that presidencies vary from institution to institution, it is nevertheless important to the understanding of the community college presidency to deal with those elements that, although unique to the individual in the sense that the individual perspective is always unique, are nevertheless common to the presidency when viewed from a broad perspective.

Joseph F. Kauffman, an astute observer of the college and university presidency and former college president himself, was concerned enough about the differences between the image and the reality of the presidency to conduct a research project devoted to the subject of expectations and realities of the new college president. The general conclusion reached by Kauffman is that the new president is in for a number of surprises, many of which were not even hinted at during the search interviews, and some of which the governing board did not even know about. Time constraints were much greater than anticipated by most new presidents, as were the personal commitments to the position and the expectations of others (Kauffman, 1977; 1980). A study of the presidency, sponsored by the Association of Governing Boards (AGB) and directed by Clark Kerr, found that community colleges have gone further than much of the rest of higher education in spelling out what the new president can expect, including formal contracts and job descriptions. Nevertheless, the report points out that many misunderstandings exist in all of higher education regarding what is expected of the college and university president, including a misunderstanding of the role of the president's spouse (AGB, 1984, pp. 33–40).

Arthur Levine has written often and well about the issues facing American higher education. On July 1, 1982, he assumed the presidency of Bradford College. A presidential colleague wrote him a good-natured letter suggesting that it was now time for Levine "to put up or shut up." While Levine took the letter with the good humor intended, he points out that the letter "captures my most private, middle of the night doubts" (Levine, 1984, p. 11). Certainly Levine sums up the fears and doubts that many presidents must feel upon assuming the presidency. *And what is often not understood by the faculty, the students, the trustees, the public, and in some cases even the spouse of the president, is that fears and doubts exist, no matter what exterior countenance the president presents.*

Community college presidents are no different from any other college or university president when it comes time "to put up or shut up," although there is some evidence to suggest that the new community college president might not experience as much shock upon assuming the presidency as is experienced by the new president of a four-year institution. This is particularly true if the community college president has planned his or her career with the presidency in mind and if the four-year president has assumed the presidency from the professorial ranks as "a first among equals." Nevertheless, most community college presidents find that the role of president is different from anything they have experienced before.

The Chronicle of Higher Education published a brief article entitled "Guidelines for New College Presidents: Getting Started is No Simple Matter." One of the individuals interviewed for the article was a new community college president whose comment tends to summarize one of the dilemmas associated with assuming the presidency. He states: "Even though I've been in senior positions in higher education for many years, suddenly the perspective changes" (Heller, 1984, p. 15). One of the presidents interviewed noted that as dean he was *very* close to the president he succeeded. Nevertheless, during his first week on the job the former dean had to deal with three cases of sexual harrassment, an area he had absolutely no experience with; he had not even realized that the problems were brewing. Another community college president suggests that presidential candidates should decide if they do indeed want to be a president and, if so, why. They should ask themselves what they expect to get out of the position, and, perhaps most important, find out all they can about the position prior to accepting it (Sims, 1978–79, pp. 16–19).

One of the most incisive analyses offered to the new college president comes from Harold W. Stoke, former president of Queens College in New York City. Stoke tells the story of an old college president greeting a new one in the following manner: "Young man, you have changed your profession." Stoke goes on to comment, "No new president is ever quite prepared for the complete shock of this truth" (Stoke, 1959, p. 21). The following provides some insight into how community college presidents view their position.

The community college presidency, probably more so than any other presidency in higher education, is a profession unto itself. That is, as suggested earlier, individuals prepare for the presidency through academic programs and through assuming the right positions within the community college. Unlike many potential four-year presidents and especially university presidents who wait to be "called to the presidency" or *at least* to be nominated for the position, individuals apply for community college presidencies in large numbers. If they do not get the position they apply for, they then seek another one. It is not unusual for presidents to apply for as many as eight or more presidencies before obtaining one, nor is it unusual for deans and vice presidents to apply for just as many presidencies without obtaining one. Moreover, most individuals who assume the community college presidency do not change professions in the sense that Stoke's young man changed professions. Indeed, most community college administrators "changed professions" from teaching to administration when they assumed their first major administrative job, even if the position was that of academic division chair. This situation did not always exist, however, as was demonstrated by those presidents who assumed the presidency because of serendipity or opportunity.

Almost without exception and regardless of what route they had followed to the position, the presidents interviewed were basically satisfied with the position. Even those presidents who qualified their answers were generally positive about their role, including one who "dropped out" of the presidency at the height of his career. Faculty and board members also felt that the presidents of their institution were happy with the office, as did other administrators interviewed. It should be added that this perception of satisfaction existed even if the president was "actively looking" for another position. This situation does not necessarily represent a contradiction since the satisfaction is with the presidency itself and therefore is not limited to a given location.

When asked if they enjoyed the presidency, many of the presidents responded with phrases such as "I love the position," "Happy, very," "Yes, if not I'd get out," "Extremely so," and so on. There were some presidents who, while generally satisfied with the post, qualified their answers. One responded, "Reasonably so, depending upon the day." Another was more explicit: "I have been less happy over the past few years than earlier. But that is a combination of a little burnout, major personnel decisions on campus, and factors in my personal life. I am ready to move on to new challenges." One person who had left the presidency a few months before he was interviewed noted: "I was happy in the good years; I was unhappy during the traumatic times."

One president's response is enlightening because it shows how the role of the community college president is changing: "Here I am going to give you an answer that does tell you that the job is changing. When I took this job I felt I was getting the best job available. I still feel it is among the best, but I now see us choked by the public schools at one end and the universities at the other." He feels that the community college is caught in the middle in regard to funding and is restrained by the limits placed on it. His choice of professions would be as president of the same institution — if the college had the authority to offer the bachelor's degree.

In summary, the presidents were generally happy in the position, although for a very few the frustrations seem to outweigh the rewards, at least after being in office for a number of years; in these cases the frustrations were enough to cause them to consider seeking another position.

For some presidents, the image of the presidency often fails to reflect the reality of the position, a situation that is difficult to anticipate prior to assuming the role. One of the potential problems is that presidents are viewed as having more power than they actually have. While this can be an advantage as well as a disadvantage, it nevertheless means that the president may be blamed for any number of things which are beyond the control of the president's office. The president of a large urban community college feels that the public perceives him as having enormous power, a false perception. His power, he believes, is largely charismatic. As one president notes, the board generally understands the reality of the presidency; however, the faculty and the public often fail to understand its limitations.

The presidency, like beauty, often resides in the eye of the beholder. As one president observes, practically every constituency has a different image of the presidency: "I used to try to get people to see a more comprehensive view of the presidency. This caused me a great deal of problems. Then I began to sort of relax — I don't mean I quit working on it — but I began to relax and say, 'Gee, it's not possible'; you deal with the various constituencies the best way you can, given their view. I really think that is about what we can do. There are probably as many views of the presidency as there are constituent interest groups out there." A president of a large multicampus district in the Midwest fears that the faculty no longer sees him as their advocate but rather as simply an agent of the board. He believes that some of the problems the president face are a result of the different images associated with the presidency, each reflecting a series of expectations.

Fulfilling the external role of the presidency causes some image problems, especially for the new president who wants to be "all things to all people." For example, one president who found the external role demanding more and more time feels that the faculty fails to understand this aspect of his role: "They think the president is self-serving if he chairs the Chamber of Commerce board — that he wants to hobnob with the big wigs and the faculty don't see him anymore, when all I was doing was promoting the college in the community." The new president who expects a pat on the back for taking an aggressive stance on external relations may be disappointed, especially if the faculty feel neglected.

A similar potential image problem exists when the president becomes involved at the national or state levels to such a degree that campus groups feel neglected. One faculty member could have been speaking for many of his colleagues when he declared, "I don't give a damn about what the president does nationally if things on the campus are going down the tube."

Even the concept of management by "wandering around" or "walking about" on campus, popularized by Peters and Waterman in their often-quoted 1982 best-seller *In Search of Excellence,* and more recently in the 1985 Peters and Austin volume *A Passion for Excellence,* has its pitfalls. While most presidents feel that it is important to be seen on campus, visibility creates certain expectations on the part of the president. As one leader analyzed his situation: "During my seven years as president I made a big deal of this thing called management by walking around — of being seen and seeing — and I still think it is important, but I am trying to create a different expectation — a different image of the office — on the part of our faculty and staff. If they don't see me every week, for example, it's not going to be something that they'll be critical about. I'm just trying to narrow my activities down a bit so there is something left over at the end of the day for that other critical part of my life I call my family, a part I have neglected." In cases where the faculty expect to see the president regularly and suddenly he or she is not visible, the image of the president can suffer as the faculty feels ignored.

The external role of the four-year college and university president has been an important role for years, so much so in fact that at one time it was seriously suggested that many institutions needed two presidents — an "outside" and an "inside" president (Dodds, 1962, pp. 3 – 4). While community college presidents have always had an external role, it has been only recently that the external role has assumed its current status, especially in regard to working with so many constituencies, particularly the legislature.

The state legislature is a major external factor. As state funding has greatly increased, so has the president's role in dealing with legislators. The legislature's purview far exceeds its part in funding, for more and more legislatures are passing laws that have a direct bearing on virtually every aspect of the community college's operation.

Many presidents did not expect to be engaged in collective negotiations when they assmed the presidency. For some presidents, working with unions has become time-consuming and, at times, frustrating. Community college presidents also experience other pressures and influences, some of which were anticipated, such as occasional conflicts with the governing board. A later section will be devoted to the external role of the president as well as to the pressures exerted on the office; suffice it to say that, while many presidents had an idea of what the presidency would be like, few fully anticipated the multifaceted nature of the position.

(The Roman god Janus has provided a popular metaphor for the presidency. Stoke suggested that, "this Janus-like relationship of the president to a board of trustees on the one hand and to the faculty and staff on the other imposes upon him a complicated and sobering responsibility" [Stoke, 1959, p. 77]. Another source refers to the community college president as a "contemporary Janus" with one face turned to the past and the other face looking toward the future [Stalcup and Thomson, 1980]. Even the god Janus would be short a few faces today.)

In spite of certain "blind spots," those presidents interviewed generally agree that the presidency is about what they had anticipated, if indeed they had a concept of the role, which was not the case with some who used the opportunistic or serendipitous avenues to the presidency. As one president who "backed into the position" put it: "I had no idea of what a community college was, much less any concept of what the president was supposed to do." This person entered the presidency in the mid-1960s and would be far from the typical president today; most who assume the office today have a strong concept of the broader aspects of the presidency.

Something of a special breed entering the presidency were those who served as executive vice presidents or in similar positions prior to assuming the presidency. Often these individuals had an excellent concept of what the presidency was like, for in some cases they were "running the college." This situation often occurred if the executive vice president was "groomed" for the presidency by a president who was contemplating retirement.

While most presidents had a broad concept of the presidency prior to assuming it, three aspects of the position were not anticipated by a number of presidents or at least to the degree that they emerged as an important part of the position: (1) they did not anticipate the inordinate amount of time they would have to devote to external affairs, including the somewhat recently added function of fund raising; (2) they did not anticipate the rise of collective negotiations, especially if they had assumed the presidency prior to the arrival of collective bargaining in their state; and (3) they did not expect the pressures on them to come from as many sources or to be as intense as they often were. Many were especially surprised to learn that *their* governing board often emerged as "the loyal opposition." From a more personal perspective, most presidents agreed that the presidency consumed far more time than they had anticipated.

As might be expected based on their backgrounds, community college presidents often fail to fit the stereotype many people have of the college presidency. The pragmatic side of the presidency, as well as this "falling short" of its public image, are illustrated by the following quote. "I never viewed it as some people might as 'a peer among peers' kind of position or as an academic-type walking across campus talking to students. I expected it to be a rather pragmatic, down to earth kind of position." Another president echoed the practical aspects of the office. He felt that most presidents, including himself, were a bit too idealistic and naive when they assumed the presidency but were soon brought back to earth by the demands of the job. Assuming the presidency is only the beginning, however. The real test will lie ahead.

CHAPTER 4

◆

The President in Office

I recall four years ago when a newly appointed member of our college board asked me during our first luncheon meeting what a community college president does. My immediate reaction was to tell him that *everyone* knows what a college president does. On second thought, I gave him a rather weak answer regarding the leadership role of the president. The incident has never left me, however, and since that time I have asked myself, "What does a college president do?"

In an attempt to answer the question, I asked presidents, board members, spouses of presidents, faculty members, and others associated with the community college to describe the role of the president as they interpret that role. Obviously, some of the answers were to be expected: the president should be a leader, a manager, a good administrator. In almost every instance, however, the answers took on a "community college flavor" and thus the following interpretations of the role of the community college president are more than a restatement of the obvious. It is instead a description of the community college presidency by some of the people who know that role from first-hand experience and by people who have a vested interest in the success of the community college president, especially "their" president.

The Four-Year Presidency

Before looking at the role of the community college presidency, however, it might be worthwhile to examine how the role of the four-year presidency is viewed by certain scholars. Kauffman sees the president as performing three primary functions: (1) providing leadership, which keeps both internal and external constituencies aware of the central purpose, values, and worth of higher education to society; as its leader, the president must constantly influence and shape the goals of the institution; (2) communicating the value of the institution to those persons crucial to its support; and (3) overseeing the management and control functions, many of which are delegated to other members of the institution's management team (Kauffman, 1980, pp. 13–14). The president's major responsibility, according to Kauffman, is to "articulate the *potential for service* of our institutions of higher learning" (p. 3).

James Fisher clearly sees the role of the president as that of leader. In his call for a strong presidency, he states that there are five types of power available to college presidents, all of which they should use in promoting themselves as institutional leaders. The five categories are coercive power, reward power, legitimate power, expert power, and charismatic power, the most effective form, according to Fisher, being charismatic power (Fisher, 1984, pp. 29–42).

The 1984 AGB report states that the most important constituency with which the president must deal is the governing board; therefore, each president must create and maintain an effective relationship with the board. Also important is the president's relationship with the surrounding educational institutions (AGB, 1984, pp. 89–93). Theodore Hesburgh, president of Notre Dame University, while agreeing with the AGB report that the board is an important constituency, believes that "from an educational point of view, the faculty are the president's most important constituency. . . . Every day of every year, year in and year out, the president must prove himself to the faculty" (Hesburgh, 1979, p. 46).

In 1959, Harold W. Stoke made the following observations about the role of the college president: "If I were to make a general observation about the qualifications of college presidents, it would be this: in recent years the factor of educational distinction has declined while factors of personality, management skills, and successful experience in business and administration have increased in importance. This fact reflects the gradual transformation of the college president from an intellectual leader into a manager, skilled in administration, a broker in personal and public relations" (Stoke, 1959, p. 15).

Harold W. Dodds, former president of Princeton University, while noting that presidents cannot hope to match the faculty in its areas of specialities or to stay abreast of what is happening in their own disciplines, must nevertheless preserve educational leadership as their first priority, including developing and carrying out policies that enhance teaching and research. He notes that some of the reasons given by presidents for not functioning as educational leaders result from a lack of interest in the educational process or from a fascination with other aspects of the presidency such as management and public relations (Dodds, 1962, pp. 2, 8, 21).

Benezet, Katz, and Magnusson, in their volume entitled *Style and Substance: Leadership and the College Presidency,* deal with the question of whether the president is a leader or a manager. Their conclusion is that whether presidents wish it or not, they are leaders. The president affects curriculum, organization, student services and the morale of the institution. The authors go so far as to conclude that the mood of an institution, through its effect on students, can indirectly help determine the mood of society (1981, p. 20). (Can anyone doubt the truth of this observation after living through the 1960s and early 1970s?)

Writings on the Community College Presidency

When community college presidents write about the presidency, which is not very often, they tend to discuss the president's role in rather broad terms. The April 1978 issue of the *Community and Junior College Journal* is devoted to a rare discussion by seven community college presidents (edited by an eighth president) on the role of their office. The thesis of the issue is that the president is the "Man in the Middle." As the editor of the volume notes, the president is faced with sorting out the dilemmas of the past two decades, including lower numbers of 18-to-22-year-olds, declining dollars, and lessening public support. "Bound by these Gordian knots, the college president of 1978 has become 'The Man in the Middle,' needing an expanding repertoire of talents and skills to maintain the initiative within and on behalf of his institution" (Berg, 1978, p. 3).

And what did these "men in the middle" see as the role of the community college president in 1978? One saw the role of the president as a manipulator, a term that has no nefarious implications as used in the article. Another president called for the president to fulfill the role of educational leader with the responsibility of setting the "tone and pace" of the institution; a third described the president's role as one of marketer, including interpreting the college to its many constituents; a fourth emphasized the role of the president as "money manager" and noted that the successful president understands pedagogy as well as finances and that through managing the money the president engages in creative planning; another saw the role of the president as shifting from "educational entrepreneur" to manager, a term used to connote that the president is "a leader, forerunner, director, and guardian"; the last article dealt with the role of president as politician, a role that the president must play with both external and internal constituencies.

The October 1980 issue of the *Community and Junior College Journal* was devoted in part to the role of the president. One essay written by a president asks, "Can the President Be All Things to All People?" The answer is, of course, no — "not if he or she wants to maintain sanity and avoid serious conflicts" (Wenrich, 1980, pp. 36–37). The author concludes that the most important role of the president is to maintain institutional integrity through his or her own ethical behavior. Another article in the same issue claims that "the community college president has no more important task than that of continuously clarifying and emphasizing the mission of the community college" (Parnell, 1980, p. 44). The statement takes on added significance today, for it was written by Dale Parnell, current president of the AACJC, and thus the acknowledged spokesperson for community colleges at the national level.

In one of the few attempts to deal with the presidency in any detail, Joe B. Rushing, Chancellor of the Tarrant County Junior College District in Texas, discusses the changing role of the community college president. The author claims that the president may expect "intensified pressures in finance, governance, public confidence, the employee's search for security, and governmental control . . ." (Rushing, 1976, p. 1). Rushing discusses the president's role in relationship to the economy, public attitudes, collective bargaining, and government relations.

With the above as background, how is the community college presidency viewed from the perspectives of those interviewed? The most important role assigned to the community college president is that of leader. While a later chapter will be devoted to presidential leadership, a brief examination of the subject is desirable at this time.

LEADERSHIP

Leadership follows several patterns, although four dominated the discussions. Prominent among the leadership roles identified by those interviewed was the role of the president as the person responsible for establishing and interpreting the mission of the college, or, as Kauffman puts it, articulating the potential for service of the institution. As one president observes: "The most important responsibility of the president, along with the board of trustees, is to establish a mission for the college; the president is responsible for spelling out that mission in terms of goals and objectives and seeing that the goals and objectives are accomplished, thereby fulfilling the college's mission." Another president observes that a major part of the president's job is to obtain and manage the resources necessary to carry out the mission of the college. He notes that "the president must educate his most important constituency, the board, about the mission." Since about 15 to 20 percent of the community college trustees are new to the position each year, according to the executive director of the Association of Community College Trustees (ACCT), the task of educating the trustees never ends.

One national leader feels that leadership must not stop at the campus but must extend to interpreting the community college at the national level; he calls on local presidents to promote "the movement" nationally. Most of the presidents interviewed suggest that, although the role of the president has changed, one constant has been the need for the effective leader to define the community college mission and to assume responsibility for seeing that the mission is carried out and understood by the college's many publics. As will be discussed later, *presidents as well as others associated with the community college feel that the community college president has been less than successful in interpreting and promoting the community college mission.*

A second aspect of leadership that came out in the interviews was the role of the president as educational leader, although the definitions of educational leadership went well beyond dealing directly with the curriculum, teaching, and learning. "I interpret my role as president as a leader who is responsible for providing every access possible for the learning of students," claims one president. Another notes that the primary role of the president is educational leadership; however, he sees educational leadership not just in academic terms but as manifesting itself through obtaining external support which will permit the faculty and staff to perform their educational role effectively. A veteran college board member who served as president of the ACCT and is a former member of the Board of Directors of the American Association of Community and Junior Colleges (AACJC) declared that "the role of the president is first and foremost to provide educational leadership. My guess is that it has always been educational leadership and will always be that. While demands change, good campus builders, good financial managers, good communicators, good external persons, and good internal persons are all important, but I feel that educational leadership transcends all of these."

Several of those interviewed feel that it is unrealistic to cling to the somewhat romantic idea that the president is the institution's educational leader, especially if educational leadership is narrowly interpreted to mean only academic leadership. One, a board member, stated, "I would like to think that academics are the president's most important concern, but realistically they are not. He must spend too much time with people outside of the college such as politicians, community leaders, managers of businesses, in getting dollars, and in projecting the image of the college" to be an effective academic leader. The trustee noted, however, that educating external constituents is an important part of the president's role. One 13-year veteran president observed, "We are not as involved in the instructional role as we think we are." Another president, while not rejecting the role of instructional leader outright, notes, "When I started out as president 20 years ago, I thought the role of the president was one of instructional leader. After working with collective negotiations for seven years, I had to make a decision as to whether I was going to survive. To survive, I had to take on the role of educational manager rather than academic leader." Seen in this light, the president might be viewed as the "manager" of the educational environment rather than as the "manager" of the curriculum and of the teaching and learning process.

Most of those interviewed agreed that the job of "managing" the environment is a realistic one today and one that meshes with the role of the chief academic officer rather than competing with it. This was the case on many campuses in earlier years, especially on those campuses where the president was the founding president and as such wanted to play academic dean (and business dean, and student services dean, etc.) as well as president. In this regard, it is worth noting that a study published in January of 1969 found that even then most presidents showed little evidence of providing leadership to the teaching and learning process (Cohen and Roueche, 1969). The findings of the study were published at a time when many of the presidents were founding presidents and, as one president declares, "not only knew where all of the broom closets were but knew how many brooms each contained." As is well known, the 1960s were a time of unprecedented growth in community colleges, a time when the opportunity to be involved with course and program development, learning and teaching styles, and other aspects of the educational program was available daily. Since 1969, things have become much more complex for most presidents, especially in regard to external demands. One result is that the opportunities to become involved with the learning process are not as readily available as they were in earlier years. Today, with a few notable exceptions, there is little evidence to suggest that presidents are active instructional leaders. Yet, as will be seen in the chapter on leadership, the image presidents have of themselves as educational leaders ranks very high on their list of important functions. Obviously, educational leadership is not limited to academic leadership.

A third aspect of the leadership role that emerged from the interviews dealt with setting the campus environment or mood, as Benezet and associates (1981) refer to it. A number of those interviewed expressed the need for the president to set the tone for the institution: "I have been a president for twenty years. In the last five years I have come to realize that my most important function is maintaining institutional vitality," claims one president. A faculty member feels that the morale of the faculty and staff is vital to the success of the college. The president must always exercise vigilance to see that all members of the college community work to produce a climate that assures a quality educational program. "Setting the thrust," "leadership by example," and "setting the climate," are some of the terms used to describe the president's role in establishing the college's environment.

The successful president may lead by example, set the climate of the institution, and do the other things normally required of the leader. Without motivating others, however, the president will not only march to a different drummer but will march alone, a march that cannot be long sustained. A number of presidents gave their formula for motivating others. The answers varied from one extreme to another. One president claims that one does not motivate people; rather, one creates a "climate of love in which naturally good people do the right thing." Another president went to the other extreme: "I motivate people by nagging, through guile, greed, and fear. I look for people who can be motivated. I am being a bit facetious, but the methods do work. However, overcontrol and a lack of communications can destroy motivation."

Some presidents motivate others by example. As one president declares, "I show commitment, enthusiasm, and am an example. I try to be intellectual enough to provide new and clear thoughts, by being a catalyst which conditions the surrounding environment." A national leader and former president works to give a clear vision of what the college is all about and to convince others to buy into the vision. "No one wants to fight in a war they don't understand," he says in describing the need for presenting the vision.

Almost all presidents turn to a number of time-tested methods for motivating others. In this category are such things as delegating as much responsibility as possible, giving people enough authority to carry out the responsibility, and then rewarding them for a job well done. Also important in motivating people is to ensure that they "have a piece of the action," according to a number of presidents. One president summarizes this line of thinking: "Your problem as a leader is to provide overarching leadership to the college in such a way that all of those people with talents wander down a particular trail. This is the difficult job of managing professionals. If you are going to do that, you have to send authority out there to do the job and you have to have measures to see that the job is getting done." Another president, and one identified in the peer review process as one of the leading presidents in the nation, describes his approach to motivation: "I have seen over my life how important a little recognition is to a major official who I thought was being recognized all of the time; for people further down the line, recognition is of great importance. I give some room to try new ideas, new directions, and not just those I think are going to work. Good people flourish under these circumstances. Finally, listen to your people, not always to take their advice, but listen."

The fourth aspect of leadership centered around the president as external leader. As the external leader, the president is responsible for working with state legislators, business leaders, special interest groups, other educational institutions, local politicians, and other groups that are unique to the area served by the college. A major function of the president as external leader is to articulate the college's mission in such a way that the necessary support is forthcoming from the external constitutent groups. The external leadership role is a major one for most presidents and is seemingly becoming more important with each passing day. Indeed, without exception, those presidents interviewed

who were identified as leaders by their peers see dealing with the
external community as a great part of their role. As one president
observes: "There is no doubt in my mind that the whole area of
dealing with public relations — the general public, the business
public, and trying to work with the legislature — is a whole new
set of skills that were not really required by my predecessor." An
aspect of external leadership that showed up often was the need
to work well with the media. One leader notes: "You must know
how to deal with the newspaper. If you see them as the enemy,
you will have an unending amount of difficulty." He suggests that
presidents take the advice which he attributes to Mark Twain:
"Never argue with anyone who can buy ink by the barrel and
paper by the ton." But, he adds, "A lot of my colleagues never
learn."

THE PRESIDENT AS MANAGER

Another perception of the president's role is that of manager.
Management as used here is not a response to the call in some
quarters for academic institutions to adopt the "industrial
model" of management. Nor is management used here in the
sense that one manages a Sears store or some other such enterprise; rather, management refers to bringing together the various
segments of the academic community in such a way that they
create a whole much greater than the parts and in a way that is
conducive to the teaching and learning process. Planning is a
facet of management, not an end in itself. In regard to management and planning, the community college president is fulfilling
one of the roles of the president as defined above by Kauffman
and Stoke, keeping in mind that Kauffman believes that many of
the management and control functions should be delegated by
the president to other members of the administration.

Feelings were often strong about the role of the president as
manager of the enterprise, especially among trustees who, by the
nature of their position, want to see things running smoothly on
the campus. One trustee states unequivocally that the president's
job is to organize the college, and notes that without organization
the other aspects of leadership cannot be fulfilled nor can the

educational mission of the college be accomplished. Another board member lists administrative skills first on her list of qualifications for the president. A number of presidents also viewed administering the college as vital to their success. A president who has developed a national reputation for his views on higher education management, especially management of community colleges, sees the president as a manager of values, a manager of change, and, just as important, a manager of the routine. One president sees the president's primary responsibility as planning and development; another states that the biggest responsibility of the president is planning. References to planning include keeping up with the routine as well as having a vision of the future of the institution and a plan to achieve that vision.

THE PRESIDENT–BOARD RELATIONSHIP

Another grouping of responsibilities of the president centers around board–president relations. Agreeing with the 1984 AGB report on the presidency that maintaining a good working relationship with the board is essential, several individuals spoke to the president's role in the classical board–president relationship. The president must follow and administer the policies of the board, claims one board member. Another board member notes that "the president is the chief executive officer, of course, who implements the policies of the board." One president observes that the president is employed by the board and charged with carrying out the mission the board has established. Another president declares that the role of the president is "first and foremost to carry out the policies of the board of trustees."

THE PRESIDENT AS MEDIATOR

With one exception, no one emphasized the primary role of the president as that of mediator, although mediation is seen as important by all of the individuals in establishing a positive campus environment. Faculty members are especially concerned that the president play a major part in bringing the various campus groups together to discuss issues and then, after the issues are discussed, to make a decision. The lack of major emphasis on the role of the president as mediator is significant when one considers that the 1972 volume, *Governance for the Two-Year College*, the one book on the community college devoted to the subject, saw the role of mediator as dominant (Richardson, Blocker, and Bender, 1972). It is likely that during the late 1960s and early 1970s the disturbances on many college campuses and the mood of the nation caused some community college leaders to seek ways of avoiding conflict and thus emphasized the role of mediator more than might have been necessary considering that calmness prevailed on most community college campuses. Or the call for mediation might have been an attempt to moderate the role of the founding presidents, many of whom were of necessity highly visible on campus. It does seem, however, that the emphasis on the mediator's role during the 1960s and early 1970s laid the groundwork for the community colleges to become more collegial in their governance. On the other hand, times have changed: Clark Kerr and the task force that looked at the college presidency for the AGB ignored the mediator role in their call for a strengthened college presidency. This was quite a contrast to Kerr's stance in his Godkind Lectures given at Harvard University in 1963, which set forth his idea of the multiversity and in which he advocated that the primary role of the president be one of mediator. In his 1972 postscript to the Godkind Lectures, Kerr stated that he regretted using the word "mediator" to describe the primary role of the president since the word created a great deal of misunderstanding. Kerr's 1982 postscript fails to mention the role of the president as mediator, thus implying that Kerr has put the issue to rest, at least from his perspective (Kerr, 1982, pp. 151–184). Certainly the role of mediator is important today as has always been the case; however, in regard to the community college presidency today, mediation is just one facet of leadership, not a focal point.

The above roles of the president are fairly well accepted as important ones for all college and university presidents; however, they have not been discussed in any detail as they relate to the community college presidency. By examining these somewhat traditional roles in relation to the community college presidency, one is better able to understand the position. The following explores some of the frustrations and pressures the president must deal with, many on a daily basis.

Frustrations

Positions of leadership bring frustrations as well as rewards, and college and university presidencies are no exceptions. *As used here, frustrations are the daily irritants that go with the position of president, that rarely reach the explosion point — either within the individual or externally — and that rarely have a direct influence upon the direction of the institution.* Frustrations are associated more closely with the day-to-day administrative tasks of the presidency than with the broader leadership functions. Frustrations, whether originating externally or internally, tend to be either beyond one's control or not seen as worth the time and effort required to eliminate them.

Some observers of the college and university presidency have written about the frustrations associated with the position. Carbone refers to the presidency as "splendid agony," with a great deal of emphasis placed on the agony (Carbone, 1981). Stoke recalls Charles Eliot's remark that one of the necessary qualifications of a college president is an infinite capacity to inflict pain (Stoke, 1959, p. 52). Stoke notes that he knew one president who maintained a Go-to-Hell Fund which consisted of enough money to permit him to move on if need be and have enough to live on for at least six months (p. 19). (Higher education folklore has it that Stoke himself invented the fund and the term used to describe it.) Warren Bennis wrote a book devoted largely to the frustrations associated with the presidential search process (1973). Michael Cohen and James March's reference to American colleges and universities as organized anarchies is well known, as is their reference to the "garbage can" theory of decision making (Cohen and March, 1974, pp. 2, 81–91), terms that tend to emphasize some of the uncertainties associated with the presidency. Research aside, common sense tells one that there are frustrations associated with the community college presidency, although an occasional president unabashedly claims that there are no frustrations associated with the position worth mentioning.

It is not surprising that many of the presidential frustrations came from sources outside the institution. One president from California, a state that has had its share of economic turmoil recently as far as the community college is concerned, identified "the inability to do long-range planning in view of the changing parameters of legislative activity statewide, both in curriculum and in financing" as the most frustrating aspect of his position. Another reference to frustrations associated with the position went as follows: "As president, I am frustrated by the political structure that surrounds us. I mean capital 'P' and small 'p.' Capital 'P' means the structures that engulf community college presidents at the state and national levels, people who meddle around in the affairs of the college. By small 'p' I mean the insiders who still play the old smoke-filled room game of 'you scratch my back and I'll scratch yours.' Neither of those has anything to do with the quality of instruction or helping people to learn." Another president theorized: "The most frustrating aspect of the job is trying to coordinate and mediate among the diverse publics that surround the institution. Because the college is so close to the people, so responsive, it generates a certain amount of conflict. At one point you may find yourself dealing with a board that is elected by public mandate and all that entails, with representatives of the medical profession on the one hand and blue-collar workers on the other. One finds conflict between the current job market and traditional values as these values relate to education. On campus you have the conflicts between the various unions and the administration, and state regulations make you go into conflict with needs of the local campus." Another president echoes a similar theme: "The most frustrating thing is the politicalization of the community college. Not only the board, but the state and others feel they have an oversight responsibility. Keeping it all in balance is very frustrating."

Those presidents who saw themselves as academic leaders found it very frustrating not being able to fill that role effectively. Several presidents confirmed what Dodds observed as early as 1962 — that is, it is very frustrating that faculty now look to the academic dean or academic vice-president rather than to the president as instructional leader.

Time constraints are a constant source of frustration. The common complaint of "so much to do and so little time" is heard often among presidents. The issue of time — the lack of it — is so common among executives that there is little to add here, other than to note that many community college presidents tend to fill their daily calendars so full that little or no time is left for deep thinking and reflection, a situation that runs counter to an institution committed to such activities.

Frustrations associated with personnel decisions seem always to be present; however, they reach a peak during the spring months when decisions must be made on most campuses regarding promotions, tenure, dismissals, and new positions. The tension level becomes especially high when resources are scarce. While the problems associated with personnel decisions are so diverse that it would be impossible to categorize them, one comment by a president explains why they are so frustrating: "Personnel decisions are tough whether you are in a small college or a large one. You have to be aware of interpersonal relationships, not just yours, but others. By necessity, as president, I do a lot of refereeing and make the hard decisions when the refereeing doesn't work; so you make the decision as to who goes and who stays. Just by my temperament and the way I love people, it is very difficult for me to make those decisions; they are the hardest part of the job." Personnel decisions, if not kept in perspective, become more than frustrations and are prime candidates for causing stress, the subject of a later chapter.

Another aggravating aspect of the presidency is financial constraints. It is interesting to note that faculty and board members feel that inadequate financing presents greater problems than actually seem to exist among the presidents. Presidents tend to see financing as a means, not an end; consequently, the lack of· funds contributes to larger frustrations which often build to major pressures such as inability to accomplish the college's mission and to force personnel and program terminations, thus changing the direction of the college. Some presidents see funding as a means of control and a source of external interference by the legislative and executive branches of state government, which thus exacerbate the situation and often generate pressure on the presidency that goes well beyond the realm of daily frustrations.

While the presidents alluded to internal conflicts with the faculty and staff, none found the conflicts particularly troublesome when on a one-to-one basis. This may be the case because most presidents delegate the actual personnel decisions and only discuss the problem at hand with the faculty and staff rather than actually deciding the issue — a situation that makes "one-on-one" conversations less tense for the president. Of course, when conflict manifests itself through group action such as unions or special interest groups, the problems are magnified many times and become sources of pressure. Two faculty members singled out internal conflicts as being very discouraging. One stated: "I imagine that it must be very frustrating to the college president to give 110 percent of your effort to something and still have people who are not satisfied with your work. You can never satisfy all of the faculty or all of the staff. There will always be some alienation between the president and the faculty. This must be very frustrating." Another faculty member saw the ongoing battle between faculty and students and faculty and administrators as an irritant. "It is an ongoing frustration, depending on the magnitude of the complaint; I think it is always there. You will never be able to satisfy everyone." Perhaps the presidents see day-to-day disagreements among faculty and administrators not only as routine but often as healthy.

Pressures

The community college occupies that middle ground between the rest of higher education and the larger community. As a result of its relationship to its community — a relationship that Edmund Gleazer refers to as symbiotic — the community college is expected to be responsive to community needs. The ability to be attuned to the larger community, while recognized as an important part of the community college's mission, often brings pressures to bear on the college president. *Pressures, as used here, have the potential of influencing the direction and well-being of the college, and dealing with them calls upon the broader leadership skills of the president.* Pressures and influences are exerted by state legislators; the governor's office; faculty and staff; local political leaders; business leaders; the governing board; various coordinating bodies and boards; unions, where they exist; and any number of groups and individuals with special interests in the college and what it can do for them.

In addition to the forces exerted by the larger community, community college presidents are constantly faced with internal constituents with their own agendas. The pressures may be positive as well as negative; they may cause the college to do some things that it ought to do but, for whatever reason, is not doing; they may cause the college to devote more time and energy to things it is already doing; they may cause the college to cease doing some things that it is currently doing. On occasion, pressures may cause the college to do some things it should not do, such as overcommitting itself to serving a single industry or to employing someone who is not in the best interest of the institution. These forces can cause the college to move in directions that may be positive or negative, depending upon one's perspective, such as engaging in collective negotiations. Regardless, the majority of the pressures are ultimately brought to bear on the president's office. The following is an examination of some of the sources of pressures and influences with which the community college president must deal.

PRESSURES FROM BUSINESS AND INDUSTRY

Most community colleges pride themselves on the relationship they have with business and industry, and indeed they should, if the criterion by which success is measured is a harmonious relationship. Several presidents noted that the college has a responsibility to work with business and industry in training and retraining workers; in attracting business and industry; and generally in making the community a better place to live, work, and learn. Curriculum advisory committees made up of business and industrial leaders are important to most community colleges and are encouraged by the presidents. In *every* instance, the presidents interviewed see the influence exerted by business and industrial leaders as a positive force. One result is that, in many cases, presidents aggressively court the favors of business and

industry. Of course, since most colleges are funded on an enroll-
ment-driven formula, it is natural that presidents are interested
in enrolling the large number of student-employees present in
the private sector of the economy. But the desire to work with
business and industry is seen as an important part of the college's
mission and appears to be far more than a self-serving ploy to
obtain students. The business–industry partnership is not without peril, however.

Although community college presidents view their relationships with business and industry as positive, this does not mean
that the relationship is free from pressure. Literally thousands
upon thousands of representatives from business and industry
serve on curriculum advisory committees and normally exert a
positive influence on the community college; yet certainly the
potential for generating pressure on the presidency is there.
While the president in the role of suitor courts the favors of
business and industry with evangelical vigor, the accompanying
music to the courtship can have the same effect as the singing of
the Lorelei. The resulting pressure generated on the presidency
is often so insidious that it is hardly noticed until it reaches the
stage where action is required. Ironically, this insidious pressure
is often brought about by the presidents themselves in their attempts to consummate the business–industry marriage and in
general to promote the community college mission.

The "selling of the community college" became a national
pastime for community college leaders during the 1960s and
early 1970s. At the heart of the movement to sell the community
college were its top officers. Most presidents were on the stump
selling the community college with a neopopulist rhetoric that
would have warmed the heart of William Jennings Bryan. The
message was taken to Rotary Clubs, to Kiwanis Clubs, to Ruritan
Clubs, to Lions Clubs, to the League of Women Voters, to
Chambers of Commerce, to garden clubs, to mid-America, to
rural America, to urban America, to suburban America and to
corporate America. The presidents' message was simple: the
community college is the people's college; it is the community's
college; it is corporate America's college; it is flexible; it is responsive; and it will work to meet the needs of all members of the
community, with special attention given to training workers for

business and industry. The presidents' message was well received and was accepted at face value by many in the audiences. Presidents told their story; however, as many found out, they also had promises to keep.

Most presidents did not realize that their message would be taken literally. They did not realize that promising too much to too many could bring unexpected pressure to bear on the president's office. *They did not realize that they were primed to become victims of their own rhetoric.* For example, in the late 1960s and early 1970s a large number of colleges across the nation began to work with the American Institute of Banking (AIB) to offer college credit for courses falling under the rubric of the AIB training program. It was not unusual for AIB to want the college to use AIB textbooks, AIB courses of study, and even employ AIB-approved instructors.

The AIB example is not an isolated case. Local examples of pressure on the president's office abound. For example, often the major industry in a community college's service region makes demands that lead one to believe that the community college is just another part of the industry's fiefdom. And why not? Some presidents have led the major employer in their area to believe that the college exists to serve the employer's needs first and the individual's needs primarily as they relate to the needs of a particular industry. This type of rhetoric was more prominent during the years of rapid community college growth than it is today and it often showed a certain naîveté on the part of the president; however, in an era of declining enrollments, scarce resources, and competition for new industry, the song of the Lorelei still entices presidents toward rocks of, if not destruction, certainly increased pressure.

The president who has spent much time and energy explaining the community college philosophy to business and industry is often faced with three choices. The first is accepting a package program from business or industry and informing the college community that the program will become a part of the college curriculum. This approach is likely to alienate much of the college community and has the potential of compromising institutional integrity. The second choice is informing the business or industry that he or she was "only kidding" about the community college's responsiveness and flexibility. This task will probably call the president's credibility into question and to put off much of the community, thus causing the college to lose forever the chance to serve it fully. Third is a compromise whereby the community college can serve AIB, the dominant employer, and the individual without compromising institutional integrity. This is the approach that is ultimately arrived at on most campuses. *Regardless of which choice is made, however, the president created pressure on the office of the president which could have been prevented had he or she used a more realistic approach in describing the community college's mission.* Of course, there are numerous examples where the president has gone far out on the philosophical limb in an attempt to be responsive to special groups only to have to crawl back to the safety of the more stable trunk of the community college philosophy. Presidents should keep in mind that the crawl back can be lonely and that it almost always takes its toll on the president, both physically and psychologically.

The major impact on the president resulting from the business–industry relationship, then, is the pressure to "produce." As one board member observed, producing means more than serving on committees; it means that the graduates of the college have the competencies to perform well in their chosen field upon graduation from the community college. Producing for the president also means interpreting the college's mission in such a way that it is understood by business and industry and in a way that does not cause unnecessary pressure on the president's office.

PRESSURES FROM LOCAL POLITICIANS

Another potential source of pressure on the president's office is that exerted by local political leaders, including those individuals who serve the local political process such as county executives. In most cases, however, little pressure from local political leaders materializes. To the contrary, presidents are often appointed to important committees by mayors and other local leaders. Nevertheless, presidents must remain sensitive to the potential pressure resulting from local politics.

It is not surprising that, when pressure does come from local political leaders, it comes in situations where the local government contributes a sizable amount of funds to the college budget or when local political leaders want someone appointed to the college faculty or staff. In one extreme case, the president's nemesis — pressure to make a personnel appointment — showed up in country government. The political leader of the county government wanted his daughter appointed to a position at the college for which the screening committee determined she was not qualified. The president received the customary phone call from the angry father who, incidentally, was one of the first graduates of the college, wanting to know why his daughter was not at least given a courtesy interview. The president had learned his lesson; the next time the interview would be granted. Three or four years later, the daughter again applied for a position with the college. This time the president asked the committee to give her a courtesy interview and the committee agreed. The committee found that she was not qualified for the position, and the president went back to the father with the decision. The father was furious and showed his anger by pounding on the table. He wanted to know, "Why did you interview her and get her hopes up?" The phrase "Catch-22" took on new meaning for the president; the father "ever since then has not really voted our way and says things about the college behind our backs." As the president said, "That is pressure."

Local political pressure often manifests itself through local leaders contacting members of the college's governing board. One trustee relates how she was called by a newly elected county supervisor who wanted to know why more faculty members had not been employed from his county. The trustee, in passing the message on to the president, wryly observed, "I can see that this new supervisor will make this call frequently." As with other constituents, the president has a responsibility to make local political leaders aware of college policies, especially in regard to employment. Failure to do so may result in unnecessary and unrelenting pressure being placed on the president.

In one state, where the county government makes the final determination on what budget goes forward and can shift funds from one category to another (i.e., from the president's office to instruction), there is always some pressure resulting from what county officials *can* do, although the fears of the president have been largely unrealized. On the other hand, at another college in the same state, a board member confided that prior to approving the budget the county executive forced the college to increase tuition, apparently not satisfied with the college's tuition in relationship to the other colleges in the state. The point is that, where a large portion of the operating budget comes from local tax dollars, the pressure from local sources on the president is likely to be greater than if the college is primarily state funded. While the virtues of local funding and the resulting local control are extolled in the literature on community colleges, local funding can be a double-edged sword. In the latter case, an external agency set policy through a tuition increase, a function that is normally the right and responsibility of the college's governing board. The negative side of local funding is rarely noted in the literature on community college funding, however.

PRESSURES FROM MINORITIES AND WOMEN

The rapid growth of community colleges in the 1960s and early 1970s coincided with a number of important political and social movements in society, including the civil rights movement and the women's movement. For many minorities and many women, the community college is the port of entry to higher education. For example, in 1982, 56 percent of the Hispanics enrolled in higher education in America attended community colleges, as did 55 percent of the American Indians, 45 percent of the Asians, and 44 percent of the blacks. In 1983, women made up more than half (53%) of all credit enrollment in community colleges (ACE, 1984, p. 3). These groups rightfully feel a certain sense of "ownership" in the community college, and it is not unusual for them to exercise their rights of ownership. When they do, pressure is created on the president's office and often results in a reshaping of the mission of the college.

One president described the relationship with the black community at his college in a way that illustrates some of the complexities that surround such relationships. The black community, he points out, was very active in wanting the college to do more to serve it: "As president I felt the pressure because we were a community-based college with an open campus and had a lot of ties with the total community. I did feel that the black community was constantly pushing, and it was interesting, for we did more for the blacks than did any other institution of higher education. The local university virtually ignored them and they virtually ignored the local university. So it was a kind of love-hate situation, possibly because they felt we were there to serve them." In the same vein, the president of a large Eastern inner-city community college, with a predominately black student body and a predominately white faculty and administration, noted the sense of ownership on the part of the black community: "The college is viewed as the city's college; therefore, black leaders keep a watchful eye on the college." The pressure to employ more blacks, while subdued, is always present, according to the president.

The former president of an urban community college which has a student body that is predominately black and an administration and faculty that are approximately 70 percent white noted that the black community kept constant pressure on the president's office to employ more blacks in all positions, offer more black studies courses, and in general to be more sensitive to the needs of blacks. Philosophically, the president agreed with the demands; practically, they generated a great deal of pressure on his office, for he found some of the demands difficult to comply with for a number of reasons. This is not an isolated example but rather was repeated to one degree or another on most campuses, especially during the late 1960s and early 1970s. As a result of the pressures from the black community, many presidents established an ongoing dialogue with groups such as the NAACP, a dialogue that likely would not have taken place without pressure being put on the president's office.

If the community college is more subject to pressures from more local community groups with special interests and special needs than are most four-year institutions, this is as it should be,

For a discussion of the president's reaction to black student activism during the late 1960s and early 1970s, see John Lombardi's discussion of the subject in his *The President's Reaction to Black Student Activism*, Topical Paper No. 16, ERIC Clearinghouse for Junior Colleges, Los Angeles, 1971.

for the community college is committed to serving all segments of the local community, a commitment rarely found among four-year schools. A trustee noted that groups with special interests do indeed bring pressure to bear on the president's office and that he sees "that as a real positive kind of thing because presidents need to be sensitive to those needs." He feels that the president who is insensitive to pressures is doomed to mediocrity, if not failure.

While the community colleges have been relatively free from marches on the president's office (one faculty member stated that he had tried to organize several marches, all of which failed) and from "sit-ins," the pressure from special interest groups can become intense. One president of a large urban community college district has to deal with an organization whose membership is almost all Hispanic and which, according to him, is "trained in the Sol Alinsky techniques of confrontation." The group showed up with 400 members at a college board meeting and made their demands. The same president noted, "At one point we were trying to select a president for one of our campuses and I had every black minister in the city in my office." However, this president also observed that sometimes the pressures are positive as well as negative. (Incidentally, he was one of the presidents who stated that he loved his position.)

Several presidents alluded to the demands made by women's groups such as the National Organization for Women. The pressures often come from within the college community and often center around wanting more women in key administrative positions as well as more courses and activities that emphasize the role of women in today's society. One president notes that he came into a situation that was basically an "old boy's club," with many of the members still around. As president, he hired a number of capable women who wanted to move up in the administrative hierarchy; the result: "Every time there is a vacancy they are right there lobbying and pressuring me to see that the next position goes to a woman." Occasionally, internal women's groups made up of faculty and students join with external groups to lobby successfully for certain things such as a child-care center on campus, thereby causing the college to move in new directions.

PRESSURE FROM THE LEGISLATIVE AND EXECUTIVE BRANCHES

Asking why working with the legislative and executive branches of state government is important to the community college president is somewhat like asking the bank robber why he robs banks; the answer is often the same: because that's where the money is. A majority of the community college presidents interviewed consider working directly with the state legislative and executive branches as an extremely vital part of their role.

Working with the executive branch, while viewed as less important and less personal than working with the legislative branch, is nevertheless necessary. In addition to the fact that the governor appoints all or some of the community college board members in many states, the executive branch plays a major role in the budgeting process. But the governor's influence extends far beyond budgeting and board appointments. For example, interacting with the various state agencies that fall under the executive branch — industrial development, for example — is often an important part of the community college presidency. Moreover, rules and regulations from the executive branch often affect the operation of the college and thus are frequently a source of pressure on the president's office, even to the extent of forcing the elimination of activities.

In working with legislators, especially those who serve on the "money committees," community college presidents in many instances have become acutely aware of just how important and powerful the legislative staff members are, and devote time and energy to getting to know key staff personnel as well as legislators. All presidents should realize that the legislative staff members often influence the thinking of legislators, and that dealing with them is vital to successful relations with the legislature.

What pressures do legislators bring to bear on the president's office other than the obvious one of not providing the funds presidents feel are needed? Many presidents, at one time or another, have had requests from legislators to employ someone, or to enroll someone in a highly selective program, or to provide a scholarship for someone. Normally, requests to employ someone at the college are, at the worst, minor irritants; however, if the request comes from a powerful legislator, there is a tendency for the request to produce strain on the president's office, especially if the legislator is intent upon seeing someone employed. An interesting fact is that more than a few presidents simply tell the legislators that they have an affirmative action plan (a pet of many legislators) which they must follow in regard to employment, thereby, if not totally eliminating the problem, certainly diffusing it. While these requests generate some pressure, most presidents view them as "part of the game." One president who, based on his record of success and longevity in office, plays the political game well, offers the following analysis of the president– legislator relationship: "I know that in 95 percent of the cases when I get letters from legislators it is just to get the monkey off their back; I quickly respond to their request and inform them that the issue has been settled in the best interest of the college; they tell their constituent that they did all they could do; the issue is closed."

The president–legislator relationship is not always as simple as passing the buck, however. Legislators can and do get deeply involved with the president's office, as happened recently in a highly publicized case in Florida. Florida Junior College at Jacksonsville (FJC) was criticized for the use of public funds for international education, travel, and entertainment. The state senator who chairs the Duval County (FJC's home county) legislative delegation appointed two members of the delegation "to review college records and conduct hearings to 'settle some very serious concerns that have been raised by the media.'" The committee was also directed to examine how well the college was governed by the trustees and operated by the administration. Adding a bit of irony to the situation was that the person chosen to head the committee was FJC's third student body president and recipient of its first outstanding alumnus award. His words nevertheless serve to remind presidents of how great the pressure can become when legislators become involved and where legislators ultimately place their priorities: "I don't believe there is anyone who has felt more closely aligned to the college than myself," declared the committee chairman. "But my allegiance and loyalties to an institution never override my concerns for efficient use of taxpayer dollars" (*Florida Times-Union*, May 31, 1984, pp. 1, A-12).

The fallout from the FJC investigation caused strain for the other Florida community college presidents, including the introduction of a bill that would tighten the state's fiscal control of its 28 community colleges. The bill was introduced in spite of the fact that the audit that sparked much of the controversy showed no evidence of wrongdoing (*Florida Times-Union*, April 20, 1984, p. 1). In addition, a college-by-college study of funds spent for travel and summer working hours was undertaken and the results published in one of the state's leading newspapers (*Florida Times-Union*, March 9, 1984, p. A-12; May 31, 1984, p. 1).

The controversy surrounding FJC drew the governor's office into the fray. Governor Bob Graham's chief of staff warned the FJC trustees that they would be held responsible for the management of the college and that their performance would be taken into account when it was time for their reappointment (*Florida Times-Union*, April 8, 1984, p. B-1). Reference to the FJC situation is not made to draw further attention to it but to serve as a reminder that intense legislative force can be exerted on *any* president's office, and, when it is, the ramifications are often far-reaching.

A sidebar (to borrow a journalistic term) to the FJC case is the role the press played in highlighting the situation. While only a relatively small number of the presidents interviewed pointed to the press as one of their major sources of pressure, every president is or should be aware of the role the press can play. (Incidentially, one president who cited pressure from the press as a major concern was from a small rural college — one does not have to be in a metropolitan area to be caught in the press's glaring eye.)

For the most part, the FJC situation aside, the governor's office puts little weight directly on the president's office other than through the budgeting process (which can be considerable, as witnessed by the governor of Virginia's 1985 plan to eliminate approximately 500 positions from the state's 23 community colleges in one year) or, occasionally, through board appointments. Often, however, the executive branch's influence is felt through numerous rules and regulations. Most presidents accept these as minor irritants rather than pressures, although several presidents expressed dismay over the seemingly endless red tape and the additional layers of bureaucracy created by additional regulations.

Finally, most presidents feel very little pressure from statewide coordinating bodies, governing boards, or state-level community college offices in those states where they exist, other than that emanating from the constant fear that state-level bodies will usurp local authority. For the most part state-level operations are just another part of the bureaucracy, sometimes helpful, sometimes another hurdle to jump. In those states where the central office is relatively new or its role greatly expanded, it is seen as more of a threat than in those states that have a long history of central office control.

In summary, there are a number of pressures and influences community college presidents must deal with and, while they vary from state to state and from campus to campus, the variation is largely one of degree: the issues are essentially the same. The major sources of pressure and influence come from business leaders, politicians, and special interest groups, with some pressure from faculty, who on occasion are members of special interest groups. (Collective negotiations and governance will be discussed in the next section in terms of their effect on the president's office.) One final note on pressure from one of the individuals interviewed: "The college president who does not know how to deal with and be comfortable with conflict resolution is not going to make it today."

CHAPTER 5

◆

The President, the Board, and the Faculty

Is the community college president subject to undue pressures from the governing board? Are more boards participating in the daily decision making on campus, as suggested by the ABG report on the presidency? And are trustees who are members of special interest groups especially prone to meddling as suggested by the AGB report (1984, p. 99)? Are governing boards "in charge," or has control slipped into the hands of politicians and bureaucrats? What is the relationship of the board and the president?

Without exception, those interviewed did not feel that state laws or board bylaws give the college board too much authority over the institutions they govern. The answers were uniform on the subject, whether the board was the elected or appointed governing board, a state-level board, a local board, an advisory board, or a board such as the board of regents that governs all of higher education within a state.

Concern was expressed, however, that board authority at the local level is being eroded by such external factors as the state legislature, rules and regulations from the executive branch, statewide coordinating or governing boards, and central office staff in those states with state-level offices for community colleges. In two states, both with major commitments to community colleges and both states where control has historically rested with the local college board, the trend seems to be away from board control at the local level and a shift of control to the state level, either to the legislature, to a statewide coordinating body, to a state office for community colleges, or some combination of the three. For example, in one state the college board in the past had taxing authority and authority to establish new programs. Currently, both actions must be approved at the state level, thus greatly diminishing the power of the college board. In another state, there is fear among some presidents that a recently established state board for community colleges will diminish the authority of the local board, although evidence of how this is happening was not presented. In some states (e.g., Virginia and Minnesota), control has rested with state-wide governing boards from the time two-year colleges became a party of the state systems.

In almost every case, elected trustees were more likely to become involved in the daily affairs of the college than were those appointed to the board. The reason seems to be that elected trustees are likely to be more politically oriented and therefore see their election to the college board as a stepping-stone in their political careers. Visibility on the board can be parlayed into political visibility, so the reasoning goes. Nevertheless, there is little evidence to suggest that any large number of board members were involved or wanted to become involved in the day-to-day affairs of the college, although exceptions exist.

The exceptions are discussed here not because they make good copy, but to illustrate what can happen, especially when trustees are unaware of, or insensitive to, their role, or when a president and board accepts what is normally viewed as abnormal involvement on the part of board members (e.g., the situation where a board chairman had an office next door to the president and had two staff members assigned to the office). In the latter instance, it should be noted that the current president demanded that the situation be corrected prior to assuming the position.

In almost all cases, the presidents interviewed felt that board members were sufficiently aware that the role of the board was to make policy and that the president's was to administer the college. Moreover, all presidents and trustees realized that it was the boards who hired and fired presidents. This knowledge did not prevent an occasional showdown between the board and the president; nor did it always prevent individual board members from attempting to get their nephew, friend, or acquaintance appointed to a position with the college. As a community college leader who has worked with literally thousands of board members across the nation notes, a very small percentage of trustees meddle in the daily operation of the college on purpose; the majority who become involved in administration do so because they do not know any better. He admits that the line between policy and administration is often a thin, wavy one resulting in grey areas where authority is ambiguous and varies from college to college. Strong boards and strong presidents are absolutely necessary if the board members are to understand their role and the presidents theirs, he feels. Educating the board to its responsibilities is the key to a successful board – president relationship, for "if the boards don't know what they are doing, they are going to be one of the president's greatest sources of pressure," he concludes.

When trustees dig too deeply into administration, it is often in that fertile breeding ground of conflict — personnel appointments. In most cases the request to the president to consider someone for an appointment to the college faculty or staff simply consists of the board member passing on a name that he or she has received from a friend, or, in some cases, a legislator, and is, at worst, a minor irritant to the president. However, when the attempt to influence personnel decisions is serious, a crisis of sorts occurs. One president found that on a few occasions during his 12 years as a president, his career, or at least his longevity in his current position, depended on the outcome of a personel decision: "One perfect example for me centered around a personnel problem. We have a very orderly personnel-hiring policy and we all — the president and the board — agreed to live by it. That went pretty well for four or five years and then a very important person, who is now a national figure who owns baseball teams, etc., sent down the word that he wanted one of his people hired. Two or three of my board members were rather beholden to him. There seemed to be no way of finessing it or negotiating it; a battle ensued for a year and a half; I finally won because our policy was clear." This type of interference is unusual and clearly should be understood as representing one case, at one college, at one particular time; it does not represent the normal situation at that college, and certainly not at most other colleges. The example is given not only to show that a board *can* become involved in the day-to-day operation of the college through the efforts of a single board member, but, more important, to remind the president that *no one* who works in the ever-shifting environment of the presidency is immune to this type of pressure.

Another example which is also atypical serves to illustrate what boards can do, if the members desire. When asked if his board members meddled in the daily operations of the college, one president responded, "Yes, constantly." In this case, the majority of the board attempted to prevent the completion of an internal audit. The president noted: "I battle with a portion of the board all the time. The battle is over keeping lines clear and the lines drawn between policy making and administering the college." The president realized that his situation was, as he put it, "bizarre" and that things had to get better "for there is no way the board can become more involved."

It is important that presidents and board members realize that usurping authority is a double-edged sword: presidents can and sometimes do exceed their proper role. One trustee who is very active with the Association of Community College Trustees (ACCT) described a situation where both a board member and a president moved beyond the pale of their authority. She noted that it can be "horrendous and very dangerous" when a trustee "walks the halls, visits the buildings, interviews people, and makes snap judgments" about the operation of the college, a situation this trustee and her board have dealt with. Yet she feels it is equally dangerous for the president to attempt to assume too much control, a situation with which her board is currently struggling. She describes her current president as an autocrat who wants to consolidate all of the power in his office. The board, she feels, must serve as a countervailing force to the power moves by the president. "We have to work very hard to make sure that the situation does not get away from us. The board feels that it must be vigilant, must study the president's proposals in detail, a right we have." With objectivity and sensitivity she put her finger on the delicate board – president relationship: "However, there is always the danger that we want to move over into the administrative arena and there is danger in that too."

Although the above examples represent extremes, no president or board can afford to sit back and assume that either the board or the president will always function in an acceptable manner. Several presidents noted that it is imperative that board members be informed on all issues and that the president provide the leadership required to educate the board. Those trustees interviewed feel that the ACCT can and should play an important role in educating board members, especially in helping them distinguish between their role in making policy and the president's role in carrying out policy. The ACCT has recently decided to provide assistance to colleges conducting presidential searches, thus placing the organization in a strong position to influence the future of the community college presidency.

What about the charge that trustees who are members of special interest groups want to become involved in the daily decision-making process on campus? One president claims that his board was taken over by the unions; another states that the union influence is very strong on his board and that the union bias influences board decisions. These attempts at board control are rare, however. Indeed, one knowledgeable leader asserts that, although special interest groups (unions being a prime example) try to influence board policy by having their members serve on the college board, the attempt to influence board policy often backfires. Members of the special interest groups get caught up in board activity to such an extent that the trustee role dominates whatever special interest the trustee was originally placed on the board to represent.

In summary, college boards generally fulfill their policy-making role; generally stay out of the daily operation of the college, including personnel decisions; and generally have a good relationship with the president's office. When erosion of board authority takes place, it is often seen as coming from external sources, although presidents should be careful not to overreach their authority. Most presidents see a good relationship with the board as contributing to their success; this relationship includes keeping trustees well informed and educating them, especially new members, to the mission of the community college and to the role of the board in making policy. When the board gets into the day-to-day operation of the college, it is usually an individual who gets involved and the situation is dealt with on an individual basis, although the entire board can be sucked into the situation, especially if a power struggle ensues between members of the board and the president. When an individual gets involved, it is likely to be over a personnel decision. As one president put it, "We have a board member who thinks that the college should be populated with people whom she thinks are deserving of jobs." *A point to remember is that the board–president relationship is delicately balanced. Situations can and do change: the president and the board must be sensitive to changes and work to see that the board–president relationship is clearly understood by all parties, a relationship that places the board in charge of making policy and the president in charge of administering policy.*

Campus Governance

Mention community college governance and the thing that comes to mind for many people is a bureaucratic pyramid with the president enshrined at the top. Mention collective bargaining and the thing that comes to mind for many community college leaders is an adversarial atmosphere in which collegiality cannot exist. Academic governance is a complex affair, and probably no aspect of the community college presidency has changed more in the last two decades than the president's role in campus governance. Changes can be traced to two major sources: the arrival of collective negotiations on campus and the demands on the part of faculty members to be included in the governance process. While the inclusion of faculty in the governance process has been a part of much of American higher education since the founding of Harvard, it has been only recently that they have had a significant role in the governance of many community colleges. The following observations, while by no means an exhaustive analysis of the governance process, should nevertheless add to the understanding of the relationship of the college president to this process.

As early as 1965, it was noted in a volume that has become

something of a classic in the field that relationships among the governing board, the administration, and the faculty were undergoing significant changes. "The roles of these three groups are going to shift from a hierarchical pattern to one in which there is a constant and effective interaction. . . . This, of course, means that one of the increasingly important roles of college presidents will be the mediation of conservative and liberal streams of thought" (Blocker, Plummer, and Richardson, 1965, pp. 197–198). Some seven years later it was argued that "the president of the future will need to possess a far greater expertise in managerial competencies and at the same time exercise such competencies in a manner that will make his position far less central to institutional functioning than has been true" (Richardson, Blocker, and Bender, 1972, p.127). It is interesting to note that the 1965 volume did not mention collective negotiations whereas the 1972 volume devoted nine pages to the subject and made reference to it on an additional 11.

Concurrent with the movement away from the autocratic presidency toward a "shared authority model" of governance was the trend toward collective negotiations on the two-year campus. It was reported in 1975 that 223 community college campuses were unionized (Blumer, 1975). While it is not clear if by "campuses" the author means individual colleges or campuses within multicampus districts, the number is nevertheless significant and represents a giant leap forward for collective negotiations on the two-year college campus since 1965, when Henry Ford Community College and Jackson Community College became the first comprehensive community colleges to be organized (Ernst, 1985). By 1978, 230 public two-year institutions were unionized (Richardson, 1979), and it was reported in 1984 that 275 two-year colleges had collective bargaining agreements (ERIC Digest, 1984). The latest count of unionization on the two-year campus reveals that there are 284 two-year colleges with 491 campuses having collective bargaining agreements; 12 of the agreements exist on 14 private two-year campuses (Ernst, 1985). Perhaps the movement toward collective negotiations spurred on the movement toward participatory governance; or perhaps participatory governance gave faculty members the courage and freedom to seek an outside bargaining unit. It is also possible that the 1960s and early 1970s, with their seemingly unlimited supply of students and teaching positions coupled with the many "rights movements," made it easy to do whatever one wanted to do on campus, including bargaining and governing collectively. Regardless of what the driving forces were and are, collective negotiations and participatory governance have had a major impact on the community college presidency.

College governance and the relationship of unions to the governance process bring forth mixed images among members of the higher education community, including some community college presidents. One community college president, writing in 1975, argues in favor of collective bargaining as an aid in identifying and clarifying the various roles on campus. He warns that "if the community college is to continue to flourish we must not return to a losing model — participatory governance" (Helling, 1975, p. 17.). This illustration is used to show the "either-or" attitude that often existed on campuses during the 1960s and early 1970s. What was missing in this type of thinking and what is still missing in the minds of some is the understanding that having unions on campus is not an "either-or" situation, but rather a "both" situation on many campuses whereby the union is a force in the governance process and academic governance tends to follow a "participatory model."

Governance and Unionization

Terms, if not always actions, such as participatory governance, shared authority, and the collegial model of governance made their way to most community college campuses during the 1960's and 1970's. In an attempt to understand better the role of the community college president in the governance process, those interviewed were asked to determine who actually makes the decisions on campus and were they, the presidents, in favor of participatory governance and shared authority; if so, who participates in the governance process and with whom is the authority shared?

"If you ask me, we were very participatory in our governance process; if you ask the faculty, they might say that I was totally autocratic." That quote was from a person who just left the presidency after 14 years; how do other presidents view the governance process? Without exception, all the presidents interviewed felt that the president must share decision making and governance of the college with a number of people, thus giving lie to the myth that still lingers in some academic circles that the community college president sits atop the organizational pyramid and makes all of the decisions. There is now some evidence to suggest that perhaps some community college presidents have spread the decision-making process so thinly that the role of the president as college leader has been eroded. On the other hand, almost without exception, the presidents declared that they are the final stopping point for decisions on campus, unless, of course, there is an outside agency or state office for community colleges that must be consulted. Faculty members and trustees see the president's "buck-stopping capacity" as being more potent than do presidents, probably because the presidents' perceived power is greater than it actually is in many cases. In regard to the decision-making process, most presidents adhere to the textbook and delegate decision making to the lowest possible level, although, when pushed on the point, several of the presidents admitted that they delegated matters to the deans or vice president and assumed that decision making continued to flow downward.

Several presidents noted that the faculty was involved in most academic matters through committees (such as the curriculum committee), on collegewide councils, or both. Where a faculty senate exists, almost all presidents interviewed consult it on major issues. In one instance, the president of a nonunionized college was able to get the faculty senate to come up with a plan for "riffing" (reduction in force) faculty; the plan was accepted by the president and the board and is currently in use. One president noted that he now shares his authority much more than he did in the past; this suggests that the picture of the autocratic president was not without merit in earlier years.

Two quotes, one from a faculty member who also has administrative duties and one from a trustee, point out how they view the governance process on their campus and give some indication of how far some presidents have gone in "letting go of the reins."

The faculty member states: "I think faculty members have gotten comfortable with being able to express themselves and to identify areas of concern and need, not necessarily with the idea of forcing the president's hand on any issue but just to communicate with him our areas of concern. Together, we have faced the issues. The way we have resolved them is through dialogue and other means of communications." According to the trustee: "We know as a board that a decision has gone through this council, that council, and finally the administrative group. I have never seen such participation from the lowest-paid, or lesser, position, to the highest position. I have never seen anything like how it works. It is just fantastic, very effective." Certainly many campuses still have autocratic presidents who deny others the right to meaningful participation in the governance process, but the pendulum has swung in the direction of more faculty involvement in governance. Just as certainly, faculty members on some campuses see as their role to "bring as much pressure on the president as we can," to quote one faculty member. But in most instances faculty members, while objecting to unilateral decisions by the president, or by anyone else for that matter, are quite willing to abide by the decision of the president, assuming their points of view have been considered prior to the decision. Indeed, one theme that came through in several faculty interviews centered around the belief that the president not only has a right but indeed an obligation to make the decision within a reasonable amount of time. Or, as a long-time national leader observes: "The effective leader must not procrastinate, must not vacillate, but must be able to say this is something we ought to do and get on with it."

Once the decision-making process has gone through the various channels, someone must make the final decision; and even some of the decisions that have been delegated to "the lowest possible level" have a way of making their way to the president's office and occasionally to the board. In this regard, several presidents made it clear that the community college campus is not a pure democracy thriving on a "one person – one vote" mode of operation nor are decisions made by consensus, as is popularly and falsely believed to be the case on the campuses of many four-year colleges and universities.

The historical development of the community college has

contributed to the image, and in some cases the reality, of the autocratic president. An individual who worked very closely with presidents and trustees across the nation for a period of 23 years, and who was recognized as the national community college leader during those years, places the autocratic presidency often associated with the community college in historical perspective: "I don't know if you would call the early presidents autocratic; they were very determined in their ways. One reason for that was because a lot of people, board members included, knew very little about the community college. Trustees used to call me and say they wanted to open a community college but knew nothing about them. They wanted somebody who knew something about them. So there was an expertise they were looking for at that time; the president was supposed to know, beyond anyone else, what the institution was supposed to be. Today, of course, most of the trustees feel that they know at least as much about the institution as the president. The role relationship has changed. I think there was another thing too. I think to some extent there was recognition of the public school background of a lot of the early presidents, a background where they were strong administrators. Call it autocratic. I call it strong administration."

Another long-time, highly successful community college presidential leader who has spent over 30 years of his life in community college administration, most of it as a president, does not hesitate to use autocratic to describe the early presidents. His observations also help place the evolution of the presidency in historical context: "Yes, I believe you could say that they were autocratic. I think, however, that they reflected the type of leadership that was expected at the time. I don't mean that the individuals were autocratic, period, but I think they were responding to what boards expected in terms of leadership. You tended to identify the prevailing practice and try to fit in and make it fly the way they wanted it to fly. Now there has been an erosion of authority and there is much more coordination, cooperation, and broad-based decision making."

Community colleges are often viewed as less than collegiate and the president as autocratic in part because of the very nature of the community college and its need to respond to community needs. If a new industry wants a training program, there is often precious little time for making a decision and often never any time for the full decision-making process to come into play. Most four-year colleges would never put an academic program into place, no matter how short in length, until the academic senate and other appropriate parties and individuals had been consulted. Often the community college president must make a quick decision and iron out the details later, a very "uncollegial" approach and one that leads to charges of autocracy from both within and outside the institution. A community college president who has a national reputation for the "participatory governance structure" at his college contrasts the approach to decision making at the community college with what he perceives it to be at four-year colleges and universities. He notes: "One of the advantages we have over four-year colleges and universities is that we *can* make a decision here. Most universities are really confederacies made up of departments and schools; we are not, and we can make decisions that stick." In no way did the president imply that *he* made the decisions alone, or that he was involved in most decisions; however, his statement could easily be interpreted as autocratic.

Have community college presidents become victims of their own rhetoric and become caught up in the community college's democratization philosophy to such an extent that they have lessened their ability to lead? While there is not enough evidence based on the interviews to reach that conclusion, there are enough signs to warrant asking the question. Most presidents interviewed were *very* careful to point out how they involve others in making decisions; rarely did anyone say that he or she, as president, makes the decision. One president described his college's administrative organization as "flat," implying that there is no hierarchy through which decisions flow. The flat organization works well for him, for he built a strong national and local reputation during the 1960s and 1970s and could probably make any organization work rather well on his campus. One must wonder, however, if his successor can provide the leadership required in the future if that successor has a "flat" organizational structure. At least one important national community college leader thinks that perhaps community college presidents have gone too far in "democratizing the decision-making process": "Most faculty and staff members are not interested in becoming involved in every decision on campus. What they are interested in is knowing how to become involved if they want to. We have bent over backwards trying to involve people in every decision when what we ought to be doing is bending over backwards to make sure people know how they can become involved, how they can get their oar in the water."

The above comments on governance indicate strongly that community colleges have a participatory governance structure that involves a number of people in the decision-making process. While presidents and others recognize that the president has the right and responsibility to make the final decision on campus as long as rules, regulations, and contracts are followed, everyone interviewed believes that the president should not attempt to make a large number of decisions alone, especially decisions that have an impact on personnel policies and educational programs.

The presidents, then, with pressure from various segments of the college community, seem to have meshed the bureaucratic governance structure, in many cases inherited from the public schools, with a collegial model. This model was brought to the campus through their own educational experiences and through the educational experiences of the faculty, most of whom came to the campuses during the sixties and seventies, a time of ferment in higher education. The result is a governance model that is participatory in nature but with relatively clear lines regarding how decisions are made; yet, in some cases, misunderstanding exists regarding the role of the president in the process. *A danger is a lack of understanding on the part of some presidents regarding how to remain a strong leader while at the same time involving the appropriate people in making decisions.* Nevertheless, on the whole, community college presidents, trustees, faculty members, and others have taken great strides in developing a governance structure that involves faculty and is compatible with the community college mission.

However, the above is only part of the story since beginning in the 1960s, a new element was added to the governance process on many campuses: collective bargaining.

Unions on Campus

For those presidents who do not have to deal with collective bargaining or, in some cases, those who were involved in the process when unions first came to the campus, the mere mention of unions evokes fear similar to that in William Inge's "Dark at the Top of the Stairs." One president summed up this point of view when asked if her campus were unionized. Her reply was "No, thank God!" Without exception, those presidents whose campuses were not unionized expressed relief that they did not have a union with which to contend. For example, one president pointed with pride to the fact that the union had conducted four unsuccessful elections on his campus, with the last union defeat being by the largest margin yet.

The fear of the dark sometimes exceeded reality, however. One president, who incidentally used to be the chief negotiator for a community college district, noted that there is very little conflict between his office and the union: "We deal honestly and openly with each other and we work very well together." Another president from the highly unionized Pacific Northwest notes that the union plays almost no role in campus governance as it relates to academics. On his campus, the union is concerned with faculty rights and responsibilities and never interferes with the teaching process. "I am very pleased with the way the union has worked out for us," he declares. Another president whose college is in a city "where everything is unionized" insists that the union is involved in the governance process beyond the contract, not because the contract permits it, but because the employees demand it. He goes so far as to note that sometimes the union is embarrassed over being forced into an advocacy role that is not included in the contract. He explains it this way: "Its leaders will come and see me and say, 'look Prez, we know we have no right in this, but people have come in and asked us to look into the following.' " He further notes: "Our whole city is unionized. It is a different environment to work in and not everyone understands it."

Unions on campus tend to confuse the governance process for some presidents as well as create a sense of betrayal. As one president declared, "In recent years it has been very frustrating trying to live with your friends. Most of us grew up in a more collegial atmosphere than now exists. Collective bargaining has brought on an adversarial relationship that did not formerly exist." Successful presidents do adjust, however. A president who was in Michigan when collective negotiations came to many community college campuses in that state found negotiations quite traumatic when they first came about; however, in recent years he has been able to put collective negotiations in perspective and finds that they no longer create the conflict for him or for the campus that they did in earlier years.

Whether people do not understand the role of the union or whether they simply do not like unions on campus, the fact is that in many cases the union complicates the governance process and brings pressure to bear on the president. A flagrant example of the union's role conflicting with the more traditional collegial model of academic governance comes from a large inner-city college which, like the one mentioned above, has a history of strong unions. In this college, the union has a contract which assures that its members will share in the academic governance process. Union members are guaranteed a certain number of positions on the three major standing committees of student, academic, and business affairs. The union is also guaranteed membership on the institutionwide committee through which *all* recommendations to the president flow.

On a Michigan campus where the union has been a way of life for a number of years and where the union has gone out on strike, a cabinet elected by the union has replaced the faculty senate. A faculty member, who feels things are working fairly well at this time because both the administration and faculty are tired of conflict, is nevertheless not secure with the truce. "I'm not sure that we have not sidestepped the issues . . . for both sides have retreated and avoided the issues rather than effectively dealing with them." He believes that things are much more peaceful because the college has a new president who is not as combative as the former president, and consequently the faculty is not placed on the defensive. He observed that, based on his 13 years of experience in a unionized college, the degree of conflict on campus in many cases depends upon who is providing the leadership for the union and who occupies the president's office. On another campus, the president is careful to appoint union members to college committees, thus attempting to keep the union well informed and reducing friction between the union and the president's office.

The most common approach to unions and academic governance is to keep the two separated as much as possible. Most presidents, however, seem to realize that unions are an aspect of governance in its broader perspective and that many "nonacademic" decisions affect the college environment and ultimately affect the teaching and learning process. In some cases, the president takes an active role in seeing that the union does not interject itself into the academic governance process beyond the terms of the contract. Obviously, the involvement of the union in academic governance must be determined during contract negotiations if further conflicts in this area are to be avoided.

In one instance, a president worked very hard to keep the faculty senate alive after the faculty became unionized. The union, it seems, was viewed as a cure-all; consequently, many faculty members saw no further need for a strong faculty senate. Largely due to the efforts of the president, the senate not only survived but thrived and today is a major component in the governance process. Another president feels that, while he and the union have been able to "work things out," the union has stayed out of the academic governance process only because he and the board of trustees have kept them out by refusing to "back off" in terms of what the union's responsibility should be. Yet another president commented that unions are involved in all aspects of the governance process "a lot and want more."

A faculty member from Minnesota has no illusions about the union being a cure-all. On the contrary, he views the union contract as a weapon to be used by both the faculty and the president and, on his campus, a weapon that the president wields as often and as powerfully as he can: "Prior to a union contract, I think the president listened more carefully to what faculty had to say because there was constant interaction." Now, he believes the president uses the contract and the power it gives him as he desires. The faculty "are simply recommending bodies that go through the motions," he concludes.

In some situations, unions do indeed play "hardball," as one president calls it. After first noting that his board is prounion, he cites one example, thereby giving some credence to the claim that some special interest groups tend to become involved in the daily affairs of the campus: "The union interjects itself into the affairs of the college regularly. We had an executive committee meeting of our board and the union was there, distributed materials, and spoke to the issues. I had to refute the comments made by the union representatives." It may be of interest to note that this scene occurred in a state that has a law prohibiting collective negotiations by public employees!

The fact that unions can complicate the governance process, even when they are prohibited by law, is illustrated by a recent story in the *Chronicle of Higher Education.* Under Texas law, faculty and administrators in public institutions are prohibited from engaging in collective negotiations. Nevertheless, the mid-level administrators at Austin Community College formed their own "union-like" group, as the *Chronicle* puts it. While the organization is not a union in the legal sense of the term, its members nevertheless want to "create some kind of professional-development plan so employees who earn work-related degrees will be promoted and receive salary increases" (Heller, 1985, p. 27). Presidents must be aware that unions can make their presence felt in the governance process in a number of ways. As Father Hesburgh, President of Notre Dame University, puts it: "Sandbagging the administration by a constant threat of collective bargaining has become a popular indoor sport in colleges and universities" (Hesburgh, 1979, p. 46).

While the purpose here is to shed some light on the impact of collective negotiations on the presidency and not on the total governance process, comments from one source serve to demonstrate that the votes are still out on the role of the union in campus governance. Noting that research has been done on the role of the union in determining faculty salaries and on the educational process, one author concludes the following regarding governance: "Comparative research has been extended into a number of other areas of interest. The most prominent among these has been, from an early period, the issue of governance. Many observers believed that collective bargaining would bring about more centralized authority. While this has occurred, as predicted, the reason . . . is that centralization of authority assists unionization, which then reinforces greater centralization. In some institutions, however, collective bargaining has brought about greater institutional involvement. . . . None of this research supports the idea that collective bargaining has made drastic changes in the governance of the institution" (Cunningham, 1983 – 84, p. 17). It appears that perhaps the greatest impact has been on the role of the president in the governance process rather than on the total process, for the president is responsible for seeing that the various factions work together to produce a process that improves the college environment and thereby enhances student learning.

It is clear that unions are a factor in community college governance today. While the president's role varies from campus to campus, the dominant role the president plays when the faculty is unionized is to work to see that the union meshes with the total college governance process. For one president, this means meeting with the union leadership once a week for an hour; for another, it means making it clear to the college community that "collegial operations are outside of the contract"— his office has no official relationship with the union other than the contract and he only sees the union leadership once or twice a year; another leader meets with representatives of the support staff and faculty unions twice a month, although the union's role in governance is very small.

Community college presidents, for the most part, have learned that they are not professional negotiators. In almost all instances, those persons interviewed have a professional arbitrator to negotiate the contract for the college. In almost all cases, someone else — a personnel director, an academic vice president, an assistant to the president — is responsible for enforcing the contract from the college's perspective and for dealing with grievances unless the contract specifies that a particular grievance must go to the president. Perhaps the most important finding to come out of the information on unions on campus is that *presidents have largely removed themselves from the day-to-day dealings with the unions and with faculty issues covered by the union contract and instead are devoting their time and energy to faculty relations that are outside of the union contract.* This approach appears to be the most feasible one for creating and maintaining an atmosphere in which collegiality can co-exist with unionization. Moreover, the approach is not only practical, it is also realistic, for unions will be a part of the academic scene for the foreseeable future.

CHAPTER 6

Satisfactions, Successes, Failures, and Prestige

When the Association of Governing Boards of Universities and Colleges (AGB) established the Commission on Strengthening Presidential Leadership directed by Clark Kerr, it asked three questions. One of those questions was whether it is now more difficult to get highly qualified people to serve as the presidents of colleges and universities than it was in earlier times, especially during the 1960s. The Commission's report answered in the affirmative, indicating that only about one-half of the current top academic officers are interested in becoming college and university presidents (AGB, 1984, p. ix).

One can assume that the lack of interest in the presidency found by the AGB study results from a lack of perceived rewards associated with the position. While the AGB report included community college presidents, it did not distinguish between the observations of presidents of four-year and two-year institutions and therefore adds little to the understanding of what community college presidents value about their position. A logical way of determining what presidents and others see as the satisfactions, successes, failures, and prestige associated with the community college presidency appeared to be to ask them. Following are some of the answers.

Satisfactions

While this volume is not concerned with material rewards, it is concerned with determining what other rewards and satisfactions are associated with the community college presidency. Consequently, those interviewed were asked both what they considered to be the most satisfying and the most negative aspects of the position. The responses not only help in understanding the presidency but also give some indication of what facet of the community college philosophy is most attractive to current presidents.

The interviews revealed that relationships with the college community and community at large do indeed provide presidents with a great deal of satisfaction, thus demonstrating that the community dimensions of the community college philosophy are important to presidents as are campus relationships. Many presidents enjoy talking informally with student groups. "It is very rewarding to hear their special approach to some of the problems we have today and how they still have great faith in the educational experience to move them from one point to another," comments one president. Contrary to much of today's mythology and, in some cases, practices growing out the late 1960s, associating with the faculty is also rewarding for many presidents, including campuses that have faculty unions.

Graduation seems to hold a special fascination for many presidents (the cynic might see the satisfaction coming from the end of another year) and indeed means about as much to some presidents as it does to the students. As one 18-year veteran of the presidency explains: "Every May or June when we have our commencement and I see the students walking across the stage —I know many of them personally—I would have to say that any frustrations I have had during the year melt away. I always come away with a tremendous high. Knowing that we are adding value that many of these students could not get elsewhere, that we have really helped them along considerably, this is reward-ing." Another commented: "When I go to graduation, that is the payoff for me. When you see thousands of people walking across the stage and you just know that they would not be there without the community college, their lives would not be enriched with-out that institution, that is the payoff for me."

Faculty, trustees, and other administrators also viewed stu-dent success as a major source of satisfaction for the president as well as for the total college community. As one board member notes, "The most rewarding thing for the president has to be seeing what happens to the college's students, whether they at-tend college to transfer to a four-year college, or to take a two-year technical program, or whether it's just a senior citizen want-ing to learn to play the piano; all are a source of satisfaction."

The community college's relationship with the larger com-munity brings gratification to a number of presidents: "Clearly the most rewarding aspect of the presidency is seeing the effect the college has had on the community and on the students; watching community changes because the college is there is very rewarding." Another states, "There are very few situations like this, where you can see the results of your work daily. The results are seen in a whole range of things: resolution of community problems, laying plans that help organizations achieve their goals, building relationships with the people in the community." Still another claims: "The most rewarding aspect of my job is seeing things done that need to be done to meet community needs." According to one leader, "The most rewarding thing is to see communities look to the community college for real leader-ship. I don't mean just educating students but to have the com-munity college president be one of a half dozen people in an urban area of over a million people who can make a difference."

Community college presidents, like leaders in all areas, enjoy the position of president because it is at the top of their profession and because of the opportunities it provides to exert leadership. As one president explains: "One of the reasons for becoming a president was to implement my ideas; it is very rewarding to know that they work." Another finds it rewarding just to be in a place where one can make things happen. Another enjoys the positive image the college has in the community: "As president, I get to savor that image." Another enjoys the prestige that comes with the office as well as seeing her ideas accomplished.

It is interesting to note that community college presidents seem to gain most of their satisfactions from what they can see, touch, and experience firsthand. Rarely did anyone interviewed refer to the feeling of achievement that comes with being a part of a momentous, highly successful movement which has brought educational opportunities to so many people. For example, graduation is seen as a climactic event, not simply as a thread in the much broader fabric that makes up the life of the individual and the institution's contribution to the individual. This inability to perceive the broad scope is particularly notable since much of the rhetoric used to promote the community college is couched in sweeping generalizations so often used to describe American democracy. Missing is that feeling of being a part of something larger than one's self, that feeling of "manifest destiny" that one would expect presidents to associate with being on the leading edge of something as big and as bold as the community college movement in America.

Failure to note the larger implications of being a community college president is also surprising considering the family background of most current presidents. They seem to lack the perception of the community college as the vehicle whereby individuals — in this case themselves — could be free of the Great Depression mentality that was so much a part of their childhood, at least in the stories of their parents and others.

Presidents would surely gain a great deal of satisfaction if they would "step back" and view their role as a significant one in the development of American democracy. They are, after all, the frontier scouts of post–World War II American higher education.

In summary (and in spite of an apparent lack of appreciation of the larger drama of the presidency), every one interviewed saw the office as having a number of satisfactions associated with it. No one interviewed felt that the frustrations outweighed the rewards associated with the position, a not-so-surprising finding since only "survivors" were interviewed on this aspect of the presidency.

Successes

Since the success of a leader is ultimately judged on the success of the enterprise he or she leads, the success of the community college president must ultimately rest on the ability of the college to achieve its mission, a mission that is committed to providing educational opportunity to a broad-based constituency. Community college leaders claim that their institutions are "the community's colleges" and take pride in the claim that their colleges exist to serve students. *Indeed, commitments to teaching and serving the community are the twin towers of the community college philosophy.* How successful has the community college been in opening the doors of educational opportunity for its ever-expanding constituents? Or, casting the question in a leadership mode, how successful have community college presidents been in leading their institutions toward the college's mission?

Those interviewed were adamant in their praise of the community college for opening the doors of educational opportunity for millions of Americans who, if it were not for the community college, would have been denied the opportunity to attend college. The major contribution of the community college according to those interviewed can be summarized in one word: *access.* Cliches such as "the democratization of higher education," "equality of educational opportunity," "opportunity college," "the people's college," "the open door," "egalitarianism," and "democracy's college" abound throughout the interviews. Nevertheless, essentially everyone interviewed saw the community college's major success as enabling members of lower socioeconomic groups, minorities, women, older adults, part-time students, academically weak students, and other segments of society that have traditionally lingered on the periphery of higher education's mainstream at least to gain a sampling of that experience through the college's wide, if not totally open, door.

How is open access to higher education viewed by community college leaders and what is the responsibility of the president for the successes and failures of an open-access institution? Before answering this question, one must place the president at the center of the enterprise that he or she is leading. The institutional "we" heard so often in the interviews, like the imperial "we," must ultimately come to rest with the leader, in this case, the community college president. Consequently, when a faculty member, trustee, president, or anyone else for that matter, refers to the community college as "our" greatest failure or "our" greatest success, or notes what "we" have failed or "we" have accomplished, their perspective must be refocused. The failures and accomplishments, whether they be institutional failures or successes, or whether they be leadership successes or failures, *must be viewed as one and the same: presidential successes or failures are ultimately judged by the successes or failures of the institution.*

With the above caveat in mind, what are some of the successes enjoyed by community colleges and their presidents? A faculty member replies: "Older adults can go back to school without having to apologize." Another faculty member states: "We have been accessible; many who lacked skills in the beginning have been able to get them." According to one president, "Our main contribution has been in demonstrating to this country that educational opportunity can produce educational success." Another declares: "Democratization. The fact that we have been able to punch a hole in the classical, pompous notion about learning and learning styles; that education for working people can be on their terms. We have given an alternative to people that has never been available before." In the words of another president, "Contribution? That's easy. That is what I call the salvage function. Making successes out of people who otherwise would not have an opportunity." A board member observes: "There is no doubt in my mind that we have reached people who, in no way in the history of mankind, have ever been reached at this level of education before. It has really made America a different place. Not too many people would make this statement, I don't guess, but the community college could well be the savior of our type of government because it brings people together at levels that other organizations can't bring together."

While presidents view open access as the community college's greatest contribution to society, what do they value most as their own individual accomplishments as presidents? Are presidential accomplishments closely tied to the community college's major accomplishment, providing open access? Or are presidential accomplishments of a more personal nature? The answers to these questions provide an interesting and informative view of the presidency.

A major theme regarding presidential accomplishments or successes is the role of the president in creating an environment on campus that permits students, faculty, and staff to learn and grow as individuals and as members of the campus community and the community at large. An important aspect of creating an environment conducive to learning is in fostering a sense of community among faculty, staff, and administrators. One president believes that his greatest success as a president has been a push for "open decision making" which in turn has helped the college achieve its mission. Another president commented proudly that his employees feel the college is a good place to work, and that the morale and self-esteem of most people who work for the college is very high. A number of presidents were pleased with their ability to create a positive atmosphere whereby unions could co-exist with the other aspects of faculty governance, a situation that rarely existed when unions first came to the community college campus.

It is not surprising that most faculty members interviewed tend to see the president's accomplishments in terms of "giving the faculty a sense of participation in the governance process," as one faculty member observed. Another faculty member viewed her president's greatest success as "being extremely supportive of the faculty and not trying to shortchange them." Another faculty member sees the president's greatest contribution as being a good listener, good communicator, and having an open door to his office. And yet another faculty member admires her president's willingness to take chances while at the same time being sensitive to the needs of the faculty and staff.

A trustee sees the president's major accomplishment at his college as promoting participatory governance. Another trustee, who otherwise had very little good to say about the president, saw his establishment of a "better" relationship with the faculty as his major accomplishment. Still another trustee praised the president's "endless supply of energy and dynamic personality" and for "bringing a much needed new air" to the college, for someone was needed who could "move it on." The fact that presidents, faculty, and trustees place such great emphasis on the president's role in setting a positive tone on campus supports earlier observations regarding the importance of this aspect of the presidency. Obviously, with such a high premium placed on the college environment, presidents view their ability to create a positive environment as a prerequisite to the successful presidency.

Several presidents saw their major contribution as one of extending their influence beyond the local campus. One president who has served as a consultant to community colleges throughout the nation believes that his greatest contribution is in sharing his knowledge of community college management with others. Another president views his role as mentor as his greatest contribution; three of his former deans are now presidents. Yet another president and former chairman of the AACJC Board of Directors sees his major contribution as providing philosophical leadership to the community college movement nationally. For some presidents, their philosophical contributions were of a local and regional nature and served a utilitarian function; they saw their greatest successes in obtaining public support, including financial support, for the community college from legislators and the general public. One president points out that he has raised over $11 million in an area with a median family income of $6,500. While no pattern emerged that would lead one to conclude that any large number of presidents pointed to a single accomplishment as their greatest or most rewarding, the accomplishments and rewards nevertheless almost always come under the very broad umbrella of interpreting and implementing the community college mission.

Presidents appear to be sensitive to the need of promoting access; however, it is often unclear how this is accomplished other than through creating a positive campus environment and endorsing the concept through countless speeches on the subject. Indeed, even in promoting access, presidents often rely on yesterday's rhetoric. As this writer has observed elsewhere: "Literally hundreds of times each year community college presidents tell local service clubs and various other audiences that the community college 'is unique,' 'is uniquely American,' 'cares about students,' 'serves the total community,' and that its faculty members are 'employed to teach and not research.' These, and any number of similar statements, shed little light on the mission of the community college. Indeed, today even the local Kiwanis Club needs to hear more than glib, meaningless phrases if the community college is to be understood and supported. Legislators certainly deserve (and are demanding) more than warmed-over phrases when they are asked to appropriate the millions of dollars requested by community colleges" (Vaughan, 1983, p. 11.)

A means of promoting access (and therefore a means of achieving success as a president) in the minds of a number of presidents is through continually broadening the community college's mission by serving different segments of society. The community college, then, becomes a vehicle for easing and enhancing the life processes as one moves through the various life stages: "Kiddie Colleges," "Family Colleges," and Condo Colleges" for retirees, are just some of the ways in which open access has expanded to include ever-widening "markets."

Presidents are not alone in advocating open access. One board member sees the greatest success of the president of his institution as his continual willingness to find new areas for service. A vice president describes the greatest asset of his institution's president as "an undying commitment to making the open door work." In line with the concept of service (a cynic might say in line with the need to meet enrollments), one president views his greatest success as "turning enrollments around." Another president sees his greatest contribution in bringing about a new responsiveness on the part of the college in meeting community needs. "I want the people to rethink what we are doing. I want to cause them to see the community college as it is and what it can become," one president declares. A strong endorsement for the community college philosophy of service to the total community comes from two presidents from highly diverse backgrounds. They see their greatest successes as elevating their colleges, which were primarily traditional junior colleges when they arrive, to a stage where they are truly comprehensive community colleges with a commitment to serving all students, especially more minorities. As one of the presidents noted: "I've seen our college move from an all-white institution to a situation where the racial composition of the student body represents the racial composition of our district." It is interesting to note that one of these presidents heads a college in Mississippi and the other a college in New York, giving credence to the claim that there is *a* community college mission. The above quote, by the way, is from the president from New York.

Although a number of the persons interviewed emphasize the need for standards and quality in everything the college does, few see providing educational leadership in terms of shaping the curriculum as one of the president's greatest contributions. The exception is noteworthy: one president sees his greatest accomplishment as bringing about academic reforms that clearly placed the college on target for meeting the needs of the remainder of the century. It is also worth mentioning that the reforms placed the president and his college in the national limelight and led to reforms in other colleges. Thus it is clear that successes can and do cross local service districts, and more important, that academic leadership can still be an important avenue for exercising presidential leadership.

The routes to success varied just as presidents vary in their approaches to the position; nevertheless, the personal drives and accomplishments of the presidents, in every instance, centered around a commitment to the "open door." No one interviewed rejected open access as the cornerstone of the community college's philosophy, and everyone felt that the president had a major role to play in maintaining open access. Ironically, the "selling of the community college" is not generally viewed as one of the community college's greatest success stories, at least not at this stage in its history.

Overall Failures

Based on the interviews and personal observations, *the perceived overwhelming failure of the community college has been the inability or unwillingness of its leaders to interpret and articulate its mission effectively, thereby failing to present consistently a positive image to its various publics.* Understanding this failure provides a good perspective for viewing many issues currently facing the community college. These issues include its ability to obtain funds, to create a positive image and in general to raise its prestige in the higher education community and in the community at large; to attract well-qualified students, faculty, and administrators; and, finally, its ability to create and maintain a positive environment, an environment that is affected by all of the above factors.

Why have community college leaders, and especially the community college president, failed to articulate the mission successfully? The question goes to the very heart of the leadership question, for the discussion again must focus on the president as leader of the enterprise. The conclusion is that in those instances where the community college has failed to articulate its mission successfully, the president has by definition failed, at least in part.

Presidents and others are sensitive to the shortcomings of leaders to articulate the mission successfully. A quote by an astute and articulate leader who served the community college long and well at the national level sets the stage for exploring the relationship of mission and leadership: "Let me say that there is one persisting skill that is required of presidents. It seems to me that one of the big jobs of the president is to interpret the mission. The president presumably has a vision of what a community college is supposed to be, and he is supposed to be able to describe that vision in persuasive terms to the people who are going to be working with him and doing a job. I find now some 25 or 30 years later that articulating the mission is a continuing problem. There is still a need to intepret the community college. I think when the institutions began to grow, and when growth leveled off, you got new people coming in, but the business of probing the mission just wasn't continued. I have interviewed many legislators and I find time after time that they don't know what a community college is. What we are doing is talking to a passing parade, but we haven't acknowledged that. We seem to be addressing the mission as if we had a stable audience out there and that it is the same as it was 25 or 30 years ago. I conceive of this to be one of the basic responsibilities of leadership, particularly of the president, to have some vision of what the community college ought to be—a vision that is persuasive enough to attract other people with him or her in the task of bringing the vision into fruition."

All segments of the college community interviewed noted the failure to describe clearly the community college. One president notes: "I think of our greatest failure in terms of the community college's image. There is a failure to make consonant the reality of the image. The image is still poor, and the reality, I think, is really high quality. Society has not seen that, and I think it is our fault. It is almost a Pygmalion effect. You get what you expect. We downgrade ourselves and thus we accept this image rather than going out and doing something about it." In a similar vein, the former chancellor of one of the more successful community college districts in the nation notes that the greatest failure of community college leadership is "to communicate to a broadguage public the contributions that we make and the contributions we can make. Call it school-community relations, but we are still low man on the totem pole. We are not the prestigious level of education—in terms of service rendered to society and that should be inverted—but we have a mind-set on the part of the American public that we have not been able to overcome." A faculty member comments in the same vein: "Our greatest failure is probably a lack of ability to convince the community of what we are trying to do and not being able to change the image of just being a technical institution; also, not giving the understanding that open enrollment can be a positive thing."

Image is a problem, even to the extent that successes cause image problems. The former chancellor referred to above claims: "We have cut ourselves with a two-edged sword with our salvage function—with our occupational education, with our remedial work; we get branded as a high school with ash trays, as the academic garbage dump, and so forth. And some of the finest things we do for society come in the areas of remedial work and occupational education, yet we get blasted for them because we are not 'a real college.'" A national leader and former president comments: "Our greatest failure is the inability to communicate to the public what we are. A statement that is becoming a cliche is that community colleges are America's best kept secret. The typical state legislator who went to a university does not understand us; the typical congressman who went to a university does not understand us; many professional people who know the university well do not understand us. This is changing some — our history is not very long in the scheme of things — but at this stage we have not done well in this area."

Failure to sell the community college mission is serious business. As one president observes: "I think the major problem in the future is going to be the inability of community college leaders to convince the various publics that community colleges are valuable assets, valuable enough in terms of priorities to see that they are adequately funded and insure that they are legitimate in terms of being a part of the system of higher education." Another president says: "Our greatest failure is to convey to the public a sense of identity and to convey to the public the contributions the community college is making. There is a large segment of the public out there that does not understand what we do, who we are, or what we are all about." A national leader observes: "Our failure, we haven't talked about it much, and I have been a party to it; it has been in misleading the public regarding the meaning of the open door. We should have been more careful in our definition of excellence, in describing quality programs in different terms, and in bringing the public along with us. Unfortunately, we have given the impression that you can do anything you damn please and make it at a community college. Nothing could be further from the truth." In the words of another president: "We are going to be forced into defining what our role is. I don't think the legislature will accept that we can be all things to all people; legislators will not let us do as we have done before." A dean comments on the subject: "I think that over the next few years community college presidents will have an even more difficult time of convincing people — legislators and others — of the important role community colleges play in the educational system. It seems to me that for as long as I have been working in the community college, which is 14 years, we have been trying to convince people that we are worthwhile. We are not doing a very good job of marketing the community college. We are seen as a place you go if you don't have money to go somewhere else. I think presidents have a major role in changing that. In our state, they do a great deal of talking about it, but I see very little action." A faculty member states: "I think we have allowed a kind of unacknowledged self-contempt to take on such dimensions that on many campuses there is a rather defeated and deflated faculty — probably administrators also — who perhaps didn't achieve the goals they thought they would achieve in their youth and so they find the community college a kind of dead-end street. For too many people it has become a second choice." One final comment from a president summarizes many of the frustrations associated with the failure of its leaders to interpret and articulate the community college's mission: "Our greatest failure and greatest future challenge is our lack of legitimacy among those who provide us with funds. They all tell us, you're great, we're proud of you, you're doing well, but when it comes to putting dollars out for us they are not going to do it. It is going to be the same damn thing it has been in the past. They don't recognize us. We are still a junior college to them."

There is a second failure of the community college; although not nearly as prominent as the failure to articulate the mission successfully, it is one that nevertheless must lie squarely on the doorstep of the president. This is in promising too much and failing to deliver on those promises, a subject that was touched on briefly in an earlier chapter in relationship to pressures from business and industry. A trustee notes that the community college "has reached out and touched" but not always with quality. A president gives a sensitive analysis of the dilemma faced by community colleges in the 1960s. He feels that it is too early to tell if the community college has any great failures, but believes that if it has failed, it was in trying to change things too quickly, or perhaps in believing too strongly in the rhetoric that surrounded the community college in that radical period. His analysis follows: "Probably the most difficult thing we had to deal with in our college was the great integration crunch. The college is 30 miles from where they found the bodies of civil rights workers in 1970. During that time period and the period immediately following it, we probably relaxed academic standards some in order to accommodate the more effective social integration of some blacks. I don't think we said that we were doing this deliberately. In retrospect, I would not have done anything differently. If there was a failure, it was on the part of the larger society to create a social climate in which you could maintain standards while achieving some type of equal treatment."

Another president believes that community colleges went after too many people too fast with too little consideration as to whether they could do the work and whether they could find jobs in the community. Another president believes that the community college has failed to "deliver on the promise of open access for thousands: access is there but not necessarily completion." Yet another president notes that it is not enough just to open the door; the community college must deliver and, to deliver, support services must be available, including financial aid. One president believes that the community college went too far in permitting individuals "to do their own thing" during the sixties and as a result dropped standards and accepted average performance as being "good enough." It should be noted that dropping standards and permitting students to go their own way were common practices throughout much of higher education during that decade.

Some presidents feel that, hand in hand with the failure to articulate the community college's mission, is the leaders' failure to examine critically the entire community college philosophy. Most presidents feel that the role the community college carved out for itself in the 1960s is not necessarily the role it should have in the 1980s and beyond. "Maybe our greatest failure is that we have not been willing to listen to our critics. We have just gone barrelling ahead with this idea of being all things to all people and we believed it; we do not like to be brought to task or held accountable," one president theorizes.

Trying to "be all things to all people" was a criticism heard often in the interviews, although it was usually couched in a larger context, as cited above. One president used the "all-things" terminology to describe the community college's failure. "In spite of what we say, we try to be all things to all people and it is probably impossible. Our greatest failure is not doing everything we do to the best of our ability." Many of those interviewed felt that the community college has gone too far in lowering academic standards and must now define what quality means in terms of its mission. Looking to the future, several of those interviewed saw declining enrollments as a major problem; others saw a lack of funds as the major problem; and, while some presidents saw the community college as having no major failures or shortcomings, those presidents were a very small minority.

The above discussion of failures is, as the reader has probably noticed, at times tedious. The major reason for some of the cloudiness surrounding the shortcomings is that presidents, trustees, and faculty members are often unaware that institutional failures, leadership failures, and presidential failures are, as suggested earlier, one and the same. Until presidents clearly understand that they must assume the ultimate responsibility for whatever lapses the community college experiences, the issue of "whose failure is it anyway" will remain ambiguous, and presidential leadership will come up short.

PERSONAL FAILURES

What are seen as the greatest personal failures of the community college presidents? One president noted that he has been unable to get special interest groups together; however, he does not view this so much as a personal failure as a sign of the times. Another one believes that his greatest shortcoming is in letting a lot of his dreams "fall through the cracks of reality" and consequently not giving the students all he is capable of giving. Another simply notes that the community college lets too many students fail without deciding whether it is the fault of the students, the faculty, or the administration. A faculty member expresses the same sentiments. He asks: Whose fault is it that students drop out and fail and what role should the president play in getting answers regarding dropouts and failures? Here the question must be raised: what is the responsibility of the president when students "fall through the cracks"? Just as the presidents are ultimately responsible for articulating the mission, they are also responsible when students do not achieve their objectives, at least to the extent of finding out who is at fault and taking steps to correct the deficiencies. Indeed, with the high attrition rates at most community colleges (as much as 30–40% from term to term, and from year to year at some colleges), keeping the community college open door from becoming the proverbial revolving door is a central issue facing the community college president today.

Since student failure can be interpreted as institutional failure, the president as institutional leader must assume a share of the responsibility for students' failure to achieve their goals. Yet almost without exception presidential failures were described in terms of personal failures. In every case, the presidents were willing "to take the rap," yet the connection between institutional and personal failure was not made by those presidents interviewed. In most cases, faculty members and trustees were willing to let presidents take the blame for personal lapses but rarely criticized them when the community college fell short of completing its mission.

A sampling of perceived personal failures of presidents gives some insight into the "mind of the presidency." These deficiencies came in all sorts of packages, although, when the presidency is viewed in its total perspective, the failures are minor in comparison with the community college's inability to make open access work as successfully as possible. More important, the sampling demonstrates that no one, including presidents, seems to understand that *someone* must accept the responsibility for institutional failure.

The sampling follows. One faculty member feels that the president of his institution is intimidated by large groups; another teacher sees the president of his institution as too far removed from the faculty. Still another states: "I don't think the president understands the kinds of pressures one faces down in the trenches, so to speak." One faculty member feels that some people perceive the president of her institution as being superficial; a dean feels that a major weakness on the part of his president is his shyness. A common criticism from faculty, trustees, and presidents is that presidents "take on too much" and often do not recognize their inability to do all of the things they have taken on. A trustee notes that the major failure of her president is that he is a poor listener. She goes on to observe: "Very often college presidents do not listen." Time away from the campus brought criticism of the president from faculty members and administrators at several colleges.

Presidents view their personal failures as minor in most cases, although most are very hard on themselves when they feel they have failed in any respect. One president hates to make almost any personnel decision and feels that, when he is forced to make those decisions, he does not make good ones; another confirms the trustees' observation, at least from his perspective, for he sees himself as a poor listener; one leader thinks he gets too involved with too many details and thus hinders the performance of those who report to him; another feels personally responsible if a good faculty or staff member "goes sour"; still another believes that he has just not been able to work well with the county government; one president fails because he has dreams that cannot be accomplished in the time available; another feels she failed in that she could not fill the role of academic leader to the extent she had envisioned; one, a "two-year veteran of the presidency," criticizes himself for not having had enough experience prior to assuming his position; another president believes that she is a victim of the "Wonderwoman" syndrome and thus fails by not letting her trustees know the "price of the presidency" in terms of physical and mental stress; yet another views as a failure his inability to sell the need for a multi campus college to the public; one president states that he was unable to get "that damned foundation off the ground"; another, a veteran of three presidencies, sees as his greatest failure his inability to win over one of his trustees to his way of thinking; and the list goes on.

Another failing worth noting may be viewed as both personal and institutional and bears repeating in detail for it is the type of problem with which community college presidents should indeed be deeply concerned. The comment comes from a national community college leader: "A lot of us caved in to the collective bargaining syndrome, that it had to be an adversarial relationship. As I look back on it, I do not think it had to be that way. But you went to all of the seminars and you were taught, 'Don't let them push you around,' and the faculty went to seminars and were told, 'Don't let those administrators push you around.' We created our own adversarial relationship. My greatest failure was allowing this to happen."

What do the above perceived shortcomings tell us about the community college presidency? They provide some insight into how presidents are observed by others and the sensitivity of some presidents to their own lapses, no matter how minor they might be in the total scheme of things. They also serve to remind the president that "presidential watching" is a favorite campus sport of some faculty, administrators, and others interested in the position. The personal failures articulated above lead one to believe that some presidents may be much too involved in minor details, especially in evaluating their own performance and image. However, the most important thing to be learned from the perceived personal failures of presidents is that most presidents *do not* seem to realize, or at least to admit, that the inability of community college leaders to articulate and fulfill the mission adequately is a major shortcoming on the part of the president and that this cannot be continued if the community college is to receive the recognition its leaders desire.

Why have most presidents failed to make the critical connection between the failure of the community college and their own failures? How can a faculty member complain about a president's failure to be comfortable before large groups, note the lack of the prestige of the community college in her state *(and in her mind)* and yet fail to mention the president's failure to articulate the mission effectively? The answer to these questions appears to lie in how the development of the community college is viewed by presidents, trustees, and faculty members. *From almost all perspectives, the community college appears to be caught in a time warp.* A candid appraisal based on the interviews and on personal observations is that community college leaders are just now realizing that the mission has not been articulated clearly. Why? For over two-and-a-half decades, community colleges have experienced steady and sometimes phenomenal growth, especially when compared with the rest of higher education; every sign seemed to spell success. Moreover, not only were funds available to support the growth but they were there to encourage it. *The assumption was that the mission was clearly understood by members of the college community, legislators, business leaders, and the public in general. Therefore community college leaders, especially presidents, saw no need to do things any differently from the way they had in the past.* In contrast, enrollments are now declining in many states, funds are not flowing as freely as in the past, and almost everyone is questioning some aspect of the community college's mission. Many presidents are beginning to escape the "time warp," or at least are beginning to realize that the community college's mission is not understood by a great many people. For those presidents who refuse to or cannot escape the time warp, the failure to interpret and articulate the mission effectively is likely to prove disastrous for their presidency and, in some cases, for the community college movement itself.

While personal deficiencies were not related directly to the failure of the community college, the willingness of presidents to discuss their failures and those of the community college is important in itself. Community college presidents are infamous for their unwillingness to criticize the community college in any respect; indeed, some presidents adopt a stance bordering on paranoia when criticized (Johnston, 1980, pp. 43–45). This candid discussion of the shortcomings of the community college and its presidents has been one of the few examples of presidents' willingness to address specific problems in a critical and unemotional manner. Perhaps it will open the door for a more discerning look at the community college by its leaders in the future and close the gap that now exists between perceived personal failures of the president and the broader failures of the community college.

Prestige

How is the community college presidency viewed in terms of responsibility and prestige? Is it "equal to" the four-year college or university presidency? If so, in what respects? If not, why not? What is the "mystique of the presidency" (to use Benezet's term)?

In terms of responsibility, social impact, and stress, many interviewed see the community college presidency as equal to the four-year presidency. Indeed, the community college leader may find the position more difficult in some respects than the four-year college presidency. For example, in most cases, working with the governing board requires more time and effort because of the local nature of the board; not only does the board meet more often than four-year college boards (some community college boards meet weekly!), but community college board members are "within commuting distance" of the president's office and thus are available to bring local issues to the president's attention at practically any time. This situation does not exist when trustees are located across the nation. As one president noted, just as the public school board expects the superintendent to know everything about the public schools, the community college board expects the president to know everything that is happening on the community college campus, a scenario one would rarely expect to find on a four-year campus. Furthermore, the local nature of the community college exposes its president to community pressures to a greater degree than is true with a four-year institution that "happens to be located in the area" and is therefore somewhat isolated from the daily concerns of the community. Keeping the community college's mission comprehensive and responsive to the local community is often difficult and adds to the complexity of the presidency.

At a meeting of the Summer Forum of AACJC's Presidents Academy in July 1985, Clark Kerr alluded to the friction generated on the community college president as a result of the college's relationship with its community. Kerr notes that by their very nature community colleges are closer to social changes than is any other segment of higher education. The community college president has less protection from local pressures than do the presidents of most four-year institutions because community colleges are not as autonomous as the four-year institutions. Kerr rates the difficulty of the college and university presidency on what he refers to as an "Index of Toughness and Protection Scale." At the top of Kerr's scale, or the best position in terms of the absence of toughness and the degree of protection afforded the president, are the expanding research universities; next are academic elite institutions which have few worries about recruiting outstanding students or raising money. The list continues through the other types of institutions of higher education in America. At the bottom of Kerr's scale are those colleges and universities whose presidents have the least protection and whose jobs are the toughest — the predominately black colleges and universities. *One rung from the bottom on Kerr's scale in*

terms of the toughness of the presidency and the lack of protection
for the president are the public community colleges. Kerr observes
that these colleges are "on the social firing line."

However, while the community college president's role may
be as demanding in some respects as the four-year college or
university presidency and may indeed be among the toughest
positions in higher education in the nation, what about the prestige associated with the position? Does the community college
presidency garner the prestige that society has historically be-
stowed upon its college and university presidents, and, if not,
why not?

The answer to the above question is decidedly no; the community college presidency does not have the prestige associated
with it that normally goes with the four-year college presidency.
The reasons for the "prestige gap" appear to be because of the
nature of the community college itself and the broader responsibilities, trappings, and history associated with the four-year presidency which are almost always lacking with the two-year presidency.

Much of the prestige associated with four-year institutions
results from the world-famous discoveries that are made at major
research universities. The presidents of these institutions, many
of whom are renowned scholars, earn and receive the respect of
the academic community and the community at large. Other
four-year institutions are often able to bask in the limelight of the
university, especially in the eyes of much of the public, which
fails to distinguish between research universities and other four-
year institutions. Community colleges never bask in the same
light, perhaps rightly so, for they were not designed as research
institutions.

While some responsibilities of the community college president may be as difficult as those of the four-year president, they
are not as all-encompassing. Most community colleges do not
have dormitories, many do not have intercollegiate sports, and
most do not have the extensive dining facilities that are required
at four-year institutions. While decisions made by community
college presidents are vitally important, they rarely rank in the
category of deciding whether or not to proceed with genetic
research, invest funds in companies that do business with South
Africa, or other decisions with worldwide implications.

Big-time sports bring prestige to many four-year institutions and their presidents, a source of prestige that is missing for presidents of community colleges. Indeed, Notre Dame University, the University of Texas, and other perennial athletic powers, in spite of the giant strides taken in recent years to upgrade their academic programs, have more prestige in the sports world even today than in academics. Community college presidents cannot gain the kind of prestige that results from the publicity over fielding winning teams in major sports.

But the prestige factor goes deeper than research and athletics. There are things inherent in the community college philosophy and mission that diminishes the prestige of its president in relationship to four-year presidents. Several comments centered around the idea that society views two years as less than four; consequently, in the minds of some people, the president of a four-year institution must be twice as good as the president of a two-year institution. One national observer, who earlier had written an editorial on the subject, noted that the community college suffers from its junior college heritage; that is, some people still view the community college as being "junior" to the four-year college; therefore, the president of the community college must be "junior" to the four-year president. Another long-time president observes: "The term junior has been an albatross. If we had it to do over again we could start with community, for junior has connotations of inferiority, and we have saddled ourselves with that." In a similar vein, a president noted that the community college's prestige suffers from its earlier association with the public schools, where it was viewed as grades 13 and 14. A faculty member candidly admits that she does not view, nor does she feel society views, teaching at a community college as having the prestige one normally associates with a college professor; therefore, the presidency suffers from the same relative lack of prestige associated with the community college faculty.

Compatible with these observations is the hierarchical nature of education in the United States, with the public school superintendent at the bottom of a rather selective group, the community college president next, the president of the four-year state college and liberal arts college next, and the president of the research university at the top. (As noted earlier in reference to the

Kerr "Index," each category of education has its own pecking order.) A number of presidents and faculty members believe that the president of a small, struggling, obscure liberal arts college has more prestige than does the successful community college president. One president notes that after 12 years in his current position people *still* want to know when his college is going to become a four-year college, a real college. This misconception supports a number of other observations offered by the interviewees, namely, that the larger society just does not understand the role the community college plays, especially in relationship to its community and to serving those segments of society that have traditionally been ignored by higher education.

Moreover, the community college president may suffer from overexposure in the sense that he or she is seen often in the community in a number of roles, including serving on various community committees and doing the more mundane things (grocery shopping, for example) that are required when one does not live in a college-owned home with college-furnished help. While familiarity may not necessarily breed contempt, it does remove some of the mystique associated with the presidency.

Several persons observed that, since the community college is essentially an open-door institution, it loses the prestige that goes with the image of selectivity that surrounds many four-year institutions. As one president observes, it is difficult to view the presidency as having a great deal of prestige when students and society know that if you cannot get into *any* other college, you can always go to the community college. The argument might be as follows: If anyone can go there, then anyone can be president. Or the argument may parallel the Groucho Marx line (paraphrased here): If I'm admitted to a club this easily, then it's not a club I really want to belong to (cited in Riesman, 1978). Although the fact is that most four-year institutions are far from selective, the myth of their selectivity persists.

One faculty member touches on a sensitive nerve when he points out that society has historically looked upon the university as an bastion for intellectual ideas and to its president as its intellectual leader and spokesman. The community college, in contrast, is viewed in a much more practical light and the president as more pragmatic than intellectual. In the same vein, another faculty member notes that the university president is likely to have a degree in medieval history, physics, British literature, or some other discipline and to have engaged in scholarly research. The community college president in her state (in all states, as a matter of fact), however, is likely to have a degree in education. She attaches, and believes society attaches, more prestige to the degree in history or some other discipline, especially if the degree holder is a research scholar, than to the degree in education. She asserts: "I respect the community college presidency, but I must admit that, if I met the president of a major university, I would be very much in awe and be impressed much more by this individual than I would be by a community college president, even if I had never met that president before." The "familiarity syndrome" might influence this faculty member's concept of the two presidencies; however, her observations also indicate that her thinking was shaped by the university, which she remembers with fondness, including the symbolic pedestal upon which the university president rested.

Placing the university president on a pedestal might be a gross exaggeration of the realities of the position. What is not an exaggeration is that four-year university and college presidents enjoy many trappings of the office not available to most community college presidents. Moreover, the university traces its heritage to medieval times and the history of most American four-year colleges goes back to the founding of Harvard. The modern community college was born in the post–World War II period at best and, realistically, during the growth of the 1960s and early 1970s.

Most four-year presidents have houses furnished by the college or university; most community college presidents do not. Most four-year presidents have groundsmen, house keepers, and cooks who are paid by the college or university; most community college presidents do not have any extra help paid for by the college. Many four-year presidents have private boxes at athletic events which are shared by governors, wealthy alumni, and others who bring prestige to the college; most community college presidents have no such perquisite. Many four-year presidents can call upon a chauffeur-driven automobile or an airplane when needed; this is rarely the case with a community college

president. The list of amenities and trappings go on, but the point
is that those things not available to most members of society but
enjoyed routinely by most university presidents and many four-
year college presidents add prestige to the office of the president. Conversely, if the trappings are missing from a position, as
is the case with the community college presidency, their absence
implies that the post is not worthy of having them; consequently
its prestige is lessened.

Finally, in some cases community college presidents relegate
themselves, or are relegated by the presidents at four-year institutions, to second-class status. In one state, for example, *all* four-
year college presidents meet monthly for the purpose of discussing higher education issues; however, only about one-fourth
of the community college presidents are *permitted* to attend the
meetings during a given year. Several of the community colleges
are considerably larger than most of the four-year institutions.
One of the presidents who is a regular member of the presidents'
group is the head of the only two-year branch campus in the state.
Do the community college presidents in the state suffer gladly
the fact that three-fourths of them are excluded from the monthly
meeting of *college and university presidents?* Certainly not all of
them do. One president, however, displays an attitude that might
contribute to the lack of prestige associated with the community
college presidency in that state. His comments regarding having
full community college membership in the group are: "What we
should be concerned with is that the Council of Presidents has
strong leadership, not whether all of us are members." The im-
plication of his remark seems to be that through some magical
way community college presidents can enhance that leadership
by sitting on the sideline and staying out of the way. There is one
thing that sitting on the sidelines is guaranteed not to enhance:
the prestige of the community college presidency.

Without exception, the presidents and board members interviewed saw the lack of prestige associated with the community
college to be at worst a minor problem. The presidents declared
that they did not feel at all inferior to the four-year presidents
(one observed that the problem is that some four-year presidents
feel superior to the community college president) in any respect.

Is this lack of prestige something to be concerned about? Perhaps. Community colleges are funded by the states at a much lower rate than are public four-year institutions; community colleges do not get their fair share of federal dollars; their presidents rarely are called upon to serve on major national commissions that recommend educational policy; these leaders are underrepresented on editorial boards of publications dealing with higher education (the prestigious *Journal of Higher Education* does not have anyone associated with the community college on its editorial board); and, in general, community college presidents do not enjoy the national exposure that four-year presidents enjoy. Certainly a lack of national exposure can be attributed in part to the provincial nature of the community college; however, some blame must rest with the lack of prestige, or respect as it were, for the community college presidency. Less than adequate funding from state legislatures might be traced, in part, to the same reason.

The question seems to be: should community college presidents be more concerned with the prestige associated with their position? The answer is yes, if they are going to compete successfully with the presidents of four-year institutions and the public (K – 12) schools in obtaining funds from both public and private sources, and if they are going to play a major role in shaping public policy at the state and national levels. Although community college presidents cannot acquire many of the things which they do not currently have and which enhance the prestige of the four-year presidency, they can be sensitive to the role prestige plays in the success of the presidency and work to enhance their own position.

CHAPTER 7

Stress and Burnout

Executive stress, or burnout in the more extreme cases, is one of the "hot topics" of the 1980s. Articles on how to survive burnout abound; workshops on coping with stress are available in almost every segment of the country; advice on what to do when executives burn out is offered, whether sought or not; questions on how much stress is too much highlight the need to be sensitive to executive "overload." Jonathan Fife, Director of the ERIC Clearinghouse on Higher Education, writes in the foreword to one of the few major attempts to evaluate burnout in academia, "The issue of burnout is one of increasing importance to institutions, because it usually strikes the most competent and committed, the ones who feel strongly about the value of what they are doing and who want to do the best job" (Melendez and de Guzman, 1983, p. vii). The authors of the volume, one of whom is a professor of humanities and adjunct professor of higher education, and the other a psychiatrist, note that some people feel that "burnout runs through the teaching profession like Asian flu . . ." (p. 1). They also state, "To burn out, people actually need to have felt challenged and excited during the early years of the job," (p. 1) a description that fits most community college presidents well.

Psychologists and others are documenting what most community college presidents have known for a long time but may not have been willing to admit; presidents, just like teachers, doctors, ministers, nurses, social workers, and others in the "helping professions," are subject to job stress which, if not checked, may result in a loss of effectiveness on the part of some presidents and, if carried to extremes, may ultimately result in job burnout.

Presidential stress first came to my attention (beyond what I experience in my daily work) in the summer of 1981 while attending a week-long workshop sponsored by the Presidents Academy of the AACJC for veteran community college presidents. Since one of the purposes of the Academy's annual summer workshops is to give presidents an opportunity to get away from the stress of their daily routine (the workshops are currently held in Vail, Colorado), it seemed natural and proper that job stress was the subject of one of the seminars. What was not natural, or at least did not seem so at the time, was the preoccupation a number of presidents attending the workshop had with the fear that someday they would no longer be able to give the leadership to their position that they were currently giving. In other words, they would "slow down," "lose touch," "lose interest," or in some way show signs of losing some of the characteristics they associated with the successful community college presidency, especially their own.

As a result of attending the Vail workshop, I undertook a small research project designed to determine if community college presidents recognized in themselves any of the signs of stress which, if not placed in perspective, could result in burnout. Those presidents surveyed identified such symptoms as a lack of enthusiasm for the job, a loss of tolerance for others, a feeling of being "stuck," a loss of creative drive, a feeling of loneliness, a feeling of being "lazy," and other symptoms psychologists associate with burnout and which the presidents recognized as being potentially damaging to their performance. The major conclusion from the brief study was that yes, indeed, community college presidents are in a stressful position, something that I strongly suspected based on my own experiences and through observing the experiences of others. Moreover, in some cases the occupant of this office is a prime candidate for burnout if stress is not handled properly, something that I was not aware of in myself or in other presidents I had observed.

My limited knowledge and the brief treatment of the subject

prohibited me from drawing any major conclusions on the effects of job stress on the community college president: I saw my role as calling the subject to the attention of my colleagues and other members of the college community. I did, however, draw some conclusions about stress that I feel are especially relevant to the community college presidency: "Many of today's community college presidents achieved their presidency at a relatively young age. Graduates of the Kellogg programs of the 1960s found themselves in the middle of the boom period of community college growth. As a result, they found opportunities for leadership perhaps unequaled in the history of higher education. Today, these presidents, many still in their forties and early fifties, have been at the peak of their profession for a number of years. . . . These presidents are 'stuck at the top with no place to go' at a time when they are psychologically ready for new challenges and new 'passages'" (Vaughan, 1982, p. 12). I went on to note in the same article that a number of factors had merged to create stress on the president: just as the young graduates of the Kellogg programs had matured, so had the community college movement. No longer were colleges opening once a week, or at all for that matter; no longer could the bored (some presidents might say *board*) president move easily to a new position; faculties were stable or declining; funds that had earlier flowed so freely were drying up; student enrollments were declining; risk taking, once a hallmark of many community colleges, was now frowned upon; unions had complicated the governance process on many campuses; and the community college was no longer viewed as a panacea for curing society's ills (p. 12).

Two Special Cases

My article on burnout was published in the February 1982 issue of the *Community and Junior College Journal.* In June of that year *The Washington Post,* in a front-page story, reported that Jay Carsey, president of Charles County Community College for 17 years, had been missing for a month. Carsey left everyone and everything behind as he literally disappeared from the scene. He left a two-sentence letter of resignation to his board of trustees, the college car in the parking lot at Washington National Airport, and little else. Why did Carsey, who, according to the *Post* was "one of the most important men in the county," disappear? (Rimer, 1982, p. A-1). (He is obviously alive and, one assumes, well, since he was interviewed for the AGB report [1984, p. 122] on the college presidency.) The important question here is not why Carsey committed the "ultimate act of burnout" short of suicide, if indeed his disappearance was due to burnout, but rather what are the stresses associated with the community college presidency and in what ways are presidents combating stress? Carsey chose a very dramatic escape route. He received a great deal of publicity with his exit from his presidency, as did his spouse. Since he gave no reasons for leaving the presidency, one can only surmise, as his longtime dean did in the *Post* article, that the pressures of being in the presidency for 17 years drove him to his unorthodox decision. While the Carsey case is interesting as a human interest story, more relevant to this discussion is the president who chose another method of "disappearing from the presidency."

While attending a meeting of the AACJC Board of Directors in 1981, I had the opportunity to talk with a community college president who had become something of a legend because of his writings, the reputation of his former college, and the reputation he enjoyed throughout much of the profession. I was shocked when, during our conversation, he informed me that he was resigning his position, leaving the profession, and opening a small business in a small town in the Southwest. Why? The question haunted me and in order to get an answer and perhaps shed additional light on the stress associated with the presidency, I called him and had a 40-minute discussion regarding his decision.

The president in question assumed his first presidency in 1962; he left his third presidency in 1981. In his first presidency, he restructured the college to serve a much broader role than it was serving; in his second presidency, he was the founding president of a college that was often viewed as a pace-setting institution during the last part of the decade of the 1960s and during much of the 1970s; in his third presidency he was presented with a $500,000 deficit by the board and knew that a large number of personnel had to be released in order to balance the budget. In his spare time, he contributed a number of articles to the professional journals and did a major book on the management of community colleges. When he decided to resign the presidency, he appeared to be at the top of his chosen profession. Why, then, did he quit? The interview reveals some of the reasons.

Noting that he started the presidency at a very young age and served as president during the entire boom period of community college growth, he offered the following observations on the major sources of stress for him while president. "Everything I did from day 1 until I completed my last presidency was either upgrading, starting new, reorganizing and trying to get things in tune with the new movements, constantly developing people, retraining people, developing new organizations, and that sort of thing. That, of course, is fun for awhile, but after a time you feel that you are doing nothing but giving and you are not getting as much satisfaction as you did when you started. You need something more stimulating to you other than just retraining, regrouping, reorganizing, recruiting new talent. After about 20 years of that kind of activity, I felt that, since I was losing some of my enthusiasm for it, it was time to make a change. I don't know if it was burnout, but I had lost some of my enthusiasm for doing it. I felt then as a leader it was time to make a change if you can't pass on that enthusiasm." He noted that he had been extremely happy as a community college president for most of his career. He also observed that he was now enjoying "some of the finest moments of his life" with his youngest child, moments that had not been possible with his two older children and moments that would not have been possible if he had continued in the presidency. He felt that the older children had grown up almost without him, to the extent that he would be sleeping in the same house and go as much as five or six days without seeing his children, since he left home before they awakened and returned after they were asleep. He estimates that as many as 20 people who went on to become community college presidents had worked under his tutelage. This indicated that he took his role of mentor seriously, a role that is often physically and mentally draining.

When asked what advice he would give presidents today who are feeling less than enthusiastic for their position, he offered the following: His writing and research were forms of professional renewal that he turned to when he was bored, and he recommends them as ways of lessening stress; he feels that, with current pressures on the presidency, presidents must get away for a "period of refreshment" in the form of year-long sabbaticals at regular intervals; and he advises young presidents to be very careful that they pace themselves in a way that keeps them fresh and vital.

Reactions to Presidential Stress

The subject of job stress and burnout evoked some interesting responses from those interviewed, especially the presidents. Those presidents interviewed tended to react in one of three ways: overtly denying that stress caused them any problems; acknowledging that stress was a problem and burnout a possibility; or admitting that stress existed in the presidency but displaying such a genuine enthusiasm for the position that one might conclude stress was *not* an important factor and therefore the prospect of burnout unlikely in those individuals.

Those presidents who denied they could *ever* suffer from stress displayed something of the "Superman-Wonderwoman" or John Wayne machismo syndrome often associated with the college presidency. These presidents would be likely to follow the advice of James Fisher when he admonishes presidents, "Your people rightfully expect you to be strong; never, never discuss your problems with them"; or, "Never admit you're tired except to your secretary, your assistant, and your spouse" (1984, p. 71).

The second group readily admitted to a feeling of burning out and spoke to those factors they perceived as causing the sensation. They also discussed ways they combat stress, especially once they realized that it was becoming a major problem for them. These presidents tend to place the Carsey case in a perspective that identifies it as being far from typical of those suffering from job burnout, yet not out of the realm of possibility. This group would identify readily with the president who opened the small business.

The third group—and the majority of the presidents interviewed fell into this category — expressed an enthusiasm for the presidency that enabled them to put the stress associated with the position in a proper perspective. These presidents also seemed to take extra precautions to assure their own mental and physical vitality.

Sources of Stress

Burnout resulting from stress occurs when frustrations and pressures exceed their normal limits and interfere with one's ability to perform at a level that is acceptable to the individual and, in many cases, at a level that is acceptable to the institution. Obviously, stress comes from many sources and occurs at different stages in the life of the individual. Situations that are considered normal in the presidency can become stressful if not placed appropriately in the total scheme of things by the individual. For example, board–president conflicts are guaranteed to increase the anxiety level for almost every president; however, a certain amount of conflict is taken for granted and should be taken in stride. But if the conflict with the board is not settled in a reasonable manner in a reasonable amount of time, the situation is likely to become a stressful one for the president. Another potentially stressful situation occurs when things do not go well with the legislature. A prime example of when legislative relations move from the realm of producing normal, acceptable pressures to the realm of producing undue stress on the president would appear to be the situation at Florida Junior College at Jacksonville referred to earlier.

Every president can probably recall some situation that moved from being a normal pressure to a stress-producing one. The stage is always set for this to happen. As one faculty member observed: "The president has so many roles that I don't see how it would be possible for any human being to fill all of them. There has got to be tremendous pressure that develops from that particular aspect of the position." How the president handles the "tremendous pressure" often determines whether the situation is a productive one or whether the pressure produces an unacceptable level of stress. Of course, there are some stress-producing situations that are well beyond the control of the president, such as budget reductions resulting in the termination of personnel. What is being presented here is the thought that stress, for whatever reason, comes not only from stressful situations but also from how the individual president perceives and deals with a given situation: *one person's routine pressure may be another's stress; what is taken in stride at one time in a person's career may, at a different stage, become a stress-producing crisis for the individual.*

The Spouses' Perspective

Stress can and does influence the home life of the president; often the spouse and children feel the effects of the president under stress. A sort of "kick-the-dog" syndrome develops, with the family playing the "dog" role. The following observations by spouses give some indication of how stress in the office can result in strain in the home. The observations of the spouses also shed light on sources of stress in the presidency.

One presidential spouse who has been in the role 13 years and who is a former school board member, goes to the very heart of the matter in discussing stress on the presidency: "Having to deal with board members who don't know their role, don't know what a board of trustee's role is. That's the hardest part. They don't realize, don't recognize that they are policy makers and not administrators." While she feels that her husband handles the stress extremely well, this spouse nevertheless believes that the board–president relationship always holds the potential for creating extreme pressure. There is nothing new here except that the spouse rather than the president is making the observation. She also notes, "Most of my frustrations have to do with his problems." This particular spouse can always tell when her husband is under strains yet she notes that he always comes home and "talks it out" not only with her, but with the children as well. The president in this case can almost always put stress-producing problems in perspective and tackle them the next day with renewed vigor.

The president is not always able to "talk it out" and leave problems for the next day. One spouse observed that she can tell when her husband is under stress because he "begins to nitpick" at home. For example, leaving things on the breakfast table such as the newspaper can become "a really big event" when he is under stress. He takes his frustrations out at home because he cannot take them out at the office. The children are well aware when stressful situations exist for their father. According to the spouse, "I tell them that when he seems to be coming down hard on them that it is usually something at the college and not them." In this case, the president turns to old friends who have no association with the college in order to relieve the pressure.

All spouses interviewed referred to the tendency of their spouse-president to become a bit more short tempered while under stress, a bit sharper with the children; one uses sleep as a means of escaping the stress; on the other hand, some cannot sleep while under pressure; some spouses are the ones who lose sleep as a result of strains on the president. Some presidents share problems; some do not. Children almost always feel some effect of their father being under stress. A common reaction on the part of children, according to the spouses interviewed, is "to leave him alone." Most presidents turn to physical activity as a means of relieving stress; some tend to drink more alcohol than usual. Tennis, golf, painting duck decoys, walking, running, dirt-bike racing, building miniature doll houses, swimming, hunting, fishing, and many other activities are used to relieve the pressures.

Tension came in many forms, in addition to the board situation described above. Some stress is produced, according to the spouses, when things are not going well politically, when the staff is not getting along — one president gets anonymous letters from what is believed to be an internal source, according to the spouse; another spouse believes that the failure of the legislature to fund the college adequately causes stress. The list is long and depends upon the individual president.

While the stress-inducing factors as perceived by the spouses were not that different from those identified by the presidents, the spouses brought a perspective to the discussion that was not apparent from talking with presidents. The home environment, then, feels some of the effects of stress. When it affects the home environment, it can often set a vicious chain reaction into motion: the president feels stress; brings it home; the spouse and children feel the results; the home life then adds to the tension the president already feels; and a blow-up of sorts often occurs, either at home, within the individual president, or, in some cases, at the office.

All spouses agreed that the presidents are "past masters" at concealing stress from college personnel. On the other hand, the spouse and children are almost always able to detect when things are not going well for the president; the result is that stress is generated for all family members. As with other aspects of the problem, job-related home stress, if not kept in perspective, can become a major problem for those who occupy the presidency.

Burnout

A quote from a former president of three community colleges who, after five years in retirement, remains one of the most respected leaders in the field, serves to introduce the pernicious nature of excess stress which may lead to burnout. His quote also tends to present both sides of the burnout argument: those who see burnout as a legitimate concern and those who see burnout as a cop-out. "Did I suffer from burnout? I have to smile at that question because it is just a convenient term. But hell, that's what administration is, just one long stream of burnout. When you start, you have aspirations, ambitions, zeal, and all of those great things. And if you start thinking about burnout, you can convince yourself that you are burned out in the first month. I agree that you just can't run full bore year after year. There have to be some peaks and valleys. But I smile wryly, because you are damned right I had burnout. A lot of mornings I got up and had burnout and I went to work and worked with burnout. I would be a little afraid that that could be a convenient cop-out for a person who says, 'Oh hell, I'm tired and I'm going to pull off today.' This makes it respectable to say, 'I've got burnout.' Don't rely on it too much or the board will get someone who doesn't have burnout."

Other presidents tend to view burnout in less polarized terms.

One observes: "While I was doing a lot of the things I was doing, I didn't really think in terms of stress and burnout, knowing, however, that when I left one college presidency and went to another one there was about a month, and the difference in my feeling during that 30-day period was so different from what I had experienced before and after that I for the first time recognized the weight of the responsibility of the presidency." Another president who describes himself as a classic "type A," and one who attended the Vail workshop referred to earlier, noted that he was "worn out" and that he went to Vail to get away from a "daily schedule with too many appointments too close together." And still another president who "burned out last year," and who thought 13 years in the presidency was long enough, offers the following analysis of his situation. After agreeing to accept the presidency of a college in the independent sector of higher education, he "began to realize that it was not the attraction of that particular job as much as it was a sort of burned out, stressful feeling that I had — impatience, fatigue. It came as a great shock that I wasn't really seeking something; I was trying to leave something." Incidentally, that president had not had "10 days off, back-to-back, for three or four years."

For some presidents, longevity in the position increased the likelihood of stress becoming a problem. One president, who is currently in his second presidency and who admits to having been burned out in his previous presidency because he had been there too long and had done all he could do, now finds that after three years in his current position it is no longer as easy to leave college-related affairs at the college as he had always done in the past, even when he was feeling burned out in his previous position. "As I have gotten older, I find that it is more and more difficult to do that. I find myself waking in the middle of the night and thinking about a college problem of some kind; I used to be able to totally divorce myself from it." Another president who does not feel that he suffers from excessive stress and certainly not to the point of burning out, admits that "stressful situations are getting more intense and more frequent." And yet another one claims that she began feeling burned out after staying in one position too long, going over the same problems with the same people, many of whom were themselves suffering from burnout,

addressing graduates at 13 successive graduations, and in general
"fighting the same windmills."

While length of time in office is a factor contributing to stress
and even to burnout for some presidents, it would be dangerous
to generalize that longevity alone contributes to burnout, for
many presidents have been in the position for long periods of
time and show no signs of burning out or of even feeling the
effects of stress associated with the position. The fact remains,
however, that stress is an ever-present factor for the community
college president and failure to recognize the danger signs associated with stress can pose a threat to presidential effectiveness.

Before leaving the subject of burnout and turning to ways of
combating stress, two thoughts on the subject are worth sharing.
One comes from a community college president in Oregon; the
other is a comment on the first and is taken from personal correspondence (1982) with David Riesman. The president wrote: "A
paragraph I read in a book about China between World War I and
World War II paraphrasing the reflections of a long-time British
gunboat captain has helped me understand my feelings about my
job. The captain compares his tour of duty with a Chinese parade
dragon where up to a hundred people form the dragon and carry
it along, but only one person looks out of the eyes of the dragon
and gives direction. After fifteen years of looking out of the
dragon's eyes, the captain sometimes longs for relief from that
position" (Vaughan, 1982, p. 12). Riesman's comment: "I enjoyed the anecdote about the British gunboat captain. If you add
that the president is not permitted to fire the gun on board, but
only is there to be fired at, the analogy is even better." In the
same correspondence Riesman adds additional thoughts of his
own on some stress-causing aspects of the presidency. He writes:
"I know very few people who are college presidents, or who have
been presidents in the last few years, who are not lonely, who do
not find redundancy in the attitudes of faculty members and
students, and who, with their spouses, are not under more pressure for entertainment and community involvement than they
can manage." (Incidentally, the president from Oregon no longer
serves as the dragon's eyes on his campus; he retired on De-
cember 31, 1984.)

Combating Burnout

In Melendez and de Guzman's observations on burnout, they view coping with it as something of an ultimatum if one is to be effective in one's professional career. In their words: "It usually affects the most productive individuals, who as high achievers are slaves of constant professional demands, living at an acutely stressful pace. These bright individuals either learn to cope with their stressful lives or succumb to burnout" (1983, p. 54). All of the presidents interviewed, including those who denied that stress caused them any problems, showed an awareness of the potentially ill effects of stress, and most of them take steps to insure that they do not become victims of stress resulting in burnout. What steps do presidents take?

Presidents do a variety of things to release stress, including talking to the dog, riding a motorcycle, and "taking it out" on the piano. The most widely used approach to relieving stress among the presidents interviewed is physical activity of all types, including running, tennis, swimming, walking, yoga, gardening, and about anything else that an individual found stimulating and convenient. Most of the presidents try to engage in some physical exercise regularly.

The individual nature of stress is best illustrated by how presidents view work-related problems in relationship to their home life. One president who says he never brings college work home with him notes, "I don't ever discuss college-related problems with my wife." Another declares that he is not married to the job, that he is not a 14-hour-a-day person. Another veteran president attempts to separate his personal life from his professional life; as a result, he rarely ever discusses college problems at home. On the other side of the coin, several presidents saw the home environment as a place where they could "let go." As one president put it: "My wife is my best friend, and I tell her things I cannot tell others. Being able to talk things out with her is a big relief." Another president who believes he has as much stress in his position as any president in the nation, has simply learned to relax and laugh at most problems. He also talks about stress with his wife, whom he describes as "a great partner."

Several presidents take on special projects at the college as a way of relieving tension. One of the presidents mentioned above who was, as he put it, "burned out," rejuvenated himself by taking on a major project in the instructional area. He took the accepted route of delegating all of the personnel decisions that he could delegate; he also delegated almost all personal contact with the union. He felt it took him 13 years and a state of near exhaustion to learn that as president he had to have other people between himself and the almost daily decisions required in dealing with personnel. Incidentally, here is an excellent case of routine matters moving from a frustrating stage to a stressful one.

Some presidents moved to new positions to help relieve stress. Often they had been in their position several years before deciding that it was time to move on. In the instances where it was possible to follow up on those who had moved, the change in positions was effective in combating stress and indeed offered the individuals a new lease on their professional lives.

One rather unique suggestion came forth on how to relieve one source of potential stress. One national leader suggests that presidents be given a new three-year contract each year, assuming of course that the board wishes to retain the incumbent president. This "rolling contract" approach would assure the president a certain amount of security, thus relieving some of the stress associated with contract renewal.

Changes in scenery and responsibility were recommended as a way of reducing stress. Included were workshops for the president and spouse, travel, vacations, and sabbaticals.

Stress in Perspective

On the whole, most presidents seem to view stress as part of the job and handle it accordingly. As with all leadership positions, stress occasionally becomes too much for the community college president. Fortunately, the interviews and other research done for this study revealed very few cases of burnout, and, where it did exist, the presidents were taking positive steps to eradicate or mitigate the circumstances which they felt were causing them to burn out. In this light, several presidents mentioned the temptation to escape the pressures through the use of alcohol or drugs, but all saw this route as an unacceptable solution. It was also refreshing and a bit surprising to learn that many trustees and faculty members are sensitive to the constraints on the president's office and, in most cases, appear to empathize with the presidents, a situation that can ultimately do much to relieve some of the stress associated with the presidency.

CHAPTER 8

◆

The President's Spouse

Earlier it was suggested that little had been published on the community college presidency to help one understand the position. A major gap in delineating the post also exists because of a lack of *any* knowledge on the role of the president's spouse. With the exception of one small, rather dated handbook entitled *The President's Wife* ("The responsibilities of a president's wife are basically the same as those of any other wife. Home and family should come first. The successful wife seeks to make the home a place where all family members return with pleasure at the end of each day" [Kintzer, 1970, p. 7]), nothing has been published on the role of the spouse of the community college president. By choosing to ignore the role of the spouse, those interested in the community college presidency have been denied an important insight into the presidency, especially if one views the job as extending beyond the president's office.

There are several volumes that shed light on the role of the spouse of the university president and thereby add to the understanding of the complexities, frustrations, and rewards associated with that presidency, with life on a university campus, and, in some instances, an understanding of the larger society (Beadle, 1972; Corbally, 1977; Kemeny, 1979; Ostar, 1983; Clodius and Magrath, 1984). While none of these publications deal specifically with the community college, they are nevertheless valuable, not only in outlining the role of a president's spouse, but in

143

comprehending the presidency as well. The following pages perform a similar function for the spouse of the community college president. It is hoped that a brief examination of the spouse's role will result in a similar grasp of the complex duties of the presidency.

A Profile

The average age of the spouse of the community college president is 48; almost 45 percent are between the ages of 41 and 50, and slightly over 31 percent are between the ages of 51 and 60. Slightly over 17 percent are under 40 years of age, and approximately 6 percent are over 60. The youngest spouse is 26; the oldest, 74 (CLS). The ages of the spouses tend to match the ages of the presidents.

The spouses of the presidents have not achieved the same formal level of education as the presidents. In contrast to the approximately 77 percent of the presidents with doctorates, slightly more than 4 percent of the spouses have doctorates. On the other hand, almost 29 percent of the spouses have master's degrees; over 33 percent have the bachelor's degree; and almost 11 percent have the associate degree. Twenty percent of the spouses have a high school diploma or less; over 2 percent have "other" forms of certification, such as a beautician's license. Almost 17 percent of the spouses received a degree from a community college (CLS).

The spouse of the community college president is likely to work in a paid occupation outside the home, thus laying to rest the belief of some governing boards that they are getting "two for one" when they employ the president. Over two-thirds of the spouses are employed at least part-time outside the home: approximately 43 percent work full-time and approximately 24 percent part-time (CLS, SS). (Some governing boards *still* prefer to employ a president — one assumes a male president — whose spouse does not work outside the home. Indeed, at one institution which was visited during this study, the spouse of the president was prohibited from working in a paid position as a condition of employment for the male president. One can only wonder if the male spouse would have been prohibited from working outside the home if the president had been female.) The over two-thirds of the spouses who work for pay outside the home is more than twice as high as that revealed by an American Association of State Colleges and Universities survey of presidents' spouses in state colleges and universities (Ostar, 1983). The major goals for the spouses of community college presidents who work in paid occupations are to maintain professional status and to develop new interests, although several spouses claim they work for the income (SS).

The largest single occupation listed by the spouse (approximately 36%) is that of homemaker. The largest category of paid employment is in education, with almost 31 percent of the spouses so employed. Slightly over 10 percent work in administrative-management positions. The next largest field (almost 7%) of employment is in health-related occupations, including nursing. Less than 6 percent (5.6) work in areas of administrative support such as secretarial work. Twenty percent of the spouses have not held employment outside the home since becoming the spouse of a community college president (CLS).

The educational level and occupations of the spouses of community college presidents offer few surprises. A bit surprising may be that 20 percent of the spouses have a high school education or less, especially since they have had, through the president's profession, what would seem to be almost continual educational opportunities. A word of caution is in order, however, regarding the educational level of spouses who do not have college degrees: those spouses with a high school diploma or less may have taken numerous courses at the community college or other educational institutions. No attempt was made to ascertain this information. It is also conceivable that spouses, as is the case with some offspring of presidents, simply do not want to attend college where their spouse is president, especially for the purpose of taking degree-related courses which would tend to identify them as not having previously completed college.

While no major attempt was made to determine what effect the educational level of the spouse has on the president – spouse relationship, the stories are legion of the spouse (usually male) who has gotten a Ph.D., M.D., law, or some other advanced

degree and "left the spouse behind" both figuratively and literally. David Riesman speaks to the dilemma the spouse of the
upwardly mobile president often faces: "Those who get to be
college and university presidents are generally ambitious
strivers; in many cases, they have been upwardly mobile socially
as a consequence of their occupational advancement. As presidential partners, the couple thus may be moving in circles to
which they are not accustomed. The situation for both partners
calls for adaptability, for quick understanding of a new setting,
and for insight" (Riesman, 1982, p. 12).

One spouse gives a candid appraisal of the situation that can
result if the spouse is "left behind" by her ambitious presidential
spouse: "I have met any number of community college presidents who are unhappy with their marriage, divorced, or who
want to be. One thing that I see happening is the number of
community college presidents who seem to be divorcing their
wives because their wives have not grown with them. The wife
stays at home, has children, is supportive, but fails to grow." Her
advice to spouses: "Grow, whether by formal education, forming
your own business, by teaching knitting, or whatever you do."
This particular spouse feels that this aspect of the spouse –
president relationship has been totally ignored by most presidents, spouses, and governing boards. She observes, much as
Riesman does, that presidents are "vital, ongoing, aggressive, or
they would not have achieved the presidency." Spouses, she
feels, do not understand this drive and therefore do not understand the presidency. As a result, both partners suffer. Perhaps
the answer is for spouses to be "vital, ongoing, and aggressive"
and to have a passion for whatever they do that equals the passion
the president has for the office.

What effect, if any, does the large percentage of spouses
working in paid positions have on the spouse – president relationship? A somewhat surprising fact is that there appears to be
little career conflict between the working spouse and the president. The lack of friction may be linked to the spouses' educational level and types of employment. Their educational level
indicates that relatively few have obtained the degrees required
to reach the top rung of their profession, thus lessening the competition often found in two-career marriages when both partners

are striving to reach the top. The large percentage (31%) of the spouses employed in education, health-related fields (7%), and secretarial-type positions (almost 6%) lessens the potential for career conflicts since most of these occupations tend to provide supplementary income in presidential families rather than serve as career advancement positions. Moreover, 36 percent do not work in paid occupations; thus there are no apparent professional struggles in those marriages, although career conflicts may exist. Finally, the blue-collar homes in which the majority of the community college presidents were reared would not have placed the mother in conflict with the father as far as career mobility was concerned, a fact that may have influenced the male presidents in their choice of spouses and their attitude toward professional competition between spouses.

The Role of the Spouse

How do spouses view their role? Most of the spouses interviewed see their role as a supportive one, not as a full partner in the enterprise. As one spouse states: "I assist whenever I'm needed. I have a dinner for the board of trustees, usually at Christmas, every year. We entertain the faculty and staff about once a year." Another sees her role as simply being supportive of the college. Another stated somewhat bitterly that her role is that of "an occasional social companion" and lamented that the role has diminished over the years after she and her husband moved from a small rural college to a larger suburban one. Another spouse sees no real role for her in relationship to the college, other than to host an occasional social function or as a social partner to the president. Still another spouse sees her role as selling the college to the community. One views her role as follows: "I'm in the background and supportive of him." Another echoed a similar theme: "I don't think anyone has ever viewed the president's wife other than being in the shadows."

The "shadow side" of the spouses' role is described with chilling candor by one ex-spouse. "It should be remembered that there is a woman in the audience when the husband gives all of the speeches and gets all of the kind words said, when in reality she is the one who gives the dinners, the one who arranges the receptions, the one who says 'Hey, did you remember to. . . .' She is the one who sees that he has clean shirts, the one who takes him to the airport, the one who smiles in the right place at the right time. I think it is time *somebody* says thank you." Another spouse points out, "The spouse not only has to be a physician, she has to be 'the father' many times, she has to be the coach, and when there is a fight she has to settle it. She has to make sure that dinner is on the table at various times, depending on what the children and husband are doing at that particular time, she has to be bus driver, and make sure things are functioning properly."

Several spouses are frustrated because there is almost no definition of the spouse's role. One expresses her frustrations and probably summarizes those of others: "The president moves into a position and people know what is expected of him; they do not know what is expected of the spouse nor does *she* know. Each spouse has to decide what the proper role is to be for her. This is very frustrating."

To expect a definition of the spouse's role might be unrealistic since the role varies so much from college to college and since the majority of the spouses work for pay outside the home, thus implying that the spouse's role is less than full-time. However, while a definition may be unrealistic, the spouse of the community college president should nevertheless have some expectation (you are expected to host a certain number of receptions, accompany the president to certain social and cultural functions, etc.) of the role, which would in turn serve as a basis for each spouse in defining the proper role for that spouse for that college at that particular time. This would permit and encourage each spouse to approach the role realistically and creatively.

Other Views on the Spouses' Role

Roberta Ostar writes in *Myths and Realities* that "a competent, active, dedicated-to-the-university spouse cannot compensate for an inadequate president, but an unhappy, recalcitrant, disruptive spouse who leaves a trail of bad feelings and dislike in university and community groups can rapidly ruin a competent president's effectiveness!" (1983, p. 27). Bringing it home to the community college presidency, a 20-year veteran of the presidency believes that "a good wife will make a good president an excellent president. A mediocre wife can make a good president only good. A lousy wife can make an excellent president good at best and maybe a failure." One cannot assume the same rules would apply to a male spouse since the college community and the larger community do not view the roles as the same; nevertheless, a male spouse who offers strong moral support to the female president will surely enhance that presidency in much the same way that the supportive female spouse enhances the office of the male president.

A president notes that the good spouse must be a good entertainer. Another believes that his spouse, through her extensive involvement with the college, keeps the institution "human." At one extreme, a president sees his wife's role as serving as an occasional hostess; yet another sees his spouses as "an advocate for the college 24 hours a day." Several of those interviewed feel that the spouse's role is an individual undertaking. That is, in contrast to the spouses' role at most four-year institutions, the spouse of the community college president, as suggested, has no set of preconceived expectations, much less a clearly defined role. The amount of activity, other than hosting functions and serving as a social partner to the president, is determined by the interests, energy, and desire of the individual spouse and the president, a situation that lends itself to creativity, but one that may well add to the frustrations of the position, especially for spouses new to the role.

Faculty members tend to see the president's spouse in a rather traditional way and in a way that surely must add to some of the frustrations associated with the spouses' role. As one faculty member notes, the wife of the president is similar to the wife of the minister: "She is expected to participate." The same faculty member did not necessarily accept the role as desirable. She notes: "Oh, I have a real problem with that from a woman's lib point of view; to me that is an unfair pressure, but, from a practical point of view, I know that the traditional role is expected." A male faculty member has a different view: "In any aspect where an individual has a position of responsibility, the major force or stability behind him is a good support woman—a wife." He continues: "The social role of the spouse is very important. I think it is important because between the two of them the talkative one is usually the woman, and they can make or break the status of that individual in that particular social gathering." Certainly this male faculty member represents an extreme chauvinistic point of view. But is his view just a matter of degree?

A female campus dean notes: "I see most spouses—and we are talking primarily about females—playing the role of hostess; of kind of staying in the background but always being there to assist in whatever needs to be done." She sees this as a disadvantage to women seeking the presidency. She expresses the dilemma as follows: "I'm not at all sure that that is not somewhat of a drawback to women seeking presidencies because they don't generally have that kind of support behind them. There are not many househusbands behind the female presidents that we have. It is a very important role in bridging the gap between the presidency and the other factors out there." While most female presidents do not want or need a "househusband," they need and want husbands who offer them support, who are interested in their success, and who generally contribute to the satisfactions associated with being a community college president.

Trustees also view the spouse's role in a traditional manner. One board member expects the spouse to provide social support and little else. He admits that not having an official college residence is a drawback to the spouse who wants to play a more active role in college activities. A female trustee believes that the spouse's role must complement the president's role. The spouse — and the trustee used the female gender—must have social graces and must know how to entertain and entertain properly. She must project the image of being the college president's wife, the trustee believes. She concludes by noting that trustees "are not giving her enough status." A 17-year veteran trustee is "confident that an introverted wife would be a drawback to the president just as she is a drawback in any professional man's life. If she is not the president's best promoter, he's going to suffer. . . ."

Some spouses have assumed major roles that are external to the college. One president notes that his spouse is one of the prime women leaders in the area and has been asked to run for public office many times. She has moved from being the area's number one volunteer at age 24 to a professional person in her own right some 20 years later. Another president whose college serves an area of over a million people believes that his spouse plays such a significant role in the community that she would rank among the top ten leaders in the area. This particular spouse has little involvement with the college, however. The president's analysis: "I think people are smart enough now to realize that presidents' spouses have to be their own person just as the president must be." Another president notes that his spouse used to host receptions for the faculty and staff; now she hosts receptions for legislators. Whereas the spouse used to devote a great deal of time to getting to know the faculty and staff, she now spends a lot of time getting to know legislators. Although she used to be on campus a lot of the time, she now spends a great deal of time in the state capitol lobbying on behalf of the college. These spouses were exceptions; most spouses are not viewed as leaders in their own right. Most find that their image, and certainly their image as perceived by the college community, is tied closely to that of the president.

ENTERTAINING

As with other activities associated with the community college, it is dangerous to generalize about the role of the spouse of the community college president. As one spouse declares: "One of the best-kept secrets of the whole aspect of the community college is the involvement of the spouse." To make her point, she recalled a recent reception hosted in her home for over 100 people and for which she did the food preparation. She was madly cutting food, serving it, and in general making sure that the reception was moving along when a woman turned to her and asked, "And what do you do?" The spouse's conclusion: people really do not know what I do or what others in my position do.

A major part of the role of the spouse of the university president is devoted to hosting the various functions sponsored by the president's office. Corbally estimates that an average of 13.5 hours per week is devoted to hosting, *not* including preparation time (Corbally, 1977, p. 95). Another source reports that the 337 spouses of the presidents of state colleges and universities issue a combined total of almost 4,000 invitations to "come to our home" each year (Ostar, 1983, p. 15). In contrast, the spouses of community college presidents host approximately five college-related activities a year, almost all of which are held for the faculty, staff, and board, and most of which involve a large degree of personal handling (SS).

The cost of entertaining also gets a mixed report from spouses of community college presidents. In contrast to the five-figure budgets available for entertaining at many universities and which, while the accounts fall under the office of the president, are generally under the supervision of the spouse, only 5 of the 92 spouses returning the spouses' survey have an expense account over which they have any degree of control; all 5 of these are spouses of those presidents identified as leaders. Moreover, only about one-half of the colleges pay as much as 50 percent of the cost of entertaining. Approximately half of the community colleges provide assistance to the spouse for official functions; the assistance includes secretarial help in sending out invitations and so forth.

One community college president's spouse discovered the "hard facts of life" while attending a conference that included the spouses of both two-year and four-year college and university presidents: "They spend more on the catering bill for one event than I spend all year. They have florists, caterers, bartenders, etc. It is just a whole different world." It should be noted, however, that only approximately 16 percent of those spouses returning the survey live in college-owned homes; the lack of an official residence is a major deterrent to extensive official entertaining. One spouse noted that she and her husband have an open house about once in every five years, a far cry from the literally "open door" policy of some university presidents' households.

The presidential household seems to follow the traditional role pattern, with the mostly female spouses — even though two-thirds of the spouses work in paid occupations — doing most of the cooking, cleaning, and caring for children. It is interesting to note that those presidents identified as leaders were much less likely to help with the cooking than were those not identified as leaders. One conclusion might be that leaders have a more erratic schedule — one that permits them to help with the cleaning and shopping, chores that can be done erratically — but does not permit them to engage in cooking, a chore that must be done on a somewhat regular schedule. Or perhaps those presidents who work at being leaders feel that they must be doing job-related tasks at all times, thereby filling their schedules even after the end of the office day.

Two male spouses returned the survey, and, while it is not the intent here to distinguish between how spouses of different sexes view the spouse's role, it nevertheless seems worth noting the reaction of the two male spouses to the survey. Both of the wives of the two male spouses have been president for approximately three years. One male spouse, a professor, stated that he enjoys the social and community activities he performs as the president's spouse. Indeed, he indicated that he hosts 18 college-related social functions each year. The other male spouse was the only person responding to the survey who had anything negative to say about the survey. His comment: "I have not seen as sexist a form as this in 20 years. Update it to the 20th century." Regarding hosting college-related social functions, he comments that "my wife is the president, not me. I am not involved in these." Perhaps some males are sensitive to being asked if they host functions, work for pay, and help with the household chores. While two responses should not be taken as representing the views of other male spouses, nevertheless the responses were in such contrast to each other that they seemed worthy of a closer look. If the attitude that "my wife is the president, not me" is at all representative, however, it should serve notice to all male presidents and to all trustees to be more sensitive to the demands placed on the female spouses, demands that many males would likely find foreign if not downright distasteful.

The faculty wives' clubs have gone the way of the whooping crane and the American chestnut, few and far between. Only 7 percent (five individuals) of the spouses reported that they have a faculty wives' club; however, all five who reported that their colleges have a club indicated that they are members. Four out of the five colleges are located in the South, with three of the faculty wives' clubs existing in one state. While three of the five clubs are located at colleges the spouses describe as rural, two are urban institutions with over 10,000 students (SS). The comment of one president who has been in office five years tends to put faculty wives' clubs in perspective: "I remember back at my first assignment in the community college several years ago there was something called the faculty wives' club which is probably way out now because of the roles women are now in. It seems to me that back in the 1960s when I first joined the community college the faculty wives' club was led by the president's wife." A spouse notes: "We used to have one, but since so many wives work we found it was not appreciated or useful in today's world." Another spouse says: "It was abandoned before I came and I am extremely glad! I have not found them to be positive in any way."

There are several explanations for the demise of these clubs. The women's movement has surely played a role; the large number of working spouses has made the clubs less feasible and less attractive; the governance process has become more formal, especially where unions are involved, thus lessening the feeling of family that existed when the colleges were first founded; and, the community college movement has matured and the colleges have grown, thus making "pot luck" affairs cumbersome for many colleges.

THE SPOUSE AS CONFIDANT

Do most presidents confide in their spouses? Yes. Do they take the advice of the spouse? That depends. The spouses' survey reveals that 84 percent of the presidents confide in their spouses about problems and issues facing the college. While the presidents tend to confide in the spouse, only 22 percent of the spouses stated that the president took their advice all of the time it was offered; 66 percent of the spouses noted that the president takes their advice some of the time; 12 percent claim that the president never takes their advice. It may be recalled from the earlier discussion on the subject that the chief academic officer, not the spouse, was mentioned most often *by the presidents* as the person in whom the president confided if he or she had a major problem on campus (CLS).

Confiding in someone is not the same as seeking the advice of that person. For example, one spouse noted that her husband shares work-related problems with her, but that she only gives advice *if* her husband asks for it. Another echoes the same sentiments: "I advise him if he asks. Sometimes he asks my opinion, but that is not saying he will take it." Another notes: "He does not heed my advice often enough. He always listens! He does not necessarily heed." On the other hand, another spouse meets all dean candidates and offers her perceptions of each candidate. Her husband, she claims, takes her observations seriously when making the decision on the dean's appointment. One spouse whose husband was under tremendous stress at the time of the interview notes that her husband shares practically every problem he has had during the day with her, including phone calls from the trustees. Does she advise him? "No. Most of the time he would reject my advice on humane grounds because you can't do what I'm thinking to people and get away with it." Another spouse notes that her husband, while sharing problems with her, is very careful not to name names. One spouse took her confidant role quite seriously, even to the point of playing the devil's advocate. She quit the practice, however. "I did take it upon myself to disagree until I found that it irritated him. Now I hold back and he likes it better that way." One spouse described the confidant role as follows: "When the little things bothered him, he seemed much more willing to sit down and talk about them; but, if it were a really big problem, he did not want to share. That was something he felt he had to work out."

Obviously, the role of the spouse as confidant is as varied as are presidents and spouses. Based on the interviews and the surveys, it appears that presidents tend to confide in their spouses yet seek limited advice after "unloading" their problems, thus creating a sense of helplessness for the spouses. As one spouse asserts: "I'm at home all day thinking about what he's going through but he is there and able to take some action, doing things, doing something about it. I'm at home having to wait until evening to find out what happened." When presidents get home, it seems as if the only thing most spouses can do is listen, a role that tends to heighten the frustrations associated with the spouse's role, but nevertheless a role that is extremely important from the president's perspective, for there appear to be few people with whom the president can talk candidly and freely.

Frustrations

While not being able to take action or to offer solutions to problems is obviously a source of frustration to some spouses, it is not the only one. A major frustration results from the frequent travel of the president. Most spouses who commented on the president's travel simply do not like being left alone, especially if the couple have children living at home. The spouse as coach, physician, bus driver, and so forth has been alluded to. Other spouses referred to their roles as plumber, clerk left behind to pay bills, and any number of other jobs that must be done while the president is away. One spouse exclaimed bitterly: "I resented being left alone, night after night, with our small children. I asked myself many times if it was worth it."

Living in a "fish bowl" brought some frustrations, although most spouses agreed that their role drew no attention, much less placed them in a fish bowl; others freely admitted that they enjoyed the attention that comes from being the spouse of a highly visible president. But living in the public eye has its drawbacks. For one spouse it means "having to keep my mouth closed when I would like to say something." The size of the community surrounding the college contributes to the visibility of the spouse. One spouse who lives in a small Midwestern town, "where everybody knows everybody" and whose husband was promoted to the presidency from within the college ranks, notes, "People are nice to me who were not before; they are just trying to butter me up. I knew them in a different way before; it frustrates me to know that people recognize me as the wife of the president. They come up to me in the grocery store or at the bank and tell me something they think is wrong with the college, hoping I will tell my husband." Sounding the same theme, another spouse finds it very frustrating when "people talk with me in the hopes the message will be passed on to my husband." Another spouse resents "having to be visible for visibility's sake." A more optimistic note on the theme comes from the spouse of the president at a suburban community college in the deep South. She describes her situation as follows: "Some days I know I'm in a 'fish bowl' when community members relate all they see us do, such as 'I noticed you had visitors from — county' (car tags). 'I saw Dr. — swinging the grandchildren. How long will they be here?' 'I didn't know *you* worked in the garden!' I know the community is very small and extremely conservative *and* genuinely interested in us. It is hard at times since I'm a private person and never lived quite so publicly. I know we're liked, needed, and respected."

The "fish bowl syndrome" extends to other members of the family. As suggested in an earlier chapter, some children of presidents are reluctant to attend the community college because of the potentially high visibility they would endure. "As our children grew up on campus, they were expected to be paragons. They took visitors on tours of the campus, ran errands, helped with entertainment, and generally made themselves useful for years. We are fortunate to have three fine adults. But outside the home their life was not easy — from snide remarks about 'rich dad' to not being able to get part-time jobs with the college because of nepotism — they are only now making us aware of some of the things they had to go through just because their dad was president."

As with any married couple who care about each other, the spouse is frustrated when the other one is hurt. As one spouse notes: "It frustrates me when I see people dealing with him unfairly. It frustrates me when I see him sometimes beating his head against a brick wall trying to get people to understand." In the same vein, another spouse notes that at times she is "horribly frustrated; what is the point of it all; no one appreciates what we are doing. Why do we do this to ourselves? The legislators will not fund us." But in the final analysis she feels that most people appreciate what she does for the college.

Certainly the way presidents handle their position causes some frustrations for spouses. Several spouses noted that their husbands wanted to "play president" at home not only with them but with their children as well. As one spouse declared, "I think that the inherent power in the presidency went to his head and he just could not turn it off when he got home." Another notes that her husband is too preoccupied with his job: "The result is that my status with him is low."

A major frustration experienced by spouses results from the

amount of time presidents devote to their positions, thereby leaving little time for their families. Over and over the theme emerged that the president and spouse had little time to call their own, a subject that was discussed earlier in this volume.

There were other frustrations such as an occasional conflict in careers and in adjusting to the president's erratic schedule. The expectations the governing board has of the spouse caused some frustrations and are dealt with in some detail later. A large number of spouses stated that they found no frustrations associated with their role as the spouse of a community college president, a situation that is reflected to a degree in the rewards associated with the role.

Rewards

Many spouses feel that their role is a rewarding one. In contrast to the small number who worry about being in the fish bowl, many spouses expressed appreciation for the fact that the spouse's role placed them in a position to meet interesting people. Some spouses enjoy the status associated with the role. As one notes: "Our town is small. It is small enough that if you have your name on a check everyone knows who you are." She observes, however, that this is not always an advantage. Several spouses stated they enjoy the social contacts that go with the role of spouse. One feels she is now "with a social group I normally would not be with. The position has a certain degree of respect." Another finds it rewarding that "people think you are important and you get certain advantages from being the spouse of the president."

Several spouses take pride in the accomplishments of the college and of their husband as president of the college. One spouse whose husband is the president of a small college finds satisfaction through "the close association with the students and faculty and the activities associated with the college." Another feels a sense of pride in being associated with the college. One enjoys "just being the wife member of the president's team."

Travel with the president was a source of satisfaction for a large number of spouses. They felt they could go places that they could not go otherwise, with at least some of the expenses paid for by the college.

The Presidential Interview

Thirty percent of the spouses responding to the spouses' survey indicated that they were interviewed as a part of the presidential selection process. The question of whether the spouse should be interviewed as part of the process is subject to debate, although based on the interviews done for this study, most spouses, presidents, and trustees feel that the spouse should be interviewed as part of the employment process.

Why is the question of interviewing the spouse subject to debate? In recent years there has been a tendency on the part of some governing boards, spouses, and presidents of not wanting to give the impression that the spouse is being employed along with the president — so as not to appear that two were being sought for the price of one. The large number of spouses who are employed outside the home indicates that those boards which choose not to interview the spouse for the above reason may be acting realistically. As one community college national leader who spent his presidential career on the West Coast recalls: "I think there may have been a time when boards interviewed the spouse. I think boards have concluded that they are hiring the president; they are not hiring the spouse." A president who three years ago accepted his second presidency, this one in the Southwest, describes his interview as follows: "In my last interview for this job, interviewing the spouse was discussed, and I said, 'Let's understand that you are hiring me, and that my wife is a person in her own right. While she enjoys college activities and doesn't hesitate to take part, there is no obligation for her to do so.' And they bought it." At a very large urban-suburban, five-campus community college, both faculty members interviewed rejected the idea that the spouse should be interviewed. "Why should she be interviewed?" they asked rhetorically. "She is a professional person and has no role with the college other than occasionally to accompany the president to social gatherings and an occasional official college ceremony, functions any spouse would normally carry out."

Others interviewed, however, felt very strongly that the spouse should be interviewed. One spouse who is very active with the college believes that it is important for the spouse to be interviewed. She states: "I think the governing board should interview the spouse and I think the spouse should interview the board. I think there should be some very clear discussions on what the expectations of the spouse are and what the board proposes to do in terms of support, financial included." A number of spouses felt that they should be interviewed, if for no other reason than to meet the members of the board. A female administrator believes the spouse should be interviewed because, as noted earlier, the effectiveness of the president can be affected by the home situation. A faculty member said yes, the spouse should be interviewed: "You need to find out if they are working as a cohesive unity. Both are seen as being affiliated with the college." A female trustee from the rural Northeast whose board had just completed the search for a president noted that the board did not interview the spouse. She believes it was a major mistake not to do so. "I'll never be on a search committee again where they don't interview the spouse. I will clearly define her role and responsibilities and the need for her to complement her husband; she represents the college in the community." A highly active trustee from a major community college in the Southeast stated emphatically, "Oh yes, I'd do it in the law practice and I would do it there too." Incidentally, a year or so later, the college employed a new president, and, according to the new president, his spouse was not interviewed.

A part of the dilemma associated with the question of interviewing the spouse is captured in the response of a female faculty member from the Southeast. Her answer (in response to whether the spouse should be interviewed): "I think it would be a very good idea for a search committee to do the interview. However, from a woman's point of view, that just negatively affects me to think that it should have to make a difference."

Based on the interviews and the responses on the surveys, it is concluded that the spouse, the president, and the governing board can profit from an interview with the spouse. If little is expected of the spouse, this should be made known at the time of the interview, thereby preventing the spouse from being trapped in a perpetual state of "rising expectations." On the other hand, if the board expects a great deal from the spouse, this too should be clarified and the spouse should be appropriately supported. The board should also be willing to let the spouse know what financial and other resources will be available for entertaining, travel, and other activities which might be expected of the spouse. Most important, the interview will give the spouse an opportunity to express his or her views of the spouse's role, to ask questions, and to decide if this is a club he or she wants to join. Assuming the interview is handled properly, no one has anything to lose from the spouse being interviewed; indeed, everyone has much to gain by making the spouse an integral part of the presidential selection process. As one spouse states: "I really think, maybe not so much for me, but for some of the younger people who will be coming into the role, it should be made very clear by the board what the presidents' wives are really doing. The board should help in some way." The interview can go a long way toward identifying what is and is not expected of the spouse. Indeed, to ignore the spouse during the presidential selection process would appear to be, rather than the final, the first affront to that spouse. Common courtesy, if not common sense, would dictate a session, if not necessarily a formal interview, with that individual so important to one's prospective leader. Moreover, this initial involvement would seem to be a prime means of indicating the spouse's importance for a successful presidency, not to mention an excellent opportunity for both the spouse and board to assess one another.

Relationships with the College Community

Spouses, like presidents, normally establish relationships with the major components of the college community. These relationships vary from spouse to spouse and from college to college; how they are perceived by the spouses sheds further light on their role. Those spouses surveyed were asked to describe their relationship with the trustees and their spouses; with deans, vice presidents, and their spouses; with faculty and their spouses; and with students. Table 7.1 outlines the results.

If there were any surprises in the relationships, these centered around the high percentage of spouses who perceived their relationship with the faculty as friendly and informal, and the small percentage who saw themselves as having little or no relationship with the faculty.

TABLE 8.1. Relationships of Presidents' Spouses with
Selected Components of the College Community

RELATIONSHIP WITH	INFORMAL/ FRIENDLY %	FORMAL/ FRIENDLY %	FORMAL/ DISTANT %	NONE %
College Board	75	15	3	7
Board Spouses	70	11	4	15
Deans, Vice Presidents	88	10	1	1
Spouses of Deans, Vice Presidents	85	13	1	1
Faculty	72	21	4	3
Spouses of Faculty	72	20	3	5
Students	47	28	1	24

Relationships with the Governing Board

Although spouses described their relationship with trustees as being largely friendly and informal, that does not mean that they view it as appropriate. Indeed, some bitterness exists among spouses regarding their dealings with the governing board. To set the stage for how some community college spouses view the board–spouse relationship, it might help place things in perspective by citing an example used by David Riesman. Riesman recounts the story of the spouse of the president of a four-year institution who asked a member of the board of trustees how he would feel if she decided to get a job outside the university. "When the trustee responded, not by saying 'We need you,' but 'Why the hell should I care?' she was shaken, and when she received a nearly identical answer from other trustees, she began to look for another job" (1982, p. 6).

One spouse, who, after 32 years, has "about had enough of occupying the role," notes that at times in her career the board appreciated what she did; however, she now feels that the current board sees no value in the role played by the president's spouse. The following remarks summarize her views: "Compared to the work and effort and heartache that a spouse puts into the job, the rewards are nil or few." Another spouse, and one who is intimately involved with the affairs of the college, believes that it would help her and other spouses if "trustees would recognize the contributions the spouse makes — maybe part-time secretarial help; certainly some household help should be provided." While she does not want to be paid a salary, she thinks that the board should "occasionally pick up the tab for a trip." What the college board at her college *does not* provide became painfully clear to her when she was one of only a few spouses of a community college president in attendance at a forum attended primarily by spouses of presidents of four-year colleges and universities. Some of the spouses of four-year presidents were discussing the roles their social secretaries play; another main topic of conversation was getting their entertainment schedule computerized. *An interesting contrast is provided: the spouse of the community college president paid her own way to the conference, had no social secretary, and had no interest in or need to computerize her entertainment schedule.* The spouse of a university president, upon hearing that she had paid her own travel, noted, "If I'm not important enough to have my expenses paid, then I'm not going." Perhaps those community college spouses who are interested in professional travel should adopt a similar attitude, or at least let their views on the subject be heard. This is not now the case, based on the interviews conducted for this study.

Was the above spouse an exception, especially in regard to paying her own way to the conference? To test the assumption that most spouses of community college presidents pay their own way to such affairs, 28 spouses attending a conference for presidents and spouses (a registration fee was charged and a program planned for the spouses) were asked if they paid their own way. Twenty-four of the 28 paid their own way; the colleges paid the expenses of the other four.

Community college spouses do "keep going," however. One spouse, in response to how the college board views her role, notes that the board gives it little attention, but nevertheless expects her to "be there." "Being there" meant that in one year she entertained as many as 3,000 people on behalf of the college. Although this particular college furnishes a home and some help for the spouse when she and her husband entertain on behalf of the college, and while she is a rare exception to most community college spouses in regard to the number of people entertained, she nevertheless does not believe that the board is sensitive to the role she plays and that the board takes her for granted. "Our board expects a lot of me. . . . Not once did the board say thank you; not once did they offer to come over to help. They expect you to do things without really asking." And what would she like for the board to do? "I would just like for them to show some form of appreciation just by saying thank you. I don't expect anything else but for them to let me have the feeling that they appreciate what I've done." A discussion with the spouse and her husband some months later revealed that the board chairman finally said thanks, but *only* after the president asked him to do so.

Some boards do show their appreciation for the contributions of the spouse. Several comments indicate that the trustees view the spouse's role as being important to the welfare of the college and to the president. One spouse comments: "I am important. They make me know that my feelings and desires are important to them. They aid me in trying to get my husband away from pressures occasionally. I'm made to feel a needed part." Another observes: "I have a friendly relationship with the board members, and I think they like having me involved in the informal social activities of the college." Still another states: "I'm an important supporter of the college and one who contributes to the college; also, the board sees me as a person with a life separate from the college." According to one spouse: "I believe the board views my role as important. I believe the present board would seriously question a president who is single." A final comment on the positive side: "I think they must feel I'm important because I'm usually included — introduced around, etc. Trustees often tell me if there has been a particularly difficult board meeting, as if to imply I'll have to put my husband 'back together again'." Two spouses stated that the trustees at their college felt the spouse should receive a salary, but this feeling was not widespread nor supported by most spouses.

While some spouses were unhappy with the way the governing board saw their role and others felt gratified with the attention given the role, almost 57 percent of the spouses responding to the survey indicated that the governing board paid little or no attention to the role of the spouse. In most of these situations, "little is expected and little is given." As one spouse declares: "Little attention is given to the role other than take it for granted that when a social function needs to be held I will take over." Another spouse notes that "the board members make no demands on me at all. My husband seldom does. We both have professional commitments that require lots of attention." One replies: "I really think the board members don't consider my role at all. I think they really don't think about it." Another spouse states her perception as follows: "I'm not sure. Nothing has ever been told to me by the board members of their expectations." In a similar vein, another spouse states: "There is no obvious attention to the role, and no demands are made." One spouse sees the board's lack of interest as positive: "I don't think it matters as evidenced by four years of marriage and little interest in my husband's divorce and remarriage to me, which may be a plus; any interest, I believe, is one of a personal nature."

The Changing Role of the Spouse

One of the questions asked of the spouses was whether the role of the spouse has changed since they first assumed the role, and, if so, how. Seventy-one percent stated that the role had not changed. (One should remember that over 50% of the presidents have been in their position for five years or less.) The 29 percent who felt that the role has changed offered some reasons.

One change alluded to earlier is the demise of the faculty wives' clubs. Another obvious difference is the number of spouses working outside the home. Both are reflections of broader movements in society. A comment from a spouse who has been in the role for 17 years serves to put both of these changes in today's perspective. "Some of the younger wives indicate they feel social activity with the faculty is not as important as it was in the past. More faculty spouses work; therefore, they are too busy for social activities."

Just as community colleges do not exist in a vacuum, neither do the spouses of presidents. One major influence on the role of the spouse has been the changing role of women in society. Another influence has been the maturing of the community college itself. One spouse speaks to these transformations: "The role of the community college has changed. I found that a great deal more was expected of my predecessor than is expected of me. I am a professional person employed in another district; there is little pressure put on me in 'ceremonial situations.'" Another spouse hits on the same theme: "We used to do more entertaining. The growth of the college, the end of the wives' club, and my career and education have made my role less significant."

Spouses change, too: "I can only speak for my own situation because I've been in the same place for 20 years; if there's any change, it's because I have changed personally. I'm much more involved, of course. Now that my children are grown, there are fewer outside demands on my time. I do feel the role is more individualized than it used to be — less rigid, more informal — and, hopefully, more enjoyable now." Another spouse notes that "there is more latitude for the spouse — there is no longer the stereotype of the president's spouse; that is, the proper little person — giving teas, etc., similar to the minister's wife. Careers are now acceptable."

The woman's movement has had various impacts on the role of a number of spouses: some subtle, some not so subtle; some positive, some not so positive. One spouse who falls into the 55-or-over age category states in relationship to the woman's movement that "my generation maintains a low profile. In contrast, one of my daughters is an attorney." Another spouse notes that the woman's movement "made our wives' club obsolete but allowed me to pursue my own career." Other spouses made similar comments; each quote is from a different spouse. "I think the movement has probably given us more freedom to pursue our own interests." "If I were a professional person in my own right, it would be acceptable in this community." "It has changed from my being expected to play a major role in the community college to acceptance of my having my own career interests." "It decreased the concept of one salary – two jobs. The movement has forced people to let me be me instead of 'the president's wife.'" "I have taken an interest in finding my own place in the community and business world, rather than depending on my husband's role." "It has enabled me to be my own person." "Freed me to say 'no' and pursue some career ideas." "It has helped me recognize my own needs as valid." "It has given me courage to be myself. It has enabled me to see my contribution as valuable and substantial — even though unpaid."

Several spouses noted the impact of the woman's movement on the larger society and how it has influenced the spouse's role. One spouse who had a career "before the woman's movement was even thought of" notes some subtle changes brought about by the movement. "Perhaps it has had an impact on other people's attitude of 'accepting.' The fact that I have continued my career for 24 years has probably prepared me for the 'juggling act' of two roles." Another spouse is pleased that she is no longer "giving in to the stereotypical." One spouse evaluates the changes as follows: "I see more women in leadership roles and our conversations center around similar problems of how to organize our time and how to get the most from ourselves without compromising our family commitments. An 'if she can do it, so can I' attitude exists." Similarly, another spouse comments: "It seems people realize more readily that I have my own life, interests, desires, too. The movement has definitely helped in this area, a type of freeing me." One spouse notes that the woman's movement has "heightened the sensitivity of others in the community to the role of all women and freed me from any stereotypical responsibilities." A final comment in the same vein: "I am not 'boxed in' by rules — spoken or unspoken — about what my behavior should be."

The woman's movement has not embraced all spouses. Indeed, approximately half of those responding to the survey stated that the movement has had little or no effect on their role as the spouse of a community college president. Some few feel that they are "just as liberated as I would ever want to be," as one spouse comments. Some spouses observed that, as a result of the woman's movement, "spouses no longer have a role!"; it "has relieved me from having a role", or, "The role of the 'spouse' is nearly nonexistent. I am allowed to be an individual." One president's remarks tend to summarize the changing attitude of presidents toward the role of the spouse: "My wife plays a different role than she did. Her changing role is extremely consistent with the changing role of women in society over the past eight years or so. When I began my career—and long before I began as president—the typical role model was the president's wife who sits there and hosts teas and hosts faculty groups and goes to every occasion of the college arm-in-arm with the president; that was the role we could observe in our previous location. That was pretty much the role she filled during our early years of our presidency. But since that time she has gone back to college and got her master's degree and has her own career as a counselor in a high school. She is still supportive, but she is her own person in every respect. She lends support to me and to the office of the president when absolutely necessary in an official capacity. But her profile is much lower now than it was and will remain that way."

General Observations

There are a number of contradictions in how the spouses of community college presidents see their positions. Conflicting viewpoints are to be expected in so complex and varied a role. However, in spite of the inherent contradictions the interviews and surveys reveal that most spouses tend to fall into one of four categories. (The two males would likely fall into a category of their own and are not treated here.) They are: (1) those spouses who have carved out a role for themselves as spouses of community college presidents, yet who are not satisfied with the role as it is perceived by others, especially the governing board; (2) those spouses who accept their role and whose credo seems to be, "That's the way it is, so why fight it?"; (3) those spouses with careers equal to or nearly equal to that of presidents and who view the spouse's role as just another part of the professional person's juggling act; and (4) those spouses who feel that they have no role as the spouse of the president that goes beyond what one normally expects to find in a marriage and who show resentment and frustration over not having a more significant role. With perhaps the exception of those spouses who have careers that are professionally satisfying to them, all of the categories produce certain frustrations that go with being the spouse of a community college president.

While the four groups are far from clear-cut, the highest level of frustration, often expressed as bitterness, is among the latter group—those spouses who feel that they have no major role to play in the scheme of things, yet who would like to be more involved with the activities of the college. These spouses are not apathetic and are not willing to buy into any "that's-the-way-it-is" philosophy. On the other hand, they are unwilling to create their own role. They generally feel that the governing board, president's office, and college community should have a good concept of the spouse's role and that it should not only be defined but should be supported both financially and philosophically. These spouses, rather than settling for second-class status, opt for virtually no official role. This group may represent the greatest potential for bringing the spouse into the mainstream of college activity. The woman's movement, while far from claiming them as converts in the strictest sense of the term, has sensitized them to those aspects of society that relegate women to an inferior status. Members of this group tend to be well educated, but they do not have professional status equal to that of the president.

Those spouses who have carved out an important role for themselves, in spite of a perceived lack of support from the college community other than from the president, would do even more than they are doing *if* resources and board support were available. It seems likely that a member of this group will write the first book on the role of the spouse; they have already "fought the wars" and have a story to tell and a need to tell it. The woman's movement has tended to rub salt into some of their wounds. On the other hand, the movement has given them the courage to ask for what they want and need in fulfilling the spouse's role.

Those spouses who accept things the way they are probably will never be catalysts for change; however, should the spouse's role expand, they would accept the expanded role. This group tends to be more traditional than the others and feels little direct effect from the woman's movement. On the other hand, these spouses do what is expected of them and rarely question the person or persons calling the shots. Members of this group seem to understand their role only in relationship to the role of *their* president.

Those spouses who have achieved equal career status with the presidents tend to do what is necessary, do it well, but do little else in regard to their role as the spouse of the president. They were either professionals before the woman's movement or are now professionals and take their status for granted. They do not see their career or status tied to that of the president and would view a greatly expanded spouse's role as unacceptable.

Obviously, most spouses do not fit perfectly into any of the above categories; yet, it seems as if most spouses could identify with one category more than the others. To test the four classifications, a group of 28 spouses were asked to place themselves into one of the four classifications, if possible. Of the 28, four placed themselves in group 1, six in group 2, eight in group 3, and ten in group 4. Of the 28, only two expressed any hesistancy about placing themselves into one of the four groups.

Although the categories are not always clearly defined, they might prove helpful to spouses in deciding not only where they are in the community college scheme of things, but where they want to go. When this happens, a definition of the community college and the presidency can only be enhanced.

Being There: One Spouse's Perspective

Peggy A. Vaughan

Little wonder that community college watchers are often at a loss to fathom the educational undertaking when even those closest to its heartbeat are often perplexed when attempting to explain it. Like the mythical sea-god Proteus, once you have it in your grasp, it is likely to present an entirely different form. Indeed, what else can one expect from an enterprise that, at least at one point in time, purported to be all things to all people (whether this claim has been made by its detractors or its supporters appears to be a moot point). Unlike Proteus, however, who, if only one could hold on long enough, must in the end present his true form, the sheer vastness of the community college (its comprehensiveness, its leaders might say) precludes any stronghold from which to maintain a firm grasp while awaiting the final transformation of the giant. (Perhaps my husband would have done well to study Proteus rather than put another face on Janus in an attempt to describe the many roles the community college must adopt for its many publics.)

Nor is it only the college itself which causes perplexity. Elsewhere in this volume my husband has referred to being brought up short when asked just what a community college president does. (I can also remember a time when another community college president was brought up short when asked by my husband—who had just been appointed by that president to be the new dean at a new community college—just what a community college dean does.) Just so, then, was I brought up short when my husband asked for my perceptions of my role as the spouse of a community college president. My first response was that I had no role but, following close upon the heels of that response, was the thought that perhaps having been at four different and certainly diverse community colleges, the latter two where my husband has been president, might allow for some unique perceptions on the community college itself, if not always upon the role of the spouse. For in reflecting upon my role as spouse, I find it difficult to speak of it in isolation from the colleges themselves. As such, I have chosen to reminisce about four colleges, two where my husband was the academic dean. Indeed, if any merit lies in my remarks perhaps it will be on the basis of a continuum, seeing what is because of what has been.

Our first community college experience (beginning in 1967) was unique in several respects: the college itself had just converted from a two-year branch college into a comprehensive community college; my husband, having taught history there one year before returning to school to complete the requirements for the Ph. D. in history, became the new community college's academic dean; and, finally, I had been hired from the local high school to teach English at the college *before* my husband had been offered the deanship—more to come on that later, you can bet! Obviously, a new community college had more to worry about than conflict of interest. However, whether we were a branch campus or a community college meant little to me for, as with most teachers, my main concern was with those students I must face across the desk every day.

The faculty was generally a young one and many, like myself, had either come to the college from high school teaching or else were new to the profession itself. We were like children who had been set down in a roomful of new toys, with no adults around to spoil our fun. The administration — whether naively or innocently (they would probably say out of necessity) — placed the faculty in a huge room with our desks ranged in a circle around the wall, and that was our office that first year. Thus while faculty disagreements were apt to become communal battles, so too did any real or perceived injustices at the hands of the administration often become communal injustices. Consider, administrator, dropping by to chat with that faculty member whom you just might have been somewhat harsh or unfair with and instead of facing one pair of hurt or hostile eyes those of your entire faculty. Consequently, it took no marches on the president's office for the necessary office space to become a reality. That need was descried quickly by administrators whose innocence, naivete, or necessity wisely gave way to new found truths about the innate nature of the relationship between faculty and administrators.

While conflict of interest did not catch up with me at this college, the wisdom which led to its birth in the first place would perhaps have been all too apparent in my own situation had an objective observer been looking. While I always enjoyed a close relationship with the faculty — and still have close friends from it today, there were those moments. Criticisms leveled at the administration were taken personally by me, followed by hasty reassurances from fellow faculty that they certainly were not referring to my husband but the other administrators. Similarly, administrative complaints about faculty were received coldly by me — those were my colleagues my husband was complaining about. To this day my attitude toward community college faculty remains molded by my teaching experiences at the first two community colleges, where my husband was academic dean. Consequently, in any faculty–administrative conflict, all things being equal, my husband knows that my sentiments more often than not will lie with the faculty, a situation that he does not particularly relish but one that I think has tempered his own administrative outlook over the years.

My second community college experience was with one

which only existed on paper when in the early 1970s we moved to a new town which, although small, was noted for its cosmopolitan atmosphere. Our new community college, as one would expect, absorbed much of this cosmopolitan flavor. This time we were old hands. This time we knew what the community college was all about as essentially the same administrative team from our previous college set to work again to build a new community college from the ground up, a new start for everyone.

Personally and professionally, I took on another role at this college, a role which has generally proved in years since to be both a blessing and an albatross for the community college. Here I became a part-timer. Not intending to teach, especially since giving birth to our second son in August, in September I acquiesced to a potentially overburdened English department and began teaching 13 hours — some part-time job, you may well say — due to the onslaught of a larger than expected student body (the community college student is a unique creature in that he generally keeps his intended appearance or non-appearance at registration a well-guarded secret until the last moment).

Well, we were off again and, taking our cue from the surrounding area, we became a fairly sophisticated community college. After all, the new community college had no identity other than that which we chose to bestow upon it. We chose to produce sophisticated dramatic productions and quality movie showings with discussions afterwards. We chose new homes, more children, the Junior Woman's Club, the Garden Club, the Rotary Club, the Kiwanis Club. We chose to begin a gourmet dinner club among our own ranks. And, certainly not last, we enthusiatically welcomed the students, both vocational and academic. We had settled down. We were a small faculty who enjoyed each other and our work. We had reached maturity and we liked it. Interestingly enough, at this point in the community college development, the only difference in being a part-time rather than a full-time faculty member was that the salary was considerably lower, the last a verity today as then. I speak not only from my own experience but from those who worked with me. We attended all meetings and had the same relationship with the faculty-staff-administration as did the full-time personnel.

This situation was not to last long for me, however, as conflict of interest was coming into a maturity of its own and, in doing so, began taking a look around at its public domain and found a prime candidate to go after. To no avail were my charges of unfairness (the astute reader will remember that I was hired by the community college system as a full-fledged faculty member *before* my husband became one of its administrators). The state won out, of course, and I reluctantly retired from the community college to teach in a private college nearby.

After a two-year stint as dean at this community college, my husband became the newly appointed president of a yet-to-be-built college some two hours distant from where we were then located. And I, I became the full-fledged spouse of a community college president. One would assume that our experiences at our two previous colleges would have exerted a dominating if not shaping influence upon the direction of this newly rising one. However, the word community in the title is not there in name only. For each community college unquestionably soon acquires, and rightfully so, its own unique community identity. As with the last college, there were no buildings when we arrived—nothing but a make-shift office and one lone secretary in a tiny, previously unused building. The town itself was a small isolated mountain town with the nearest theatre (we all have our priorities) at that time being 40 country miles away and the nearest airport a considerable distance from that. The "sophisticated" approach gave way to the "frontier" approach. A young administration (my husband was still in his 30's) and a young faculty (generally speaking, both in terms of experience and age) found in themselves a raw energy fit for the time and place and unleashed it upon both the college and the community. Elsewhere in this volume my husband has spoken of the evangelical fervor often displayed in the community college movement, particularly by its leaders. Well might he speak to that fervor, for I saw it displayed openly and daily in the young years of that particular college. The surrounding area was bombarded in that first year by my husband and his fellow administrators. Every week and often every night in the week brought a new organization or a new group to confront with the community college philosophy as the team exhorted the audiences on this new gospel. And it did work: I remember one particular occasion (I was usually in the audience) being surrounded by a group from the audience after one of the presentations and being asked almost in awe "Where did you find him?" referring to my husband. The speaker went on to comment that she was so taken with the speech that several times she wanted to applaud. (Having grown up in a small isolated mountain town myself, the camp meeting flavor of some of these "one-night stands" was not lost on me.)

Private homes opened their doors for us to meet the local townspeople and explain our mission to them. I recall one particular night when my husband and his deans journeyed by car along with his board chairman, his wife, and myself to another town in the college's service area for a dinner meeting with local townspeople in a local business leader's home. Following our directions and arriving at what we thought to be our destination, we were greeted at the door by a teenager. Explaining who we were, we were invited in while the young man brought his parents. Undaunted by the all too conspicuous load of laundry lying in full view on the floor and obviously meant for the washer soon, we quickly and expertly began unloading and setting up equipment (they must see as well as hear our message). Some few minutes later we were repacking and, somewhat chastened I hope, on our way to the correct address.

Nowhere could the population of this area escape the "good news" of its community college. Local restaurants willingly accepted placemats which told of the college's mission and its educational offerings. I'm sure that on the night of the now famous episode when Elizabeth Taylor choked on a chicken bone in a small restaurant in Big Stone Gap that a college placemat lay beneath her plate.

Just as the college and the community were fertile ground for both expounding and implementing the community college philosophy, so too were they fertile ground for the spouse of the president to find many seeds, if not to plant, at least to nurture. One will no doubt have gathered that, with the nearest theatre 40 miles away, other traditional opportunities for social intercourse were limited. Impromptu parties became a way of life with us as the faculty shared this casual entertaining with us. We had many such gatherings, sometimes cramped, but no less fun for all that —a young faculty could ill afford new, comfortable living quarters and certainly these would not have been available to us at that point anyway. And just as the frontier had its own bards to record its history in song, so did we. Many nights we sat on the floor in someone's home listening to our own bard sing our own special lyrics to "Country Roads," lyrics which spoke of the college's now famous portalettes and other humorous byproducts of both our new and isolated status. No more do I hear John Denver's lyrics when I hear the song but rather our own special lyrics.

There soon became obvious the need for more organized social outlets, however, and so began our Faculty Women – Wives Club, so began a Junior Woman's Club which I had been approached about organizing soon after we arrived in town. The initial meeting to determine the extent of interest in forming a Junior Woman's Club found over 50 young women crowded into our living room. Consequently, the club was organized, and I became its first president, serving two consecutive terms. Some 14 years later, the club is one of the most active in the state's Federation of Women's Clubs.

More formal entertainment for the faculty and staff became necessary and was met, in part, by formal receptions at which the community college board participated. These receptions became successful, looked-forward-to affairs which often lasted well into the morning hours. Our first faculty-board reception got off to a less-than-successful start, however, at least in the eyes of one of the board members. Although fears that the food would disappear in the first thirty minutes did not materialize, the nonalcoholic punch was not a hit with everyone. One of our most prominent board members, finding no bar set up anywhere, told me firmly that, "Honey, if you can't afford a bar at these things, I'll take care of one for you." Needless to say, ways were found to cater to various tastes, particularly those of the board, at future functions. We were still learning our lessons, but we were quick learners.

A final endeavor for a social outlet for the faculty was MECCA — our sometimes venture into communal ownership of what in retrospect can only be described as a decrepit and decaying house whose only mode of entrance was directly through the middle of a cemetery. Since the college's acronym was MECC, it

took no particular leap of genius to arrive at the MECC Association or MECCA. Perhaps going through a graveyard to reach it
was indeed an appropriate gesture. MECCA became our retreat
for parties, for picnics, for horseshoe pitching contests, for song-
fests. While it lasted, it was indeed a mountaintop experience for
us, cemetery or no cemetery.

But change has become one of the verities of life and, as such,
change of course came to all of us, as we all moved on to new
challenges, if not necessarily to new frontiers. My husband and I
moved to our present community college eight years ago. We
live in a town where education is a way of life and where the
community college operates under the shadow of a major university with an international reputation for quality. Obviously, the
needs of this community and this faculty lie light years away from
our last experience at a community college. Here my position as
spouse of a community college president has become one in name
more than in role. There is no nonexistent Junior Woman's Club
to form; the faculty wives and women have no spare time to be
filled up with a faculty club, no need for dilapidated old houses to
retreat to. What has been my own response to this current role
—or lack of role? Lots of secret guilt. For years in our previous
position when friends would ask how I managed to juggle the
roles of teacher, spouse, club president, Sunday School teacher,
and mother of two young children, my response was always
given, I am sure, with a smug smile. Today, I also wonder how I
did it. But those various roles also brought with them a certain
amount of assurance that I was providing for needs which were
not being taken care of elsewhere. I am still startled (and, oh yes,
guilt-ridden) when friends or associates of mine not connected
with the college comment on how busy I must stay with college
commitments. While social functions for the college still occupy
a small portion of my time, and, while these are always appreciated by the college community, as time goes by they seem to be
serving less and less a vital need for the college. I am just as
convinced that, at one point in its history, this college community
no doubt had many of the same needs as other young colleges. Or
perhaps this is my method of rationalizing the need not to be a
more active community college spouse. In any event, I can remember years ago being at a gathering and being introduced

simply as the wife of a college dean, with no mention made of my also being an educator. Well, at least that is no longer the situation. Now I am more apt to be introduced as an educator, with no mention of being a community college spouse, or, if so, that is secondary information. I personally am satisfied with this situation, as I think my greatest asset at this particular community college is being seen by the faculty, staff, and board as a professional in my own right. Although I obviously do not teach at the community college, I feel that the faculty has respect for me as a colleague.

Be that as it may, however, and my present satisfactions notwithstanding, I do understand how today's community college presidents who learned their trade during the boom years of community college growth must feel at the essential loss of the community college frontier and with it their role as frontier scouts — not necessarily because of the smoke rising down the road from another community college (although, admittedly, we have the territory pretty well covered) but at the changing face of "presidenting." For I miss that new territory too sometimes. It may not have been Camelot, but for one brief moment, it *was* Mecca. But I guess you had to be there.

CHAPTER 9

———◆———

Leadership

"In the final analysis, it all comes down to one word: leadership." This statement from a community college president serves to summarize much of what has been said about the role of the community college presidency up to this point. Defining leadership in any context, however, is somewhat like trying to lasso an eel; once you feel you have it in tow, it slips away. Yet to ignore leadership is to ignore much of what the community college presidency should be about.

Observations on Leadership

Warren Bennis observes that almost everyone has an idea about good and bad leaders, but he concludes that, after 50 years of research on the subject, only one conclusion can be reached with any amount of confidence: there are no generalizations about leadership (Bennis, 1975). Nevertheless, Bennis himself generalizes about what constitutes this quality, and he does so in a rather traditional way: "Leadership is the capacity to infuse new values and goals into the organization, to provide perspective on events and environments which, if unnoticed, can impose constraints on the institution" (Bennis, 1973, p. 84). Another source uses a scientific approach in its search for a definition; a typology of four presidential styles was developed through the use of factor analysis (Astin and Scherrei, 1980, pp. 57–70).

An insightful discussion of the complexities surrounding the leadership of academic institutions is found in a volume by Richman and Farmer (1974). The authors acknowledge that leadership can take different forms and that effectiveness depends on much more than formal authority. They also note that leadership is critical to external relationships, an observation that is important in considering community college leadership. They call for strong presidents while offering the caveat that successful leaders are also successful managers, negotiators, and mediators (pp. 18–24).

Departing for the moment from academic leadership to leadership in general, one of the more comprehensive and intelligent treatments of the subject is provided by the renowned historian and social scientist, James MacGregor Burns (1978). Burns sets the stage by noting that "leadership is one of the most observed and least understood phenomena on earth" (p. 2). Leadership as a concept has "dissolved into small and discrete meanings," according to Burns. Indeed, he notes that a recent study turned up 130 definitions (p. 2). Burns identifies two basic types of leadership: transactional and transforming. Transactional leadership exists when leaders "approach followers with an eye to exchanging one thing for another: jobs for votes, or subsidies for campaign contributions" (p. 4). This type pertains in most situations, according to Burns. Transforming leadership, on the other hand, is more complex and more potent: "The transforming leader recognizes and exploits an existing need or demand of a potential follower. But, beyond that, the transforming leader looks for potential motives in followers, seeks to satisfy higher needs, and engages the full person of the follower. The result of transforming leadership is a relationship of mutual stimulation and elevation that converts followers into leaders and may convert leaders into moral agents" (p. 4).

The moral factor emerging from transforming leadership is the concept that concerns Burns most. Moral leadership, as defined by Burns, exists when leaders and followers have mutual needs, aspirations, and values; when leaders and followers have adequate knowledge of alternative leaders and programs and the capacity to choose among alternatives; and, when leaders take responsibility for their commitments and assume leadership for bringing about the changes to which they commit themselves. "Moral leadership emerges from and always returns to, the fundamental wants, needs, aspirations, and values of the followers" (p. 4). As will be seen, Burns's views, especially his concept of moral leadership, are helpful in understanding the community college presidency.

A volume that became something of a manifesto on college and university presidential leadership in the last half of the 1970s is Michael D. Cohen and James G. March's *Leadership and Ambiguity* (1974). Indeed, in 1980 one study identified the volume as the book most frequently recommended for college presidents (Drew and Schuster, 1980). While Cohen and March did not include community colleges, and while many of their conclusions do not apply to most community college presidencies, it is nevertheless worthwhile to consider the volume's major thesis; it had a great impact on how leadership is now viewed in higher education. Cohen and March see the American college and university presidency as belonging to a class of organizations called organized anarchies. Not only do American colleges and universities belong to the class, but the authors see them as the prototypes of organized anarchy. Speaking of an organized anarchy, they note that "it does not know what it is doing. Its goals are either vague or in dispute. Its technology is familiar but not understood. Its major participants wander in and out of the organization" (p. 3). The president is relatively unimportant in organized anarchies: "The world may collapse tomorrow; it may not. The university may survive another ten years; it may not. The differences are important, and the problems are serious. But the outcomes do not much depend on the college president" (p. 5).

Cohen and March were "coming out of the 1960s" with their discussion of the presidency. The mood of the nation has changed since then; no longer are people willing to accept and indeed demand "leaders" who do *not* lead. The image often imposed on the Carter White House of no one in control has been replaced by an image of strong leadership; the suspicion of the Carter years has been replaced with the Boy Scout virtues of the Reagan years, no matter that many of Reagan's appointees would hardly qualify as scouts themselves. Carter the layman could not seem to fulfill the nation's hunger for leadership; Reagan the actor, however, has succeeded in creating the desired image. The mood of the nation has indeed changed. College and university presidencies are not immune to these changes.

The most visible symbol of the changing view of the college and university presidency is James L. Fisher's volume *The Power of the Presidency* (1984). Fisher's book is currently in its second printing and seems to be on its way to replacing Cohen and March's volume as the new bible on the presidency. One reviewer refers to Fisher's work as follows: "Arguably the best book yet published about leadership in American colleges and universities." The reviewer continues: "Fisher's book bids to become the text for workshops and conferences among new presidents and for mid-career seminars with veteran incumbents" (Robinson, 1984, p. 50). Whether the volume will be as important as the reviewer believes is subject to further interpretations. Regardless, the mood of the nation is such that the time seems right for a strong statement on presidential leadership in academia; Fisher has made that statement and has made it rather convincingly.

True to its title, Fisher's volume concentrates on the power associated with the college and university presidency and the use of that power. He writes, "The thesis of this book is that college and university presidents' power motivation is 'socialized' (for the common good.)" (p. 29). He asks rhetorically, "What is power?" and then proceeds to define his concept of power under five headings: coercive power, reward power, legitimate power, expert power, and charismatic power. The most effective and therefore the most important type of power a president can wield, he believes, is charismatic power, although the effective leader must combine charismatic power with the correct portions of expert, legitimate, and reward power. For the most part, leaders should avoid the use of coercive power. To Fisher, charismatic power is derived from the admiration, trust, and affection people feel for the leader; the followers of the charismatic leader believe that the leader will make things better; thus they not only feel good about the leader but also about themselves (pp. 39–41). Painting a regal picture of the presidency ("Never, never get off the presidential platform"; "A small entourage can be important with off-campus groups . . ."), Fisher believes that three conditions must exist in order for the president to develop and use charismatic power effectively: distance, style, and perceived self-confidence. The most important condition for charisma, Fisher believes, is distance (p. 43).

How important is Fisher's interpretation of the college presidency to understanding the community college presidency? Community college presidents are reading the volume. During a discussion of the Fisher book with some of my colleagues, one claimed that he carries it in his brief case at all times; another noted that he owns two copies, one for the office and one for travel. The volume is probably appealing to the community college presidents in part because it brings a perspective to the presidency that says, yes, participatory governance is highly desirable but so is strong presidential leadership. A word of caution is in order, however. There is some danger that community college presidents might interpret Fisher's stance as a need to return to the autocratic presidency associated with the community college during the 1960s and still associated with it today in the minds of many.

Fisher is not alone in his call for leaders to lead. The AGB report on the presidency is entitled *Presidents Make A Difference,* a title that flies in the face of Cohen and March's thesis regarding the relative unimportance of the presidency. The report outlines ways of strengthening the college and university presidency and calls upon all segments of the campus community to become involved in the conditions of leadership (AGB, 1984). Joseph Kauffman, a member of the AGB Commission on strengthening presidential leadership and a source referred to often in this volume, while noting that presidential power has been eroded by "a decade of anti-establishment fervor with its concomitant hostility toward our social institutions" (1980, p. 109), suggests that the tide might be turning. He writes: "I believe, however, that the pendulum is swinging to a more positive view of the need for leadership and for the renewal of our social institutions (1980, p. 110).

Louis Benezet, Joseph Katz, and Frances Magnusson's *Style and Substance: Leadership and the College Presidency* (1981) deals almost exclusively with the role of the president as leader. The authors conducted interviews with presidents, senior administrators, faculty, and students at 25 colleges and universities (community colleges were not included), with the express purpose being to explore the dynamics of the college presidency. Among the conclusions reached by the authors: (1) presidents do make a difference; (2) the position requires an enormous amount of time and energy; (3) in spite of the importance of dealing with economic and political issues, most presidents aspire to be educational leaders as well (p. 9). In addition to being a good leader, the president must also be a good manager, conclude the authors. Ending their volume on an optimistic note, the authors hold out the belief that presidents, whether they wish it or not, are leaders, and that strong presidents can and will make a difference in the future role of higher education in shaping society. These are conclusions that should capture the attention of all community college presidents.

Presidents Who Are Leaders: Personal Attributes

In an attempt to identify those community college presidents viewed as leaders by their peers, those presidents who received the Career and Lifestyles Survey were asked to name the two top presidential leaders in their state, excluding themselves. Any president receiving as many as five votes from his or her peers was considered to be a leader in a given state. In addition, any president from a state with fewer than five presidents returning the survey (some states do not have as many as five community colleges) and who received as many as two votes was accepted as meeting the criterion for leadership in that particular state. The result was that 75 presidents across the nation were classified as leaders within their respective states. These 75 were then asked to complete the Leadership Survey (LS). Eighty-four percent of those surveyed satisfactorily completed the survey. Personal interviews dealing with leadership were conducted with 13 of the 75 individuals, in addition to several other individuals who are, or have been, community college leaders at the national level.

Among other things, the survey asked the leaders to rate the personal attributes, skills, and abilities required of the successful president. The rating scale used on the survey, and the one used throughout the remainder of this discussion when reference is made to a scale, was a 3-point scale ranging from 1 to 3, with a rating of 1 being of little importance and a rating of 3 being of extreme importance. Figure 9.1 shows the relative mean ratings of the personal attributes associated with being a successful community college president as ranked by those presidents identified as leaders by their peers.

As shown by the scale, those attributes receiving the highest ratings are integrity, good judgment, courage, and concern for others, characteristics one would expect to be associated with educational leaders whose role is to promote values in individuals and in society and who would be expected to fulfill Burns's concept of moral leadership.

Ranking at the bottom of the scale but still of considerable importance is charisma. It would be a mistake, however, to confuse the ranking of a personal attribute with Fisher's more complex theory of charismatic power, although Fisher contends that charisma in the person, whether natural or developed, is a prerequisite to the development and use of charismatic power. While no president interviewed actually used the word charisma to describe the presidency, the use of such terms as "high energy level," "personable," "exciting," "inspiring," and "dynamic" strongly implies that charisma is important in fulfilling the role of the presidency. Most administrators interviewed view this quality as a desirable characteristic for the community college president. One trustee claims that the most important thing she wanted in a president was for "the president to look and behave like a president," thus connoting images of the charismatic leader.

It is interesting to note that a tolerance for ambiguity is seen as less important by leading community college presidents than by Bennis, Cohen/March, and others who view the college and university president's role as, at best, ill-defined. It is likely that there is less ambiguity associated with the presidency in community colleges, most of which have a bureaucratic organizational

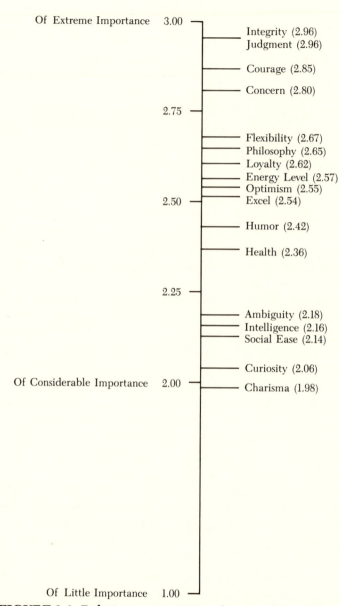

FIGURE 9.1: Relative mean ratings of personal attributes.

structure, than is the case with the more complex organizational models found in the large colleges and universities with which Bennis and Cohen/March have been primarily concerned.

Personal attributes required of the successful leader are important in shaping and achieving the broader goals of the institution. As one community college leader notes: "I have seen presidents who could not carry out their own value system, and they are therefore walking wars with themselves. As a result they are never able to achieve their full potential as a leader." As Burns writes, "At the highest stage of moral development persons are guided by near-universal ethical principles of justice such as equality of human rights and respect for individual dignity. This stage sets the opportunity for rare and creative leadership" (1978, p. 42). Certainly the community college presidents' top-rated personal skills of judgment, integrity, courage, and concern for others partially equip them to fulfill Burns's call for creative leadership. But, as all successful leaders know, there must always be a practical side to successful leadership.

One highly successful former president cautions that, although certain personal attributes are necessary for successful leadership, they will not stand alone. He proclaims that "if you leave out pragmatism as a factor of leadership, you probably aren't going to make it. The idea that you have dedication, sincerity and courage — that's probably going to get you fired if that's all you've got. You've also got to have prudence, a capacity to compromise, and what I call pragmatism — a recognition that even if you are right, you can't always have it your way. It's the best you can get and not the best that there is, because if you strive for an unobtainable level, an unobtainable goal, you strive yourself right out of business. It doesn't work that way and one has to back off and say, 'Is there any assurance that I have a pipeline to heaven and know the true answer?'; it's possible that maybe the people who want it another way are right and you're wrong. And when you back off, it may shake your courage foundation a little bit because being courageous suggests that you discover what you believe in and stay on course, never wavering until you get it. That's courage, but a fatal type of courage, particularly in the current arena."

The Community College Presidency: Skills and Abilities

Moving from personal attributes to skills and abilities, Figure 9.2
shows that the ability to produce results is the top skill associated
with the successful president. When the top-ranked skill is considered along with the top-ranked personal attributes of integrity, judgment, courage, and concern for others, one finds that
potential conflict is inherent between the moral-laden personal
attributes and the more external, results-oriented top personal
skill. Burns describes the potential frustrations associated with
conflicting values: "Perhaps the most disruptive force in compet-
itive politics is conflict between *modal values* such as fair play and
due process and *end-values* such as equality" (1978, p. 43).

Close behind the ability to produce results are the ability to
select capable people, the ability to resolve conflicts, and the
ability to communicate effectively, all of which are skills exercised best in conjunction with the top-ranked personal attributes
of integrity, judgment, courage, and concern for others. (Incidentally, the high ranking given to conflict resolution indicates
that the role of the president as mediator is considered important
by community college leaders, but, as suggested earlier, the mediation role is exercised in concert with other skills and personal
attributes).

The relative low ranking of establishing a peer network contrasts with the importance given it by other sources. For example, Bennis, drawing on the work of Henry Mintzberg, ranks the
ability to establish and maintain a peer network as one of the
eight essential leadership skills (Bennis, 1975). The compara-
tively low ranking given to peer skills by leading presidents can
be attributed to the local nature of community colleges, many of
which are in rural areas and whose presidents are essentially
isolated as far as ongoing relationships with their peers are concerned.

The lowest-ranking skill or ability for both the successful
president and for subordinates is the ability to produce scholarly
publications. On the surface, one would think that the ability to
engage in scholarship resulting in publications would be a highly
valued trait in both presidents and subordinates, especially since
a number of presidents indicated that they have published an

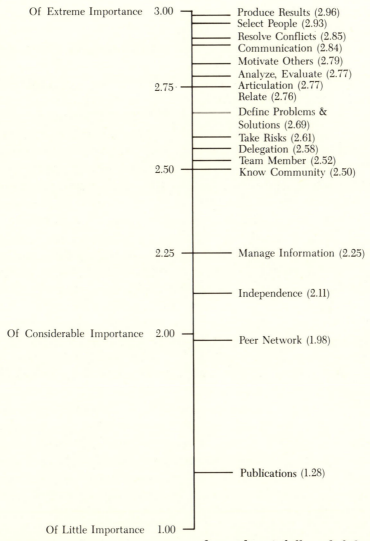

FIGURE 9.2: Relative mean ratings of presidents' skills and abilities.

article within the past five years. Why do presidents rank the ability to produce scholarly publications so low? This might be explained in part by the community college's credo of being a teaching institution, thus implying that teaching and research are at opposite ends of the continuum. Another reason might center around the number of community college presidents who have their highest degree in education, a field that normally does not emphasize research resulting in publications. There are, however, more practical reasons for the low ranking.

When asked why presidents rate the ability to produce scholarly publications so low, most leaders noted that the position required the incumbent to be an activist, thus leaving little time for scholarly research and even less time to translate research into publications. Another line of thought involves the practical aspect of the presidency, a concept that is seen by some presidents as conflicting with producing scholarly works. One presidential leader noted that presidents are judged on what they accomplish and not on what they write in journals. Governing boards, he noted, pay little or no attention to research in published form or any other.

It is not surprising that the president's old nemesis — a perceived lack of time — is given as a reason for not producing scholarly works. One president probably expressed it best: "Presidents have the feeling that everything else is more important. They feel that scholarly publications should be the work of professors on university campuses." For whatever reason, the ability to publish learned articles is not seen as an important part of the president's role by most presidents.

There were some exceptions to the notion that presidents should not engage in scholarship, however. One national leader notes, "I do not think we have enough good scholarly research going on in our field that is sponsored by us, promoted by us, and acted upon by us. All of our research seems to come from somewhere else." At least one of the top-ranked presidential leaders in the nation takes his role as a scholar seriously: "Most people tend to think of their jobs as internal to their institutions; I think of my job as steering the institution within the framework of the world, the nation, and the community. Therefore, I believe it is my job to continue to learn, to do scholarly work, and to publish the results."

Also rated among the top skills and abilities required of the successful president is the ability to select capable personnel, an ability that draws heavily on judgment, integrity, and courage. The next highest ranked skills — ability to resolve conflict and ability to relate well with others — are not in conflict with the highly graded personal attributes.

With perhaps the exception of conflicts that could occur between the top-ranked ability to produce results and certain top-ranked personal attributes (concern for others, for example), the ratings given both the personal attributes and the skills and abilities appear to be highly compatible. This might help to explain the relative satisfaction presidents have with their positions since such a combination that would seem to provide a fertile breeding ground for Burns's transforming leadership.

The rankings given to personal attributes and skills provide some basis for understanding what leading community college presidents consider important in fulfilling their role. These gradings might well serve as a yardstick for presidents who wish to engage in introspection, as far as their own values and skills are concerned. Moreover, the ratings should be extremely valuable to governing boards seeking presidents, especially if they wish to employ someone who has the characteristics and skills associated with community college leadership.

Skills and Abilities of Subordinates

Ability to select capable people was one of the top two skills the leaders identified with the successful president. What do leaders look for when they select people? Do they want clones of themselves? Or is there a different set of skills that leaders perceive to be required of deans and vice-presidents from what they require of themselves? In order to answer these questions, the leaders were asked to use the same criteria to rank the skills and abilities they consider important in subordinates as they used in evaluating themselves. Figure 9.3 illustrates the results.

As can be seen from Figures 9.2 and 9.3, there is an important difference between the mean ratings of six of the 18 skills and attributes of presidents and those of their subordinates. However, the ability to produce results is the top-ranked ability the leading presidents see for their subordinates as well as for themselves, leaving little doubt that "getting the job done" has the highest priority for the successful president.

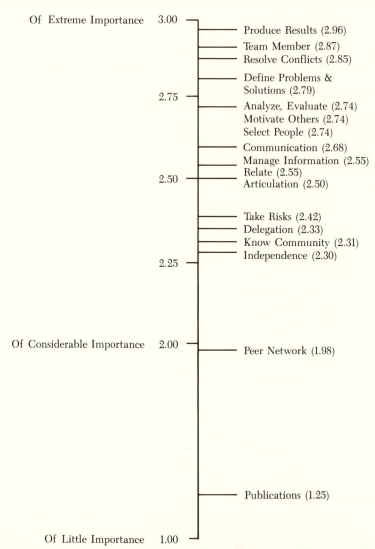

FIGURE 9.3: Relative mean ratings of subordinates' skills and abilities.

Another significant difference in the ratings is seen in the ability to work as a team member, an ability that is viewed as more important for subordinates than for presidents. The successful president thinks that being a member of the team has considerable weight but not as much for presidents as for subordinates. The implications are that, as leader, the president can and should be able and willing to break ranks with the team when required, an act that is likely to call upon the highest-ranked personal skills of integrity, judgment, and courage. The higher ranking given to the presidents' ability to select people and delegate functions versus the ranking of those abilities in subordinates implies that presidents see themselves as capable of "letting go" of responsibilities and, one would think, of authority.

Clearly, the president is viewed as the person with the primary responsibility for effectively articulating the college's mission and goals, a subject discussed in some detail in Chapter 6, although this role is also important for subordinates. Presidents appear to rely heavily upon subordinates for processing and managing information. On the other hand, it is more important for presidents than for subordinates to relate well with a broad range of people, a skill that is required with the expanding external role of the president.

A significant point is that the leading presidents consider producing scholarly publications an even lower priority for subordinates than for themselves. This ranking implies strongly that subordinates are not rewarded for publishing. While very few presidents and deans will continue to write books and articles on the community college, the majority of the publications dealing with the community college will continue to come from universities and other sources. This situation, while not necessarily undesirable, indicates that scholarly analysis resulting in publications is unlikely to be any more important for community college leadership in the future than it is at the present or than it has been in the past.

In summary, presidents tend to see essentially the same skills and abilities as being important for their subordinates as they see for themselves, although the degree to which they are viewed as being important is significant in some areas. The reader should keep in mind, however, that the scale shows most skills and abilities as being either of considerable or of extreme significance for both presidents and subordinates. In both cases, the only exceptions are in regard to establishing a network of peers and in the ability to publish, two abilities that are highly valued in many professional fields, and especially in much of the rest of academia.

Leadership and Relationships

What do those presidents identified as leaders perceive to be their relationship with the faculty? With those who report directly to the president? With trustees? With students? The following presents these perceptions.

Over 43 percent of the leaders perceive their role with the faculty as that of educational leader. This high percentage is at first surprising since only a few of the presidents and others interviewed identified academic leadership as a major function of the president. The contradiction seems to be in the definition of educational leadership, rather than between the survey and the interviews. For example, a number of those interviewed see educating the board, faculty, staff, legislature, and the general public on the mission of the community college as of extreme importance. One can conclude that the role of educational leader as perceived by most presidents and others associated with the community college is much broader than working with curriculum and instruction, the more traditional roles associated with educational leadership. For instance, by far the second largest percentage (41%) of the presidents see their second most important role vis-à-vis the faculty as articulating and advocating the college's goals and mission, clearly a function of educational leadership as far as the president's office is concerned. One 20-year veteran president expressed strong sentiments regarding his role as an educational leader: "I teach more in a day than a faculty member teaches in a week; I am constantly teaching people either how to adjust to a situation, how to understand better the philosophy of the college, how to understand the policies and procedures, how to handle a situation they are concerned about. I think 99 percent of my work is in teaching."

Only 2 percent of the leaders identified their principal role with the faculty as that of colleague. This low percentage tends to support the earlier discussion of the presidency as a clear-cut career choice and a rejection of the "first among equals" concept associated with many four-year college and university presidencies. The failure to see faculty members as colleagues also makes it difficult for the president to return to the faculty, a topic that will be discussed in the next chapter. Indeed, some of the leaders not only did not see themselves as colleagues of the faculty but saw themselves as its supervisor. Five percent of the leaders considered themselves the symbol of the college and 5 percent as the person with the primary responsibility for motivating the faculty.

None of the 62 presidents identified as leaders who responded to the survey perceived their primary role as a mentor or role model for the faculty. These statistics seem especially significant, since these 62 presidents were identified by their peers as representing the outstanding leadership within their given states, and since several of the presidents interviewed referred to a mentor as being important to their own development. The conclusion might be that there is a greater distance between the president and the faculty than one might think, especially considering the involvement of faculty in the governance process.

What is the perceived role of the president in relation to those who report directly to the president? The largest percentage (32%) of the presidents believe their principal function with those who report to them is that of motivator. Second is the responsibility for articulating the goals and mission of the college; 23 percent see this as the primary role the president plays with those who report to the president. Approximately 17 percent of the leaders view their major role with subordinates as that of colleague; 13 percent see it as supervisor. Seven percent of the leaders consider their primary job to be mentor and 3 percent, role model. This represents a significant increase from the zero percentage given these roles in regard to relationships with the faculty but is still relatively small considering that the president as leader would normally be expected to serve as the mentor and model for those persons who report directly to the president, many of whom have aspirations to become presidents themselves.

The importance given to the roles the leaders identified in their relationship with the governing board provides some interesting insights. In regard to the board of trustees, 53 percent of the leaders see their principal role as one of educational leader who provides direction to the board. This perceived relationship with the board would explain, in part, the high percentage of leaders who see their primary role as that of educational leader. It would also support the earlier conclusion that educational leadership extends well beyond curriculum and instruction.

Twenty-three percent of the leaders perceive themselves as the chief executive officer who carries out the policies of the board; 17 percent see their principal function as consulting with the board when appropriate. Thus, 40 percent describe their relationship with the board in much the same way as chief executives in business or industry view the executive–board relationship. This is not surprising in light of the definition of presidents provided earlier.

The perceptions of board–president relationships varied greatly, a situation one would expect considering the various types of boards, that is, advisory, local, state-level, and so forth. No attempt was made to distinguish between the responses of those presidents reporting to one type of board versus another type.

In regard to students, 55 percent of the presidential leaders perceive their principal role as that of being responsible for articulating the college's mission and standards; 20 percent see the role as an interested, concerned adult; and 13 percent as a symbol of authority. Only 3 percent of the presidents saw the principal role with students as supplying a role model, a very small percentage since, historically, college and university presidents have been viewed as role models for students and in some instances for society in general. Certainly the large number of part-time, older adult students who attend the community college would explain in part the low ranking given the student role model function of the community college president.

Are Leaders Different?

An attempt was made to answer the question, "Are those presidents who were identified as leaders by their peers different from other presidents?" In order to gather information relating to this question, certain demographic variables used on the Career and Lifestyles Survey (CLS) were included on the Leadership Survey (LS). Among the variables were the state in which the president was currently employed, the college's full-time equivalent enrollment, number of years in current position, marital status, and age. These variables made it possible to identify those leaders who completed the Leadership Survey and who had previously completed the CLS. Of the 63 leaders completing the Leadership Survey, 49 were "matched" as having completed the CLS. Based on the matches *and keeping in mind that the 49 leaders were included in the results of the CLS*, the following are some of the ways in which leaders differed from their colleagues.

Those presidents identified as leaders serve as presidents of larger institutions than do those not so identified. Indeed, the median size of the college headed by a leader is 4,501, whereas the median size of the college for all presidents is 2,030. What does it mean that the leader comes from a college over twice the size of the school of a president not identified as a leader? It would seem quite natural that the "pecking order" of size would be important in identifying leaders within a state, since, in public higher education, as with much of the rest of American society, bigger is often seen as better.

There are other factors relating to size, however. In one state, the college whose president was identified as a leader by his peers enrolls almost one-third of all of the community college students in the state; in another state, the perceived leader's college enrolls 50 percent of all community college students in the state. Since budgets follow enrollments, these colleges' budgets would approach almost one-third and one-half, respectively, of the total for all of the community colleges in their states. It is also easier to catch the national eye if one is located at a large institution; thus the opportunity for the president to be in the national spotlight is greater than for the president of a smaller institution, a position that tends to impress colleagues and the public alike.

A comment about state leadership versus national leadership is in order. In *every* instance except one, anyone identified as an outstanding national leader in this study had previously been named as a state leader by his or her peers, thus giving additional credibility to the peer ranking of state leaders. The one exception is a president who occupied a highly visible national position at the time of the Leadership Survey and who had served as president of the current institution for slightly over a year.

Presidents identified as leaders have been in their current positions for a median of 9.4 years, versus a median of 5.3 for all presidents. The median number of years leaders have been in their current position indicates that, if there is a point of diminishing returns for providing effective leadership, it is certainly longer than the five-to-seven years that is a popular part of higher education's mythology.

Leaders are more likely to have held more than one presidency than are those not identified as leaders. Although 56 percent of those persons identified as leaders were in their first presidency, 75 percent of the total number of presidents responding to the CLS were in their first presidency. Thirty-three percent of those identified as leaders were in their second presidency, versus 19 percent of those answering the CLS. Eleven percent of the perceived leaders have held three or more presidencies, whereas 5 percent of the other presidents have held three or more. The assumption is that a number of leaders started their presidential career at a smaller institution and moved to a larger one. On the other hand, some presidents identified as leaders "started at the top," as far as size is concerned. (For example, one such president started his presidential career at an institution that enrolls approximately 50,000 students.) Several of the presidents identified as state leaders have simply "grown up" with their colleges and their presidencies, either as founding president, as the president who took over soon after an institution first enrolled any large number of students, or as an executive vice president who was groomed for the presidency.

In regard to the highest degree held, those identified as leaders are more likely to have a degree in education, especially higher education, than are those presidents not so identified. Sixty-three percent of those perceived as leaders have degrees in higher education and 32 percent have degrees in other areas of education; 46 percent of the presidents responding to the CLS have degrees in higher education and 30 percent have degrees in other areas of education. Only 5 percent of the leaders have degrees other than in education, whereas almost 25 percent of those not so identified have degrees in other fields.

Those designated as leaders are more likely to have published something within the last five years than are those who were not so classified. For example, 62 percent of the leaders have published something within the last five whereas 35 percent of those not identified as leaders have published something within the same time period. Since leaders consider the ability to produce scholarly publications of little importance in relation to the other skills and abilities they ranked, there appears to be a contradiction between their actual publishing and their gradings. The next chapter discusses publications by presidents in more detail and perhaps sheds some light on the seeming incongruences inherent in their views on the subject.

While perceived leaders are more likely to have held multiple presidencies than their colleagues, the analysis between leaders and those not so identified reveals that leaders were no more likely to move within the next five years than were other presidents. It is likely that perceived leaders are more satisfied with the role they are currently playing than are other presidents and thus see no reason to move. As one long-time leader explains: "I think we have to be very careful about criticizing someone who doesn't want to be something else or who doesn't want to be some other place. Maybe you worked hard and got to be exactly what you want to be, do what you want to do. I know that when I got to ———, I said after three years that I had the best job in the world. It fits. It is where I want to do it, what I want to do, under the circumstances I want to do it. There wasn't any job in the world I would trade for that. I didn't regard that as a lack of ambition. I regarded it as a very fortunate professional and personal break to find a situation that combined all of these things."

Those identified as leaders are not any older than other presidents, indicating that leaders may have accomplished more professionally in less time than their colleagues. Other variables such as marital status, location of the high school from which they graduated, position held before becoming a president, service organizations, lifestyles, and other variables showed no major differences between perceived leaders and other community college presidents.

State Leadership: Some Observations

Those identified as leaders within their respective states were asked why they thought they were so designated. Although the answers varied, the interviews confirmed that size is important for establishing a leadership base; as one pointed out, when an institution enrolls 50 percent of all community college students in the state, it is almost impossible to ignore the role the president of that community college plays in the state. The most important single ingredient identified by those interviewed, however, was the leadership the president had given *within* the state. Again, size may be a key factor in influencing who is considered a leader within a state. The president of the smaller colleges quite naturally take certain cues from the president of the larger institution. Also, legislators and the public in general are likely to accord more prestige to the president of the bigger school, especially if it is considerably larger than the other community colleges within the state.

Presidents show a great deal of respect for colleagues who are willing to assume state positions of leadership regardless of the size of their institution, especially in areas that affect all community colleges in the state, such as legislative lobbying. The positions may consist of chairing the state organization of presidents, chairing the legislative action committee of presidents or other state-level committees, or in some other way serving in a capacity that distinguishes them from their colleagues. One president in a state with three different types of public two-year institutions feels that the reason he is viewed as a leader within his state is because of the key role he played in bringing all the institutions together in order that they could speak with "one voice" to the legislature and to the public. Another president believes he was chosen because he was chair of the state association of presidents; chair of the legislative committee, which includes trustees as well as presidents; and was soon to assume the chairmanship of the state higher education association made up of all college and university presidents in the state.

Second to assuming leadership at the state level was the reputation of the college within the state and, in some cases, nationally. The successful president must assure that his or her "own house is in order" before assuming leadership positions at the state and national levels, so conclude a number of leaders. Put another way, *successful leadership begins at home.*

Several presidents note that they have held positions of leadership at the national level, thus enhancing their image as a leader. A number of them publish articles regularly and some have contributed to books. In some cases, those identified as leaders have become household words, at least within community colleges. Almost none of the leaders showed any surprise at being rated a leader by their peers, which implies that they are conscious of their relationship with their colleagues and that they are aware of their own leadership efforts.

National Leaders

Just as the CLS asked all presidents surveyed to name the two individuals, other than themselves, they considered leaders within their state, the Leadership Survey asked the resulting 75 to name the two individuals, excluding themselves, whom they consider to be the outstanding community college presidents in the nation. While a relatively large number of presidents showed up on the list of national leaders, only 10 presidents were named by three or more of the 63 presidents returning the survey. Only five of the 10 received five or more votes. It is interesting to note that, of the 10 presidents receiving three or more votes, only three are located outside the Sunbelt and all three of these are from large community college districts in the Midwest. Of those receiving five or more votes, only one was from a state outside of the Sunbelt. The two presidents receiving the largest number of votes serve as presidents of colleges located deep within this region. While any extensive analysis of why the Sunbelt presidents are held in such high esteem nationally is well beyond the scope of this study, it is nevertheless worth noting that most Sunbelt states have gained population and new industries, while much of the rest of the nation has been losing both. Maybe the Sunbelt presidents are just fortunate victims of their environment. Or perhaps being in the region relieves them of certain pressures faced by their colleagues in other parts of the nation, thereby leaving more time for leadership activities.

It is also worth noting that the two presidents receiving the largest number of votes are extremely active in national organizations and both contribute to the literature on the community college regularly. More important, perhaps, is that both of their institutions are recognized nationally for the work they have done and are doing with students, both in the instructional and student services areas. It is significant that both presidents have been active in charting the course of their college in these areas.

Leaders on Leadership

What do those presidents identified as leaders by their peers have to say on the subject of leadership? Are leadership skills and attributes universal, in the sense that there are certain characteristics common to the successful leader, regardless of the time and circumstance? What leadership skills are required by the successful community college president today that were not required in the past? And what new ones will be required in the future? Are the same leadership skills required in a multicampus operation as on a single campus?

In general, most of the individuals interviewed believe that certain personal characteristics know no boundaries as far as time and situations are concerned. Sound judgment has always been a characteristic of the effective leader and one assumes always will be. The same is true of the ability to plan for the future, to anticipate problems, and to motivate people. But even time-honored personal skills may take on new dimensions as time and circumstances change. For example, most of the people interviewed believe that the ability to work well with people, while always important for leaders, is more vital today than in the past. Several of the presidents interviewed referred to the "Theory Z" philosophy of management and to *In Search of Excellence* by Peters and Waterman (1982), both of which place major emphasis on the individual's role in successful institutional management. As one presidential leader notes, in the past the emphasis was on techniques such as management by objectives, program budgeting, efficiency, and accountability; while these are still important, there is a great need today to consider them in the context of what they mean to the individual's relationship to the institution. "People skills," as this leader calls them, are required in dealing with pressure groups who want to move the college in some direction other than what the president and board wish; yet the support of special interest groups and others who want "a piece of the action" is essential to the successful president.

Most of the leaders interviewed agree that the development of new management and organizational skills is critical today. One quote from a presidential leader tends to summarize the thinking of most of those interviewed: "I think you could get by in the past by just being a good model, a good intuitive leader, a seat-of-the-pants leader. I think it is more difficult to get by in today's world. In fact, I have a hobby of asking what happened when a president gets knocked off. In my mind, I see a lot of leaders getting knocked off who do not have those organizational skills required today; they make costly blunders that would be avoidable if they had the necessary skills."

Management of change is viewed as essential to today's successful president, according to every president interviewed. The presidential leaders were talking about the rapidity of change in society, for they acknowledged that the management of change has always been an essential part of the president's role. Works by Toffler and Naisbitt were referred to often as sources documenting the accelerated pace of change. At the heart of the change process is the "information age." Today's successful presidents must understand what computers can and *cannot* do; they must envision the role of technologies in the learning process; they must be able to interact with change in a manner that promotes the interest of the institution without sacrificing the welfare of the individual, without compromising institutional integrity, and without aborting the college's mission. As one president comments: "In the future, the leader really has to have a strong understanding, not so much of how technology works, but of what it can do and where we go from here." Another expresses his views on leading in today's society: "I think the leader of the future is going to be someone who stands between his field of research and the institution and one who becomes an active translator of research into process. Change is coming much more rapidly; you have to translate research into action; otherwise you lose your effectiveness as a leader."

The external role of the successful president will continue to expand, according to every leader interviewed. One states: "I see leadership in development, in working with business and industry, in fund raising, in working with politicians, and in other external areas growing rapidly. We have never had to deal with these areas to any large degree until recently." Dominant in external relations for the leader of the future will be working effectively with the legislature and the executive branches of government at the state level.

A number of presidents believe that the charismatic leadership required to build colleges may not be what is needed to maintain them today. One president sees the role transforming: "I think that, as I look back at when we were in a building stage, we could isolate ourselves because we had the resources in terms of money and students. We were very provincial then; we had a lot of turf we were protecting. Now I think the skills are very different. We need to be more cooperative and involve ourselves more with other organizations, including other educational institutions, as well as government, business and industry, and other external agencies. I find it to be quite a different role than when I started 12 years ago." Another leader notes that it was relatively easy to lead or at least to give the appearance of leading when community colleges were riding on the crest of growth; he observes that few people questioned the effectiveness of the leader when enrollments and faculty were doubling in size each year, and when new buildings were springing up everywhere. However, he notes that today the successful leader must be more flexible, more creative, and more willing to involve others in making decisions. The chancellor of a large Midwestern community college district suggests that the successful leader of today and of the future must come to grips with collective negotiations: "The effective leader must show a willingness to quit fighting collective bargaining where it has occurred. This acceptance means recognizing that there is a counter leadership force that must be accommodated and hopefully turned in the direction of mutual concern for the advancement of the institution in terms of what it can do for its students."

Leadership has altered in other ways. The aura that often surrounded the founding president has all but vanished in most cases; consequently, presidents today must use new approaches to establishing their legitimacy, including involving others in decision making. Founding presidents by and large had all of Fisher's (1984) forms of power — coercive, reward, legitimate, expert, and even charismatic up to a point — handed to them on a silver platter. Today, however, each form of power listed by

Fisher has to be earned in one way or another, including legitimate power which is shared with the board, faculty, legislators, and practically anyone else who can establish a power base. As one national leader observes: "There was a time when as president of the institution you automatically had the respect and loyalty of almost everyone within the institution. I don't think that happens anymore; there are many claims on faculty loyalty today, unions for example. Today, you find that faculty don't automatically accept what the president says. You are challenged; you must earn respect; it does not come automatically with the position." Another president remarks: "We must compromise today, and compromise does not mean weakness. To the contrary, the ability to compromise often means a great deal of strength. The authoritarian approach to management of the past does not work today; you may win the battle but lose the war." Or, as Coca-Cola Chairman of the Board Roberto Goizueta believes: "Often the quality of one's compromises is much more important than the correctness of one's position" (Griessman, 1985, p. 2B).

Almost without exception, leaders believe that the successful president must have a greater understanding of financial affairs today than was the case in the past. One president observes that financial decisions are in truth educational decisions; where one places the funds determines which educational goals will be emphasized. The successful leader can delegate the placing of the funds but must know where they are placed. To a lesser degree, the presidents feel that knowledge of legal matters is more important now than it was in the past. Probably the most important thing a leader can know about legal matters is when to consult an attorney, maintains one president.

Are different leadership skills required to lead a multicampus or multicollege operation than a single campus operation? Yes and no. Again, the personal characteristics required of the successful leader are essential to effective leadership, regardless of the organizational structure of the campus. There are differences, however. Generally, the leaders concede that while the same skills are required, they may be applied differently. For example, it was conceded by most of those interviewed that the multicampus or multicollege district requires more coordination but contains fewer potential people problems. One president speaks for many: "The successful president in a multicampus college must give the total institution direction while giving the individual campuses the freedom to do things; you must also keep the balance among campuses; you must decide when you can deal directly with the faculty without interfering or making it difficult for the campus head." Another head of a multicollege district, who formerly served as president of a single-campus college, agrees that the skills required in his situation are different in degree and not in kind. For example, all of the presidents interviewed experience some degree of the "lonely-at-the-top syndrome" and agreed that certain skills are required for coping with the isolation of the office. The isolation that often occurs with the head of a multicampus district may be more intense than on a single campus, however. One president describes a danger inherent in multicampus operations: "One of the things that concerns me is the easy way a person in the district administration can lose sight of the human aspects of the operation. This happens because you are dealing so much with legislative activities, with budgets, and with relatively impersonal things that you can have a problem, which has been the case with me. As a campus president, you were at least face-to-face with faculty and students." All of those interviewed agreed that the president of a multicampus or multicollege district must be willing to "let go," that is, to delegate more than might be the case with a single-campus presidency.

From the interviews, it is clear that presidential leaders do not see the role of the president as "business as usual," regardless of the organizational structure of the institution. While most personal attributes associated with leaders are as relevant today as in the past, new skills are required today that were not required before; even newer skills will be required in the future, many dealing with the impact of high technology on the educational and management processes and new concepts of the role individuals play in the governance process of the institutions. Most of the presidents agree that "keeping up" means more than simply keeping up with what is happening in education. Keeping up for the successful president means keeping abreast of shifts in the larger society and adopting and adapting those changes in ways that are most beneficial to their colleges and communities. A highly respected presidential leader observes: "The leader needs to continue to study world economics, the development of world society and American society and begin to look forward and see what all of this has to say about what the institution should be and where it fits, plus the successful president must keep up with what is happening in education." One president laments: "I think that some of my presidential colleagues have not realized that changes have occurred and have kept on the same way." One can hope that these presidents are in the minority and that most community college presidents are interacting with change in a positive way.

Perceptions of Leadership

Do presidential leaders perceive themselves as others perceive them? Can you tell a leader when you see one? If so, how?

Most presidential leaders interviewed believe that they are perceived to have more power than they actually have. At the same time, the general consensus is that the faculty do not— cannot—know the full extent of the pressures the president faces. One prominent president observes: "I think others look at me as always being up front pulling the team along. I don't think that is the case at all. I think the most effective leader is the one who gets the most satisfaction out of the successes of others. I think that is strong leadership." Another perception from a president in a large southeastern institution: "We always judge others by their actions and we judge ourselves based on our motivations and intentions. I know what my motivations and intentions are and I think they are the best, but I have to recognize constantly that others don't know that and the only thing they can judge me on is what I do and say. I think it is important for every leader to understand that people are not judging us by what we are thinking or by what our motivations might be. Trying to narrow the gap between what the leader perceives and what others perceive is one of the big roles of the leader, it seems to me." Another president notes that "there are probably as many views of the presidency as there are constituents out there." Most leaders agree that those with whom they work most closely tend to see them more nearly as they are. Some leaders put forth a great deal of effort to be what they are perceived to be. On the other hand, if one buys into Fisher's concept of charismatic power, the images associated with the presidency should serve the effective leader well.

The reader should keep in mind that the foregoing perceptions of leadership only describe certain aspects of the presidency, albeit very important ones. All presidents must continually work with the board effectively and efficiently, must effectively articulate the mission, must plan for the future, must inspire others, must see that the governance process is carried out fairly and effectively, must maintain positive internal and external relationships, and must perform the many tasks associated with the day-to-day operation of the college. Leaders, on the other hand, must do all of these things well and must do more. Perhaps that is why such a small number of presidents are rated as national leaders.

A Postscript on Leadership

Missing from the interviews with the leaders was any reference to articulating the community college mission effectively and consistently, an issue discussed in some detail in Chapter 5. One would think that the high ranking given to the desirability of a strong philosophical commitment to the community college and to the desire to produce results, communicate effectively, and articulate what the college is about, would cause leaders to give more attention to interpreting the community college mission, especially when one considers the consequences of failing to do so. Those presidents identified as leaders do not seem to be any more sensitive to their shortcomings in articulating the mission than the other presidents interviewed.

CHAPTER 10

———

Tenure, Professionalism, and Life After the Presidency

The average age of today's community college president is 50.7 years (CLS). It is interesting to note that the average age today is almost identical to that in 1964, when it was 50.3 years; a 1970 study pegged the average at 48.8 (Wing, 1972, p. 2). Over half (51.6%) of the 591 presidents responding to the survey are 50 years of age or younger. The great majority (45.5%) of these are in the 41-to-50 age group (CLS). Assuming that the presidents work until age 65, over 50 percent of today's presidents could conceivably occupy their position for at least another 15 years, and many considerably longer. This picture might be a bit discouraging for the many young deans and vice presidents who have their eye on the office. On the other hand, 37.4 percent of the current presidents are between the ages of 51 and 60 and 11 percent are over the age of 60, thus cutting the waiting time considerably for those who would be president.

The above statistics aside, those who are interested in becoming a community college president can take heart. The average number of years today's presidents have been in their current position is 7.2, a figure that is somewhat misleading because some presidents have been in their current position for long periods of time. The 7.2 compares with a mean of 4.2 years in 1970 and 1971 and is exactly the same as the 7.2 average reported in 1964 (Wing, 1972, p. 3). When the current average number is compared with the 1964 and 1970–71 averages, a conclusion might be that the average number of years in office for presidents had leveled off prior to the period of rapid community college growth (opening one college a week required a new president a week), declined during the years of rapid growth, but has now reached the plateau that was reached prior to the boom years. If this observation is correct, it is conceivable that the average number of years in office will continue to increase, assuming the community college scene remains stable.

The average time in office seems to be the figure that has dominated the literature on the college presidency. However, for the purposes of this study, the more significant figure is the median, for over 50 percent of today's presidents have been in their current position for five years or less; another 21.5 percent have been at their present job for 10 years or less. Only 11.7 percent of today's presidents have occupied their current post for longer than 15 years (CLS). As with most statistics, these can be read more than one way: either many of the vacancies have been filled by relatively new presidents who will be around for a rather long time, or community college presidencies have a high turnover rate, and therefore the young dean or vice president who wants to be a president need not worry; there will be plenty of room at the top. Certainly the median number of years in office, in conjunction with the almost 300 current presidents who responded to the survey who are over 51 (65 are over 60 years old), leaves plenty of room for upward mobility if one aspires to the presidency.

During the 1960s and early 1970s, the image often prevailed that the favorite game of community college presidents was "musical chairs." Do presidents, once they enter the "magic circle," bounce from presidency to presidency as seems to be the case? In the period 1970–71, slightly over 15 percent of the presidents came to their current position from another presidency (Wing, 1972, p. 4). Today, almost 25 percent (149 of the presidents responding) have held more than one presidency; of those who have held more than one presidency, 6 percent have held more than two, and seven of these have held four presidencies (CLS). As one trustee noted in an earlier chapter, those presidents with presidential experience "have a leg up" in the search process when vacancies occur. This implies that those individuals who are willing to accept a less-than-desirable presidency may be correct in assuming that the important thing is to become a member of the club and then seek a more desirable position.

Risks of the Presidency

Frustrations, pressures, burnout, long hours, high turnover rates: are these the things of which presidencies are made? If these considerations were all there were to the position, one could readily conclude that today's community college presidency is indeed a high risk job. In an attempt to determine how presidents view the dangers involved in the position, those identified as leaders by their peers were asked if they considered the presidency to be one of high risk. Although risk taking and being in a potentially hazardous position are not the same, those particular presidents were queried, rather than the others, because one of the characteristics often associated with leadership is risk taking; this implies that leaders would not shy away from such posts.

The 63 presidents responding to the leadership survey represent an 83 percent return rate of those surveyed. Of the 63, 19, or 30 percent, view the presidency as a high-risk position. The great majority, 68 percent, see it as having moderate risks; only one president feels that it is a low-risk job (LS). What image do the presidents project regarding the perils associated with the presidency? Do they tend to dramatize the dangers involved with the position? Or do they "tell it like it is?"

In an attempt to answer the above questions, the spouses of leaders were asked how they rated the risks involved with the presidency. Forty-eight spouses of leaders were surveyed; 38, or 79 percent, of the spouses returned surveys. In addition to the survey of the spouses of perceived leaders, a systematic sampling of the spouses of presidents not so identified was taken. Of the 107 surveyed, 51 percent returned the survey. Forty-two percent of the leaders' spouses view the presidency as a high-risk position; 58 percent as one of moderate risks. Of the spouses of the presidents not identified as leaders, an identical 42 percent see the post as highly risky and 55 percent as one of moderate peril; 3 percent of the latter group of spouses consider it low-risk (SS). Certainly the percentages are close enough to indicate that the presidents do not tend to overemphasize the risks involved with the position, at least not as far as their spouses are concerned.

Presidential Workload

Even the term "presidential workload" has a strange sound in academia, for the ears are more accustomed to hearing about faculty workloads. The assumption is that the president's workload is what is required to get the job done, probably a correct assumption in most cases. Nevertheless, in order for those who are not presidents to have a concept of presidential workload, it is desirable to determine if the workload is seen as heavy, moderate, or light.

Over 56 percent of the presidents (547) responding to the survey reported that they work over 50 hours a week. Almost 38 percent indicated that they work from 41 to 50 hours a week; only 6 percent stated that they work fewer than 40 hours a week (CLS). Thus, the majority of the presidents exceed America's standard of the 40-hour workweek. But what does that mean?

Leaders were asked if they considered their workload to be heavy, average, or light. Two-thirds of those responding thought their workload was heavy; 32 percent felt it to be average; and no one called it light (LS). Since that most presidents are married and a common complaint is that they never have enough time with their families, how does the spouse view the workload?

Ninety-two percent of the spouses of those presidents identified as leaders saw the workload as heavy; 8 percent as average (SS). The spouses of leaders, then, see the president as carrying a heavier workload than do the leaders themselves. The reaction of the spouses would seem to be natural; the tendency of the spouse would be to measure workload in time alone, whereas, based on my own experiences and observations, presidents tend to rate workload on activities, many of which are very exciting, rather than on time alone. The old cliche "Time flies when you are having fun" might well help to explain the different views of the spouse and the president. (For example, if the president is staying at a first-class hotel in San Francisco for five days and the spouse is back home in Big Stone Gap, Virginia, the perspective on workload may differ, with the spouse tending to see it as heavier than does the president.)

Presidents earn an average of 21 days' leave annually. However, they only take an average of 13 days of leave each year. Over 90 percent of the presidents take fewer than 20 days of leave each year and 44 percent fewer than ten days. Approximately 72 percent of the presidents take family vacations each year lasting over four days; however, 40 percent of them take work with them (CLS). The "work-while-on-vacation" percentage might well be misleading, for many presidents sandwich vacations between professional meetings, or take their vacation before or after a professional meeting; thus the vacation becomes a "working vacation," not only for tax purposes, but in reality. Apparently, then, either presidents like the heavy workload associated with their position or else they feel that it requires more hours than they can give and still take the annual leave (vacation) time they are allocated.

Professional Memberships and Activities

Professional associations tell something about a person's professional outlook. Community college presidents were asked to list the professional organizations to which they belong. While some presidents belong to more than one professional organization, the results provide some indication of where presidents place their professional loyalties. Three things should be kept in mind: (1) professional associations such as the AACJC, the Association of Community College Trustees, and the American Council on

Education are largely made up of institutional memberships and therefore presidents would not hold membership as individuals in these organizations; (2) although individual memberships are not held in the above organizations, they nevertheless are the ones with which most community college presidents identify professionally, especially the AACJC; (3) it is the practice in many states (Virginia, for example) for presidents to pay their own membership dues to their professional associations; thus membership indicates a commitment that might not be present if the college were paying the dues. Also worth noting is that 181 of the 591 presidents responding to the survey chose not to answer the question on professional memberships. This question received by far the largest number of "no responses" of any one asked; indeed, all of the 591 presidents responded to most questions. However, the "no response" does not necessarily mean that those presidents who did not answer the question are not professionally active; someone could be very active professionally with the AACJC and not belong to any of the professional organizations that require individual membership.

More presidents belong to the Phi Delta Kappa (PDK) than to any other professional organization: 62 percent (254 of the presidents answering the question); the next largest percentage belong to the American Association for Higher Education (AAHE), at 53.2 percent (218 presidents); 24.6 percent are members of the National Association of College and University Business Officers (NACUBO), although this percentage might be misleading since NACUBO offers individual memberships through one institutional membership which is likely paid for by the college. After that, the percentage of membership drops rather substantially, with 6.1 percent belonging to the National Association of Student Personnel Administrators (NASPA); 4.9 percent to the Association for the Study of Higher Education (ASHE); 3.7 percent to the American College Personnel Association; and 2.9 percent to the American Educational Research Association (AERA) (CLS).

What does membership in professional organizations say about presidents? First, the Phi Delta Kappa is an organization made up of educators from all levels of education. According to the executive director of the PDK, approximately 80 percent of its membership comes from public schools. Assuming that community college presidents are active in the PDK, they retain close ties with public school teachers and administrators. On the other hand, the AAHE is devoted exclusively to higher education and is largely responsible for the publication of the *Journal of Higher Education,* one of education's most distinguished journals. The small percentage of presidents who belong to ASHE, "a professional association devoted to the study of higher education," and to AERA, which is "concerned with the improvement of the educational process through the encouragement of scholarly inquiry," indicates that most presidents have little interest in pursuing the study of higher education as participating scholars. Perhaps the most telling thing about the presidency is the small number of presidents who belong to the organizations dealing with student services; less than 10 percent belong to NASPA and ACPA combined, enforcing the belief set forth earlier that presidents are not as close to student services as they are to academics. This point has been made several times in this volume in reference to the president's professional relationship with the academic dean.

Publications and Research

Are research and publications a part of the president's life? If presidents do research, do they publish the results? What is the most common form of publication? These questions open up a subject that is rarely given much thought, even by the majority of the presidents.

Thirty-nine percent of the presidents indicated that they have conducted research within the last four years. On the other hand, 12 percent said that they have *never* conducted research. Another 30 percent have not conducted research within the last nine years (CLS). What do these figures tell us about the presidency? The most obvious point is that the majority of the presidents do not actively engage in research. On the other hand, it is noteworthy that almost 40 percent see engaging in research as important. Whether the president engages in research is probably less significant than whether research is being done by someone on campus regarding the role of the community college. Indeed, one highly respected president identified one of the major failures of the community college as its failure to do research; he places the failure squarely on the shoulder of the president: "The community college president must correct a grave weakness which has beset two-year colleges from their beginning. Placing great emphasis on the student, these colleges have stressed the teaching function and have proudly and enthusiastically denounced over-commitment to research. As a result, institutional research has been tragically neglected. It must be an integral part of the community college of the future" (Rushing, 1976, pp. 12–13). Unfortunately, the situation has changed little since those words were written in 1976, in spite of the fact that almost 40 percent of the presidents state that they have engaged in research during the past four years.

Writing for Publication

Do presidents engage in writing that results in publications? Thirty-six percent state that they have published something within the last four years; almost 22 percent have never published anything. The most common form of publication is the article; 72.7 percent of those who have ever published anything did so in this format. Thirty-one presidents (6.7% of those responding) state that they have published a book and another 36 (7.7% of those responding) state that they have published a chapter in a book. It is interesting to note that 126 presidents (over 21%) did not respond to this question, the second largest no-response category to any question asked on the survey (CLS).

Some cautions are in order when evaluating presidential publications. First, of those presidents who have published something, several have published through more than one outlet. For example, those who have published a book have also published articles and chapters in books. Second, one cannot assume that publications by presidents are founded in research. To the contrary, many articles published by presidents are "how-to" articles based on experience. While articles written from experiences are valuable to the profession, they are not the same as the researched articles that one normally associates with scholarly publications in the academic disciplines. The same applies to articles published in newspapers. This is not to downgrade newspaper articles as being unimportant, for James Fisher may well be correct when he claims that, "for the president, a feature article in the newspaper is infinitely better than a scholarly piece in a professional journal" (Fisher, 1984, p. 154). The point is that in most academic circles newspaper articles are not included among one's publications.

Based on the rather limited information gathered on the subject, it is difficult, if not impossible, to evaluate the president's role in regard to publishing. One might conclude, based on the number of presidents who have published articles, that presidents are fairly active in publishing. The truth is that very few presidents write for publication on a regular basis, or, if they do write for publication, the manuscripts are not being published, for only a handful of community college presidents contribute to professional journals on anything approaching a regular basis. Whether or not presidents should contribute to scholarly publications is another debate for another time. For now, suffice it to say that presidents have not ruled out research and publications as one aspect of the presidency, although the role appears to be of minor importance at this time. This fact was clearly demonstrated through the rankings presidential leaders gave to the ability to produce scholarly publications for both themselves and for those who report directly to them.

Life After the Presidency

Community college presidents, as is the case with essentially all top positions in an organization, cannot always decide when to leave their position. Presidents are evaluated by their boards either formally or informally, some on an annual basis. Board membership changes and new trustees can present new problems for the president. Institutions change and, if the presidents do not or cannot adjust, they may find themselves out of touch with the faculty, trustees, and other members of the college community. When a president loses touch, trouble is likely to follow.

The great majority of community college presidents survive, however. Several questions are important for those presidents who do survive, perhaps the most important one being, "Is there life after the presidency?" However, other questions are also significant: Is the community college presidency a permanent career? Or is it a temporary one, as is the case with the four-year presidency, according to Kauffman (1980)? What image do community college presidents have of themselves other than as presidents? How do the spouses view the president's role in relationship to their own role?

It might be interesting to answer the last question first, thus providing a different perspective from what one normally gets of the presidency. While interviewing presidents, a large percentage mentioned their relationship with business and industry. The relationships were social (country club), recreational (golf, tennis), civic (Rotary, Chamber of Commerce), and professional (training, retraining of workers). Occasionally during portions of the interviews, I had the feeling of interviewing civic-minded business leaders rather than educational leaders. In an attempt to see if others saw the strong affinity between the community college presidency and the business world, I once again decided to "go in the back door" to try to find an answer.

The back door was to ask the spouses of presidents how they perceive their own role in relationship to a number of other professions. The specific question asked was, "Which of the following most closely resembles your role as the spouse of a community college president?" The choices were: spouse of a minister; spouse of a four-year college president; spouse of a university president; spouse of a successful business person; spouse of a public school superintendent; and an "other" category.

Slightly over 50 percent of the spouses surveyed feel that their role most closely resembles that of the spouse of a successful business person. In this regard, it might be worth recalling that almost 65 percent of the current presidents belong to the Rotary Club—the businessman's service club. The next highest category was the spouse of a public school superintendent and spouse of a four-year college president, with 21 percent and 20 percent, respectively. Nine percent listed their role as most closely resembling that of the spouse of a university president; 3 percent minister's spouse; and 10 percent listed various other occupations, including two who saw themselves as partners of the president, a popular image among the spouses of university presidents. Only one spouse listed the spouse of a politician as the one most closely resembling her role. Some spouses listed more than one category; thus the percentage of responses totals more than 100 percent. Nevertheless, the image the spouse associates with her role (two male spouses responded) is revealing.

Presidents too seem to have an image of themselves as business leaders. In an attempt to determine how the presidents viewed their role in relationship to other professions they might want to follow, they were asked to speculate about what they would like to do if they were not presidents. Two clear categories emerged: the presidents would either stay in education or work in business and industry. Most who would stay in education would either want to teach at a university or work in an educational organization at the state level. Those who would go into business saw themselves as executives with a corporation, often dealing with investments or marketing. The one president interviewed who left the presidency because he had "had enough" bought a small business which he now operates. I should add that some presidents simply could not see themselves as anything other than a community college president.

Those presidents interviewed were realistic about where their careers were taking them in educational administration: no one interviewed speculated about being a university president (four presidents who responded to the CLS and who indicated they were very likely to move in the next five years saw their move to a four-year college presidency), although two of those interviewed had rejected offers to be the president of a four-year private college; another president, who has published a number of articles on the community college and who has regularly taught graduate courses at the university in question, turned down an offer to become the chair of a department of higher education at an Ivy League university. The three examples, however, seem to be exceptions and should not be taken to mean that most community college presidents have a large number of options from which to choose.

Moving from the fantasy world of "doing anything you want

to do" to the more realistic question of "Is there life after the presidency?" provided some interesting insights into how presidents perceive their roles. Several of the presidents see the office as a clear career choice and as a permanent position. Most who view it as permanent note that it is so almost by definition; it is difficult to move from the presidency to another equally rewarding position. Moreover, the demands of the position leave little time to prepare for another job, including university teaching which requires a record of research and publication today, even if one has the practical experience associated with the presidency.

One thing is clear in regard to life after the presidency: in contrast to the situation at some major universities, there is no life to be had within the community college where the person has served as president. No one saw opportunities for ex-presidents on their own campus. As one president declared, "You just cannot assume a second- or third-level administrative position at your own college." One dean shared an example of where the president was "eased out" and was given a teaching position within the institution. Was the former president content to teach? Not according to the dean. The former president became very active with the union and very critical of the settlements the faculty negotiation team made with the administration. Where then, if anywhere, can former presidents turn after they leave the presidency?

Several presidents felt that university teaching was a possibility after leaving office. On the other hand, one president felt that dreaming of going back to the classroom — any classroom — was, if not a fantasy, certainly unrealistic: "One must fight the notion that wouldn't it be nice to go back to the classroom. That is probably the first sign of stress. Once the bridges have been burned, I do not think you can or should go back to the classroom; it is a nice myth, though." Another dispels the belief that, once you are a president, you have many fields open to you. He states: "Most presidents do not prepare themselves for life after the presidency. They do not publish or do the other things that would qualify them for academic positions." During the peak period of community college growth (to keep things in perspective, remember that this was a time when some universities held job fairs for their graduates interested in community college teaching and when presidents and deans traveled to the fairs by the hundreds to recruit community college faculty, including those with specialties in the social sciences and humanities), some community college presidents with little scholarly research or publications to their credit left the presidency to become professors of higher education specializing in community college education; however, simply having the experience gained as a community college president will not get one a position on most university campuses today. Curiously, a number of community college presidents cling to the myth that they could become a professor at a major university, if they desired.

One president may have spoken for many of her presidential colleagues regarding life after the presidency when she remarked: "Yes, there is life after the presidency, but it is like hitting 40, you have to figure out what it can be." Some presidents have successfully moved from the presidency to positions at the state and national levels, but they are few in number. Consulting has offered some opportunities, but only for those presidents with a national reputation or with a special skill or expertise such as marketing, management, fundraising, or some other sought-after speciality. Occasionally a president will become a "hired gun," serving as interim president as needed.

One study examined the status of former presidents. Regarding community colleges, the study found that 22 percent of the former community college presidents surveyed were retired and another 7 percent were "semiretired." The same study found that 10 percent returned to the classroom; 19 percent assumed another presidency; 4 percent assumed leadership of their own district or system; 10 percent assumed other positions in higher education; 13 percent took jobs outside the academic world; 4 percent died while in office; and it appears that the other 11 percent wandered aimlessly looking for something to do (Carbone, 1981, p. 17–19). These statistics indicate that life after the presidency is limited; 67 percent either retired, died, assumed another presidency, or wandered aimlessly. Based on the study cited above, the 10 percent who took positions within higher education assumed positions with less responsibility and less prestige than that of the presidency; and, from what can be determined from the study, the same is true of the majority of the 13 percent who took posts outside academia.

As with most positions, retirement is a possible form of afterlife for community college presidents. Indeed, of the 121 presidents who stated that they were very likely to move within the next five years, 21, or slightly over 17 percent, said they would retire (CLS). Considering that only 65 of the current presidents are over 60 years of age (CLS), the retirement route represents an important avenue out of the presidency.

In discussing life after the presidency, it is well to remember that 77 percent of the current presidents have their doctorates in education. While the doctorate in education, especially higher education, prepares one quite well for the community college presidency, it is not a degree that is in great demand in other fields. In contrast to a Ph.D. in physics, engineering, or even crowded fields such as English and history, the degree in education does not prepare one to return to the classroom on most campuses in the nation. What does it prepare one for? It can lead to the very limited number of slots in schools of education, assuming the other criteria are met; a public school superintendency, in some cases; or a "grab-as-one-can" situation for the few vacancies at the national and state levels. The prospect is not exciting if one wants to leave the presidency, but the fact of the matter is that the degree held by the majority of the community college presidents appears to prepare them well for their current role but for few other positions of equal or higher status. A glimmer of hope would seem to be that one's professional experience, rather than the doctorate, might offer some options since the practical experience of managing a complex institution would appear to open up a number of career choices in business and industry. On the whole, however, the choice to become a community college president is often a somewhat irrevocable career decision, for most signs point to the community college presidency as a permanent position, in the sense that any career choice is permanent. As one 20-year veteran president put it: "Life after the presidency, no, not at my age," implying strongly that retirement is his only option.

How Long is Too Long?

For years, a favorite parlor game among presidents has been speculating on how long is too long to occupy the presidency. As is the case with most parlor games, one's perspective on the game changes with age, availability of desirable options, and the satisfaction associated with the game itself. And, indeed, as with most games, the players are not always able to control their length of office, for there are always certain rules, referees, and others who have an influence on any one career. Indeed, for the community college presidents, the board, the faculty, and any number of individuals have some say in how long the tenure may be. One president suggests that "being a community college president is like dancing with a bear, you can't always say when its time to quit."

Perspectives on what constitutes an "optimum" time for exercising presidential leadership seem to vary somewhat with the times. The presidential giants of the past century, such as Charles Eliot of Harvard who occupied the presidency of his institution for 40 years, were often the embodiment of Emerson's observation that the university is the lengthened shadow of its president. The modern-day community college president may fantasize that his or her institution is a "lengthened shadow" or, on the contrary, may break out in night sweats at the suggestion of occupying a given presidency for 40 years. Probably either reaction would be extreme, for most community college presidents seem to have a realistic perspective on the office.

A number of scholars have written about presidential tenure. Cohen and March engage in a rather lengthy and complex discussion of the subject (1974); Fisher believes that from six to ten years in a particular presidency is the maximum time one can exert charismatic power (1984); Kauffman describes the college and university presidency as a temporary role of leadership rather than a professional career (1980). However, as suggested earlier, the community college presidency is probably a permanent career choice for most people who assume the position, at least as far as the availability of comparable career choices is concerned.

Presidents themselves were asked, "How long is too long?"

The answers are revealing and tend to reflect the attitude of the survivors, since no attempt was made to discuss the topic with those who had left the presidency other than under favorable circumstances.

One president, who has occupied a prominent place on the national scene relative to community colleges and who has been in his current position for six years, makes the following observation: "Ten years ago I would have said five to eight years was long enough. Today, I would say that it is dependent upon the situation much more than it is any given length of time. I've seen leaders stay 20 years who were effective when they left; I've seen some stay five years and they were not effective after the first year." Another 17-year veteran makes a similar argument: "A point of diminishing returns? I think it depends upon the individual, and it depends on the institution. A person can be successful over a long period of time if the institution is one that is dynamic and changing — it depends on the individual and on the institution." A president who is currently in his third presidency states: "I think it depends on the circumstances. When I first started as a community college president I thought seven years would be about the maximum time you could make a contribution. But I think times have changed now and I think the length of time you can make a contribution is longer because times are changing much more rapidly. Previously, we were in a growth-oriented situation; once you reached a level of five, six, or seven years, you had to look for different things to do. But there are so many different things taking place now that you can continue to generate vitality within the institution; I don't think the seven-to-ten-year time span is valid anymore." *It is important to remember that those presidents identified as leaders have been in their current position for a median of 9.4 years, whereas the median for all presidents is 5.3. This demonstrates that leaders are productive well beyond the five-to-seven-year time period and implies that more than five to seven years may be required to achieve leadership status.*

Most presidents agree that there is no set time for exerting effective leadership in the presidency and agree that much depends upon the individual and on the stage of development of the institution. However, the dilemma of how long one can effectively lead continues to haunt community college presidents. One chancellor of a large metropolitan district believes that "most leaders sense it when their capacity for motivating others to seek change and improvement begins to diminish. The tragedy occurs when some leaders begin to sort of kid themselves and do not realize that they are coasting, and others see that they are coasting. Tragedies occur when well-respected people who have done a lot for a district just hang on too long."

The ability to adapt seems to be a major factor in maintaining presidential effectiveness. For example, one president observes that the autocratic president would be out of place today. Several presidents concur with those organizational theorists who believe that organizations have life stages and therefore require different types of leadership at different stages; at one stage the builder-president is required, at another stage a "management of maturity," to use the words of one president, is required. Just when the various stages are reached is a matter of conjecture. One president, for example, was ready to leave his current position because he could not imagine staying in a position more than 10 years; however, in his twelfth year he discovered that the college was at another stage in its development and that he was excited about the prospects of taking the college in new directions. The cynic might view the change of heart with skepticism and suggest that it came about because the president had few desirable choices; the president, however, displayed a strong sense of commitment to providing the leadership required to move the college down new paths.

There is perhaps reason to be skeptical when asking a president who has little prospect of moving what comprises too long a tenure. One observation that provides food for thought comes from a president who entered the presidency at age 45 and who has been in his current position for 13 years. He notes that there is a tendency for presidents to be satisfied with a certain level of achievement, especially when they achieve more as president than they originally believed they could. The result, he believes, is that these presidents find it very difficult to raise the vision for their institution; they no longer have the "sharp edge" in their thinking that is necessary for effective leadership.

How does one know when the "sharp edge" is no longer

present? "I think a lot of presidents start to lose their freshness, their sense of zeal, their sense of mission, their sense of feeling good about what they are doing and feel as if they don't know if they want to go to work today. That is a bad feeling; I think they ought to look at a new vision for their life," one national leader observes. He suggests that those presidents who feel that they have been in a position too long should look around and move if possible.

In responding to how long is too long, the president of a large multicampus community college in the East, who had just completed his fifth year in the presidency when interviewed, offers his analysis. "I've asked myself that question a good deal. Matter of fact, it's one of the things I thought about my very first year — and that's a strange time to think about it, but I thought, 'If you don't think about it early you get into a position where you never do' — was how long can I stay in my position and give leadership to the institution. In regard to how long is too long, I've never been able to say here are the signals that say that is the case and triggers a person's moving. I don't know what the signals are. But if a person is to be truly effective in a leadership position it seems to me as if you cannot do it without the support of those you are supposed to lead. If you ever get to the point where your faculty, administrators, students, staff, and board no longer support you, obviously you can no longer be a leader and you have stayed too long."

David Riesman concurs that the question of when to leave a presidency is a difficult one, especially if one is not close to retirement. Noting that provincial wisdom suggests a seven-year period as optimal, Riesman offers his opinion on how long a president should stay in the same presidency: "I believe that even a decade can be too brief if one wants to have an impact on the quality and collegiality of faculty and staff" (Riesman, 1984, p. 171).

How long is too long? Are the presidents interviewed simply rationalizing in order to justify their own tenure when they suggest that the time in office depends upon the stage of development of the college and on the vitality of the president? Probably not. As strange as it may seem to those presidents who never had the opportunity to found a college, founding a college is quite different from maintaining one. During the founding stage, a president builds buildings; employs faculty, staff, and administrators; gets programs "up and running"; and in general accomplishes tasks that are visible and, indeed, in the broadest sense, can be completed. Many presidents who were founding presidents stated that they moved on because they had accomplished what they set out to do: open a college. Today, no such sense of completion exists in most situations. Rather, the job is ongoing and therefore there are no psychological triggers or completed buildings to say that the job is done.

A number of presidents, some of whom are referred to above, see the position as changing enough to keep it exciting. The external role of the presidency has greatly expanded; therefore, new challenges are available. The same is true of a very specialized external role, fund raising from private sources. Some presidents who were "set in their ways" have found private fund raising to be an exciting new challenge and have devoted much of their time and energy to that aspect of the role.

How long is too long? Most presidents probably *do* know when they have been around too long. Few, however, are willing to move voluntarily, especially if they know that the career choices after the presidency are very limited.

Postscript

What can faculty, trustees, presidents, deans, students of higher education, and others learn from the foregoing pages? The following are some personal observations.

The presidents interviewed were, without exception, intelligent individuals devoted to the community college philosophy. Even those who were disillusioned with their current situation or who felt that they had been in their current position too long, had few or no regrets about their decision to become a community college president.

Contrary to what had been my experience and that of others in the past, presidents and others connected with the community college were willing to talk about the shortcomings of the community college. The discussions were always in a tone similar to what one might use to talk about a loved child who is not always making good grades in school. Presidents were perhaps more willing to look at the community college critically at this stage in history than in the past, for even the most idealistic president now realizes that the community college cannot be all things to all people, that it is not the single answer to society's ills. These facts have become quite clear as resources, public support, and student enrollments have declined, or at best, leveled off.

The personalities of those who occupy the presidency are as varied as those one might find in any group of individuals who occupy the top position in an organization. However, regardless

229

of their personality, the presidents tended to "sing off of the same song sheet" when talking about the community college. Indeed, now more than ever I believe strongly in *a community college philosophy*, a philosophy that is similar whether one is at a community college in Mississippi, California, New York, or Minnesota. The philosophy permeates the very being of the president and centers around the belief that all individuals have the right and responsibility to develop their talents to the fullest. The most visible symbol of this belief being translated into reality is the community college's commitment to open access.

While there is a community college philosophy, the philosophy has been adapted to meet the needs and circumstances of each local college. All community colleges are different from each other, and, while one should be careful about generalizing about them, the difference is almost always in degree rather than in kind. Since community colleges differ in this way, I firmly believe that much is to be learned by discussing the community college presidency, an approach that might be more difficult and less valid if one were to talk about the liberal arts college presidency, for example. In understanding why this is true, one must again turn to the community college philosophy. The philosophy, not the environment of a single college, is the driving force around which the community college presidents rally (indeed, the short history of most community colleges would make it difficult to rally around a single college). Another factor working in favor of a broad philosophy and against identifying solely with one's own campus is the fact that most community colleges are commuter colleges and therefore do not have the traditions or personality that come with most residential campuses. These observations are not to indicate that community college presidents do not care for their particular college, for indeed they care deeply. On the other hand, these deep feelings are readily transferable, as demonstrated by the views of those presidents who are in their second, third, and even fourth presidency. Most presidents who move to other campuses very quickly care for them just as much as they did for the ones they just left. A useful analogy might be to liken the community college president to a Methodist minister who changes churches every four years or so: the minister loves *the* church, not necessarily *a* church.

On the other hand, presidents seem to have little or no appreciation of the frustrations their spouses face. Indeed, a suggestion made by me to a group of 50 presidents that there is a great deal of frustration — and in some cases anger — among the spouses brought forth a sense of disbelief on the part of many presidents and denial on the part of others. Presidents have given little thought to the role of the spouse beyond the traditional role of entertaining. On the other hand, spouses, particularly female spouses, are literally hungry to know more about the spouse's role. One rarely gets additional comments on a survey from presidents; almost every spouse who responded to the surveys sent out completed the questions requiring essay-type answers. Some wrote several pages. *Presidents must realize that spouses have few avenues to the board and to the college community other than through the president. Stated another way, the only advocate the spouse can rely on in defining and interpreting the spouse's role is the president.*

Finally, presidents do not seem to understand fully their role as leader. There seems to be a struggle among presidents to determine how they can give strong leadership without alienating the faculty and board. The struggle seems to result from attempts by presidents to shed the autocratic image associated with the community college presidency, from unionization on campus, from participatory governance, and from the obvious need for strong leadership. The successful president will have to reconcile these seemingly diverse elements. As was suggested, the community college president is often viewed as a pragmatic leader primarily concerned with the day-to-day affairs of the college. Even in interpreting the community college mission, many presidents come up short. The successful community college president of the future must provide the intellectual leadership that is currently missing on many campuses. As one individual observes: "If presidents do not provide the intellectual cutting edge for the community college phenomenon, who will?"

The Board

Trustees have strong feelings about the community college and about the presidency. This volume should aid trustees to define their own role as well as the role of their current president and should help them when they seek a new president.

In understanding the presidency, trustees simply must realize that it is a stressful position and one that requires relief if the president is to perform as effectively as possible and as effectively as most boards desire. Relief should include regular sabbaticals. In this regard, presidents are guilty of failing to practice what they preach; they advocate sabbaticals for everyone except themselves, thus promoting the "Superman-Wonderwoman" image that can ultimately be deadening to the presidency. The effective trustee can and, in many cases, should take the lead in insisting that the president take some extended time off.

Trustees must constantly be sensitive to that thin line between policy and administration and work to assure that they ma!.e policy, not administrative directives. As is the case with presidents, trustees must subscribe to the community college philosophy, thereby leaving special interests outside the boardroom door. They should examine the role of the spouse and at least say thanks to the spouse when warranted. Gratitude should be in the form of paying for trips to professional meetings for spouses and in sharing with the spouses what is expected of them.

Finally, trustees should view the president as their greatest ally and greatest asset, not as someone to be used and discarded at the whim of the board once the immediate goals of the college are accomplished. In this regard, boards should develop some mechanism for easing a president out of a position. While "golden parachutes" are impractical in the public sector, an extended contract can assure some amount of security for those presidents who are forced to leave their position. More important, extended contracts can help salvage the dignity of the individual, the least a board can do for someone who has devoted his or her career to salvaging the dignity of so many Americans.

Faculty

Faculty members displayed more empathy with the trials and tribulations of the presidency than was anticipated when I began this study. This empathy, however, often took the form of bewilderment (or even sympathy, something few individuals in high-level positions need or want) at the frustrations (not enough time, not enough money, too many questions, too many pressures, etc.) associated with the presidency. The result is that faculty see many of the problems associated with the presidency as belonging to the individual occupying the president's office rather than as college problems and ultimately individual faculty problems. On the other hand, without exception, all the faculty members interviewed expressed the need and desire for strong leadership in the office of the president. It is now time for faculty to realize that presidents cannot give the leadership desired and required without the support of the faculty. Support means keeping the avenues for faculty participation open and keeping the faculty involved when appropriate. On the other hand, faculty members should back off and encourage presidents to make decisions, without consultation, in those areas that do not directly affect the teaching and learning process and that do not affect the well-being of the faculty and students. In other words, faculty should join with presidents to determine when and where faculty involvement is needed and when and where presidents should move ahead with little or no guidance from the faculty. Faculty members should show the same concern for presidential prerogatives that presidents have shown, albeit reluctantly at times, for faculty rights. The result should go a long way toward bridging the "we–they" gap that exists on too many campuses between faculty and administrators.

Deans and Vice Presidents

In a narrow sense, this volume might be viewed as a "how-to" volume for deans and others who would be president. The most important conclusions are the obvious ones: get into the academic pipeline; get the appropriate degree; work with a mentor; be willing to move; and call attention to yourself by doing a good job and by doing more than is required for survival. Beyond the obvious, deans and others should examine the personal characteristics and skills of the successful president and evaluate themselves in relationship to those characteristics and skills. It might well be that some deans will realize that they are not "cut out" to be a president. On the other hand, deans should not become so tied to the rankings that they abandon individual initiative. For example, the relatively low-ranked ability to produce scholarly publications should not be discarded as unimportant; publications might well be the method best suited to expressing one's beliefs as well as an important way of gaining attention.

Students of Higher Education

This volume is about more than the community college presidency; it is about the community college. In the past, those persons studying the community college have done so without the benefit of an analysis of the role played by the presidents of these institutions. This study is a step toward filling the void that has existed until now. It is my greatest hope that students of higher education will consider the significant role the leader plays in the successes or failures of the community college, for, without understanding the role of the leader of an enterprise, one cannot fully understand the enterprise.

The Future

As stated in the methodology section, no attempt was made to distinguish between male-female, minority-majority presidents. This does not mean that differences do not exist. Indeed, if the present situation is any indication of the future, in the years ahead, more and more community college presidents will be women and minorities; fewer will be married; and those aspiring to the presidency will certainly be younger than the largely middle-aged group who occupy the office today. With this in mind, future studies of the community college presidency should take these changes into account, for an increasing number of presidents of the future may well be female, minority, or female and minority. They will provide a major statement on the success of the community college in serving ever-increasing segments of society. Today's presidents are visible symbols of how individuals, most of whom are white males from largely blue-collar backgrounds, can make it to the top of their profession; future community college presidents may well represent a similar statement on the ability of women and minorities to achieve these successes.

Bibliography

American Council on Education (ACE). 1984. *Higher Education and National Affairs* 33:3.

Association of Governing Boards (AGB). 1984. *Presidents Make a Difference: Strengthening Leadership in Colleges and Universities.* Directed by Clark Kerr. Washington, D.C.

ASTIN, ALEXANDER W. 1983. "Strengthening Transfer Programs." In *Issues for Community College Leaders in a New Era,* edited by George B. Vaughan. San Francisco: Jossey-Bass.

————, AND RITA A. SCHERREI. 1980. *Maximizing Leadership Effectiveness.* San Francisco: Jossey-Bass.

BEADLE, MURIEL. 1972. *Where Has All the Ivy Gone? A Memoir of University Life.* Chicago: The University of Chicago Press.

BENEZET, LOUIS T., JOSEPH KATZ, AND FRANCES W. MAGNUSSON. 1981. *Style and Substance: Leadership and the College Presidency.* Washington, D.C.: American Council on Education.

————. 1982. "Do Presidents Make a Difference?" *Educational Record* 63:10–13.

BENNIS, WARREN. 1973. *The Leaning Ivory Tower.* San Francisco: Jossey-Bass.

————. 1975. *Warren Bennis on Leaders: An Endangered Species?* New York: AMACOM, A Division of the American Management Association.

BERG, RODNEY. 1978. "The Man in the Middle." *Community and Junior College Journal* 48:3.

BLOCKER, CLYDE E., ROBERT H. PLUMMER, AND RICHARD C. RICHARDSON, JR. 1965. *The Two-Year College: A Social Synthesis.* Englewood Cliffs, N.J.: Prentice-Hall.

BLUMER, D. H. 1975. "Faculty Collective Bargaining: A Status Report." *Community and Junior College Journal* 45:27–29.

BURNS, JAMES MACGREGOR. 1978. *Leadership.* New York: Harper and Row.

CARBONE, ROBERT E. 1981. *Presidential Passages.* Washington, D.C.: American Council on Education.

CHESLER, MARK A., AND WILLIAM C. CAVE. 1981. *A Sociology of Education: Access to Power and Privilege.* New York: Macmillan.

CLODIUS, JOAN E., AND DIANE S. MAGRATH, eds. 1984. *The President's Spouse: Volunteer or Volunteered.* Washington, D.C.: National Association of State Universities and Land-Grant Colleges.

COHEN, ARTHUR M., AND FLORENCE B. BRAWER. 1982. *The American Community College.* San Francisco: Jossey-Bass.

COHEN, ARTHUR M., AND JOHN E. ROUECHE. 1969. *Institutional Administrator or Educational Leader?: The Junior College President.* Washington, D.C.: American Association of Junior Colleges.

COHEN, MICHAEL D., AND JAMES G. MARCH. 1974. *Leadership and Ambiguity: The American College President.* New York: McGraw-Hill.

CORBALLY, MARQUERITE WALKER. 1977. *The Partners: Sharing the Life of a College President.* Danville, Ill.: Interstate Printers and Publishers.

CUNNINGHAM, J. DAVID. 1983–84. "After a Score of Years, What's Faculty Union Score?" *Community and Junior College Journal* 54 (Dec.–Jan.):15–17.

DODDS, HAROLD W. 1962. *The Academic President: Educator or Caretaker?* New York: McGraw-Hill.

DREW, DAVID E., AND JACK H. SCHUSTER. 1980. "Recommended Reading for College Presidents." *Change* 12 (July–August):33–38.

ERNST, RICHARD J. 1985. "Collective Bargaining: The Conflict Model as Norm?" In *Ensuring Effective Governance,* edited by W. L. Deegan and James F. Gollattscheck. New Directions for Community Colleges, no. 49. San Francisco: Jossey-Bass.

Eric Digest. 1984. Los Angeles: ERIC Clearinghouse for Junior Colleges. June.

FISHER, JAMES L. 1984. *Power of the Presidency.* American Council on

Education/Macmillan Series in Higher Education. New York: ACE/ Macmillan.

Florida Times-Union. March 9, 1984, p, 1; April 8, 1984, p. B-1; April 20, 1984, p. 1; May 31, 1984, pp. 1, A-12.

GRIESSMAN, B. EUGENE. 1985. "Coke's Chief Values Tradition — and Cash." *USA Today*, July 19, p. 2B.

HAWK, RAY. 1959–60. "A Profile of Junior College Presidents." *Junior College Journal* 30 (September–May):340–346.

HELLER, SCOTT. "Guidelines for New College Presidents: Getting Started is No Simple Matter." *The Chronicle of Higher Education* 28 (June 27, 1984):15.

——. "College's Middle Managers Form Union-Like Group." *Chronicle of Higher Education*. 29 (Feb. 6, 1985):27.

HELLING, J. 1975. "Participatory Governance — A Losing Model?" *Community and Junior College Journal* 46:16–17.

HESBURGH, THEODORE. 1979. "The College Presidency: Life Between a Rock and a Hard Place." *Change* 11:43–47.

JENCKS, CHRISTOPHER. 1972. *Inequality: A Reassessment of the Effect of Family and Schooling in America*. New York: Basic Books.

JOHNSTON, J. RICHARD. 1980. "Community Colleges: Alternative to Elit-ism in Higher Education." In *Questioning the Community College Role*, edited by George B. Vaughan. New Directions for Community Colleges, no. 32. San Francisco: Jossey-Bass.

KARABEL, JEROME. 1972. "Community Colleges and Social Stratifica-tion." *Harvard Educational Review* 42:521–562.

KAUFFMAN, JOSEPH F. 1977. "The New College President: Expectations and Realities." *Educational Record* 58:146–168.

——. 1980. *At the Pleasure of the Board*. Washington, D.C.: Ameri-can Council on Education.

——. 1982. "The College Presidency — Yesterday and Today." *Change* 14 (May/June):12–18.

KEMENY, JEAN ALEXANDER. 1979. *It's Different at Darmouth: A Memoir*. Brattleboro, Vt: Stephen Greene Press.

KERR, CLARK. 1982. *The Uses of the University*. 3rd edition. Cambridge, Mass.: Harvard University Press.

KINTZER, RUTH. 1971. *The President's Wife: A Handbook for Wives of New Community College Presidents*. Santa Monica: Pine Publica-tions.

KOOS, LEONARD V. 1925. *The Junior College Movement*. Boston: Ginn.

LEVINE, ARTHUR. 1984. "Diary of a New College President." *Change* 16:10–17.

LOMBARDI, JOHN. 1971. *The President's Reaction to Black Student Activism*. Los Angeles: ERIC Clearinghouse for Junior Colleges, Topical Paper no. 16.

LONDON, HOWARD B. 1978. *The Culture of a Community College*. New York: Praeger.

LORTIE, DAN C. 1975. *School-Teacher: A Sociological Study*. Chicago: University of Chicago Press.

MELENDEZ, WINIFRED ALBIZU, AND RAFAEL M. DE GUZMAN. 1983. *Burnout: The New Academic Disease*. ASHE-ERIC/Higher Education Research Report no. 9. Washington, D.C.: Association for the Study of Higher Education.

NICHOLSON, R. STEPHEN. 1981. *Chief Executive Officers Contracts and Compensation, 1981*. Washington, D.C.: The American Association of Community and Junior Colleges.

OSTAR, ROBERTA H. 1983. *Myths and Realities: 1983 Report on the AASCU Presidential Spouses*. Washington, D.C.: American Association of State Colleges and Universities.

PARNELL, DALE. 1980. "Major Restraints or Grand Opportunities." *Community and Junior College Journal* 51:44–48.

PERKINS, JAMES R. 1980. *An Outcomes Analysis of the Preservice Fellowship Recipients of the W. K. Kellogg Foundation Supported Junior College Leadership Program*. Doctoral dissertation, The Florida State University, Tallahassee.

PETERS, THOMAS, AND NANCY AUSTIN. 1985. *A Passion for Excellence: The Leadership Difference*. New York: Random House.

PETERS, THOMAS J., AND ROBERT H. WATERMAN. 1982. *In Search of Excellence: Lessons from America's Best-Run Companies*. New York: Harper and Row.

RICHARDSON, RICHARD C., JR. 1979. "Can Faculty Unions Provide Leadership on Educational Issues?" *Community College Review* 7:17–21.

———, CLYDE E. BLOCKER, AND LOUIS W. BENDER. 1972. *Governance for the Two-Year College*. Englewood Cliffs, N.J.: Prentice-Hall.

RICHMAN, BARRY M., AND RICHARD N. FARMER. 1974. *Leadership, Goals, and Power in Higher Education*. San Francisco: Jossey-Bass.

RIESMAN, DAVID. 1978. "Community Colleges: Some Tentative Hypotheses." *Community Services Catalyst* 8:1–5.

————. 1982. Personal correspondence, February 16.

————. 1982. *Some Observations on the President's Spouse: Hazards and Opportunities.* Charlottesville, Va.: Center for the Study of Higher Education, Occasional Paper Series no. 11, April.

————. 1984. "Refractions and Reflections." In *The President's Spouse: Volunteer or Volunteered,* edited by J. E. Clodius and D. S. Magrath. Washington, D.C.: National Association of State Universities and Land-Grant Colleges.

RIMER, SARA. 1982. "Exit the Rainmaker: The Disappearance of a Md. College President." *Washington Post,* June 20, pp. A-1; A-12.

ROBINSON, JAMES A. 1984. A review of the *"Power of the Presidency:* Combining Scholarship, Personal Reflection, and 'Campus Savvy.'" *Change* 16 (July/August):49–50.

RUSHING, JOE B. 1976. *Changing Role of the Community College President in the Face of New Administrative Pressures.* Washington, D.C.: American Association of Community and Junior Colleges.

SIMS, DAVID M. 1978–79. "So You Want to be a President?" *Community and Junior College Journal* 49 (December/January):16–19.

STALCUP, ROBERT J., AND WILLIAM A. THOMSON. 1980. *The Community College President: A Contemporary Janus.* College Station: Texas A&M University.

STOKE, HAROLD W. 1959. *The American College President.* New York: Harper and Brothers.

VAUGHAN, GEORGE B. 1979. "The Challenge of Criticism." *Community and Junior College Journal* 50:8–11.

————. 1982. "Burnout: Threat to Presidential Effectiveness." *Community and Junior College Journal* 52:10–13.

————. 1984. "Forging the Community College Mission." *Educational Record* 65:24–29.

————. 1983. *Issues for Community College Leaders in a New Era.* San Francisco: Jossey-Bass.

WENRICH, J. WILLIAM. 1980. "Can the President be All Things to All People?" *Community and Junior College Journal* 51:36–40.

WING, DENNIS R. W. 1972. *The Professional President: A Decade of Community Junior College Chief Executives.* Los Angeles: ERIC Clearing House for Junior Colleges, Topical Paper No. 28.

Index

243